ALSO BY BILL PRESS

EYEWITNESS

SPIN THIS!

BUSH MUST GO

HOW THE REPUBLICANS STOLE RELIGION

TRAINWRECK

TOXIC TALK

THE OBAMA HATE MACHINE

BUYER'S REMORSE

BILL PRESS FROM THE LEFT

A LIFE IN THE CROSSFIRE

THOMAS DUNNE BOOKS
ST. MARTIN'S PRESS ⚟ NEW YORK

THOMAS DUNNE BOOKS.
An imprint of St. Martin's Press.

Designed by Anna Gorovoy

www.thomasdunnebooks.com
www.stmartins.com

The Library of Congress Cataloging-in-Publication Data is available upon request.

ISBN 978-1-250-14715-8 (hardcover)
ISBN 978-1-250-14716-5 (ebook)

First Edition: March 2018

10 9 8 7 6 5 4 3 2 1

For Milo, Prairie, Willow, Django, and Silas:
In a life full of wonders, you are the greatest of all!

CONTENTS

PREFACE: "DON'T TAKE NO SHIT!"

"FROM THE LEFT, I'M BILL PRESS."

For six exciting, rousing, and altogether fun years, I had the joy of saying that every night on CNN, followed by, "From the right, I'm Bob Novak"—or Pat Buchanan, or Mary Matalin, or Tucker Carlson—announcing the end of that day's edition of *Crossfire*.

I had a good run on *Crossfire*. As I learned in a number of jobs along the way, six years is a long time for television. I think I did a solid job, judging from both the kudos I received from the left and the hate mail from the right. And no wonder. I had the world's best coach: the president of the United States!

In February 1996, a few weeks before actually landing the job, I was in Washington for a third round of auditions for *Crossfire* when I got a call from my good friend Susie Tompkins Buell from Bolinas. She was in town to attend a lunch for major donors at the White House. Since I was still, at that time, chair of the California Democratic Party, I made a quick call to Deputy Chief of Staff Harold Ickes and landed myself an invitation.

After lunch in the State Dining Room, Susie and I lined up with other guests to greet President Clinton in the Blue Room. Susie and I had both met the president several times before. In fact, Susie and her husband, Mark, were among his biggest supporters and fund-raisers in California, and, as state chair, I was part of his entourage almost every time he came to the Golden State—which ocurred so often, we joked with him about his being eligible to vote in California.

When our turn came, Susie and I each gave Clinton a big hug and extended very special greetings from West Marin County, where we both have homes.

Clinton was in a particularly good mood, so after a little back-and-forth banter, I said, "Mr. President, I'll bet you don't know why I'm in Washington today."

He looked puzzled and said, "No, why's that?"

I told him I was trying out for a job on *Crossfire*.

He asked, "You mean, you're a guest on *Crossfire* tonight?"

And I explained, "Oh, no. I'm actually auditioning to be the show's new cohost on the left."

At which point, Clinton grabbed my arm, pulled me to the side, brought his face up close to mine, and gave me my marching orders: "Let me just tell you one thing," he told me, wagging his finger in my face. "Don't take no shit!"

And I didn't. Not that day. And, once I got the job, not any day for the next six years, starting with my debut as *Crossfire*'s new host on the left: February 26, 1996.

My challenge that night was defending normalization of relations with Cuba. This was just two days after Cuban MiGs had shot down two civilian aircraft belonging to the Miami-based organization Brothers to the Rescue, killing all four on board. Via satellite from Miami, arguing that this was an "act of war," which demanded a military response by the United States, was the notorious Jorge Mas Canosa. As founder of the Cuban-American National Foundation, under both Republican and Democratic presidents, he had single-handedly dictated U.S.-Cuba policy for the last thirty years. No Republican or Democratic president dared oppose him.

Especially given the timing of the incident and the death of four Brothers volunteers, it was a tough argument to make and a good introduction to the challenges *Crossfire* would offer for the next six years. I thought I'd held my own, but was shaken upon leaving the studio to receive a phone message from a close Los Angeles liberal friend, Hollywood producer Stephen Rivers.

"I can't believe it," said Rivers. "Your very first day on *Crossfire*—and you defend fucking Fidel Castro!" I realized right then and there that I was in for a wild ride.

Crossfire, which started with the launch of CNN in 1982, was the first and best of America's political debate shows. And, to my mind, canceling the original *Crossfire* was one of the dumbest decisions ever made in cable television.

I say that not just because I was cohost on the left. I was only there for six out of the show's twenty-two years, and I had moved on before the ax finally fell. I say that simply because it's true. No other show could compete with *Crossfire* then. And no other political show today is as good or compelling, nor offers the same spontaneity and passion.

For me, *Crossfire* was the latest adventure in an ever-changing career, catapulting me from Switzerland to San Francisco; from Los Angeles to Washington, D.C.; from a decade in the seminary to the California governor's office; from leading the most populous state's Democratic Party to cohosting the most popular debate program on national television.

Some people's professional lives may proceed in a relatively straight line from start to finish. Mine never did. Instead, I've zigzagged in what were often totally opposite directions: first stepping outside the world for ten years to study for the Catholic priesthood; then diving back into politics as volunteer, campaign manager, and, ultimately, statewide candidate myself; taking time out again to serve in government as legislative aide, department head, and adviser to the California governor; and, finally, jumping into the world of media, from local political commentator to host of four national TV and radio shows.

Maybe the weirdest part is that I ended up on the left at all. Yes, I proudly admit, I'm a bleeding-heart liberal: pro-choice, pro-environment, pro–gun control, pro–affirmative action, pro-immigrant, pro–gay rights, and pro-union. Also anti-war, anti–death penalty, anti-discrimination, and anti-vouchers. And yes, a card-carrying member of the ACLU.

But by birthright, I probably should have ended up on the other side of the tracks.

After all, I grew up in a Republican stronghold, south of the Mason-Dixon line. Both my parents were Republicans. In my small town, segregation was the rule. Blacks—although we routinely used the N-word instead, without acknowledging there was anything wrong with it—shopped in their own stores, worshiped in their own churches, and walked a mile outside of town to attend their own school.

As kids, we had rock fights with black kids in the streets. And as Catholics, we were vehemently anti-abortion, anti-divorce, anti-sex outside of marriage, and anti-homosexuality. We didn't use the term *gay*. We, I'm ashamed to admit, called them *queers* and *faggots* and considered LGBTQ Americans mentally ill.

Let's face it. Given where I came from and what I was taught in school, I should probably have ended up a Trump voter.

Some of my family and friends back then likely wonder: What went wrong? Where and how, along the way, did I veer off the tracks?

A better question is: What went right? Or, more to the point, what went left? How did I escape the clutches of conservatism and end up a flaming lefty, let alone the chair of the California Democratic Party, liberal cohost of CNN's *Crossfire* and *The Spin Room*, liberal counterpuncher on MSNBC's *Buchanan & Press*, and nationally syndicated liberal morning radio talk show host?

That, my friends, is what this book is all about. Of course, that transformation didn't happen suddenly or all at once, like—to use a metaphor I learned in those olden days—Saint Paul being knocked off his horse on the road to Damascus. It happened gradually, over time, through the series of events and experiences portrayed here: the story of how one misguided young redneck saw the light and made it to the promised land of liberalism.

If there was hope for me, there's hope for anyone! And throughout this often bumpy and unpredictable ride, there were three critical forces that propelled me.

First, from the time I was a kid, a drive to spread my wings and fly as high as I could in order to escape the poverty, hard times, and tough lives I saw family and friends experience in the small town in Delaware where I grew up. I loved them, and still do, but I knew there was a bigger world out there, and I wanted to be part of it.

Second, a determination, in whatever field, to excel. I've always been compelled to strive for the top. I had to be in first place. There was no second or third. It's a conviction best expressed, I believe, by famous architect Daniel Burnham, father of the skyscraper, architect of New York's famous Flatiron Building, and designer of the Chicago World's Fair: "Make no little plans. They have no magic to stir men's blood and probably will not themselves be realized."

Strangely enough, that spirit of Burnham was captured in our time by builder Donald Trump, long before he decided to run for president. Shoot for the moon, said the Donald: "As long as you are going to be thinking anyway, think big." He's right. It may be the only thing Trump ever said that I agree with. What's true for buildings is also true for lives.

Third, what some might call a recklessness, but I would call a readiness, to leap at whatever opportunities come along, no matter how new and different—and even create a few new and challenging opportunities of your own. In the end, I discovered, it's not the plans you make, it's the risks you take that count the most and advance your career the strongest. As management guru Tom Peters put it, "If a window of opportunity appears, don't pull down the shade."

That's certainly worked for me. I didn't plan to be a priest, but almost did. I didn't plan to become one of Governor Jerry Brown's inner circle, but ended up there. I didn't plan to rescue an American prisoner of war from a Nicaraguan jail cell, but somehow, I pulled it off. I didn't plan a career on national radio and television, but here I am. It's that readiness to leap into the unknown that's powered me through the different phases and surprising twists of my personal and professional life, from the church, to politics, to the media.

I've had a lot of fun and exciting adventures along the way, and that's a story I want to share with you. Believe me, it's been a long journey from the days when I walked out the railroad tracks in my hometown of Delaware City with a fishing pole and a can of worms, looking for catfish.

So, whether the world is going to pieces or not, whether you are on the side of the angels or the devil himself, take life for what it is, have fun, spread joy and confusion.

—Henry Miller

FROM
THE
LEFT

1

CANAL RAT ON THE DELAWARE

Delaware City is a little town that could have, but never did. But it's where I grew up. And I still love it.

It was originally settled as Newbold's Landing, surrounded by peach orchards, a small port on the Delaware River serving farmers in southern New Castle County. In 1829, it suddenly grew to prominence—and was renamed Delaware City—when it became the eastern terminus of the newly constructed Chesapeake and Delaware Canal, linking the Chesapeake Bay to the Delaware River, and Baltimore to Philadelphia.

Delaware City's at the east end of the canal; Chesapeake City, at the west end. As a kid, I remember being shown an old map on the wall of our town hall that projected Delaware City to grow bigger than Philadelphia was at the time. But that was not to be.

By the turn of the century, many larger ships could no longer squeeze through the locks at Delaware City. So, on January 31, 1927, the locks on the old canal shut down and a new, wider, and straighter canal opened. It was rerouted to enter the Delaware River at sea level at Reedy Point, a mile to the south of Delaware City. Grand plans for the next Philadelphia collapsed. And Delaware City remained a small town with a big name.

Today, Delaware City's much the same as it was back then: a quaint, sleepy, forgotten, little one-traffic-light town on the banks of the Delaware River, nine miles south of historic New Castle. The running joke among locals is that Delaware City's population is 1,200. At low tide, that is. Only 900 at high tide.

It was in Delaware City that I spent the first eighteen years of my life. And—for a young white boy, at least—it was a magical place to grow up: an *Ozzie and Harriet* kind of town, where everybody knew everybody else, where neighbors and family looked out for one other, where nobody had much money but it didn't really matter, and where life centered around work, church, and school. I only realized later that not all of Delaware City's residents had it so good.

I might as well admit this, too: For those first eighteen years, I was not known as Bill Press, either. I was stuck with the family nickname: Chippy, or simply Chip. My family called me that, I was told, because I had the same legal name—William Henry Press—as my father and grandfather before me. (My full name, in fact, which I never use, is William Henry Press III.) So they needed some way to tell us apart. And, besides, I was just a "chip off the old block."

I suffered that nickname gladly until the first day of my eighth grade class at Salesianum High School, when Oblate Scholastic Mr. Robert Lawler called the roll. After declaiming, "William Press," he asked, "What do they call you, son? Bill?"

At that point, I'd never been called Bill in my life, but I was too scared to contradict him. "Yes," I nervously stammered. And, from that day on, I've been Bill Press—everywhere, that is, but in Delaware City.

The Press family, part of the Cook Cousins clan, made up a big part of Delaware City, even at high tide. The family patriarch, my grandfather, William H. "Pop" Press Sr., was born on December 2, 1888, in Salem, New Jersey. He joined the army in World War I and was assigned to Fort DuPont in Delaware City, directly across the Delaware River from Salem. There, like many of my uncles and family friends, all fellow Fort DuPont alumni, he met and married a local girl, and never left.

For us grandkids, the big question, then and now, was: Where did the Press family come from? It's a question we often asked Pop-Pop Press, without ever getting a straight answer. He insisted he was a direct descendant of the Cherokee. As proof, he'd unbutton his shirt, show us his bare smooth chest, and ask, "You never saw an American Indian with hair on his chest, did you?" Not exactly a DNA test, but some of our family still believe that tall tale. Even as a kid, I always thought it was bullshit. And I am now more than ever convinced it was.

My first sign came while working at my first job in politics, as administrative assistant to San Francisco supervisor Roger Boas. One day, I accompanied Roger to a luncheon at one of the city's big synagogues. Roger, a prominent member of San Francisco's Jewish community, sat at the head table, alongside the president of the congregation, whose name was, curiously enough—Sam Press. Meanwhile, I was seated at a table in the back of the room, where everyone was speaking Yiddish. At one point, the woman next to me turned and whispered, "You do understand what we're talking about, don't you?" When I admitted I didn't have a clue, she was stunned. "What? A name like *Press* and you don't speak Yiddish?"

More evidence poured in, years later, once I popped up on television, first on KABC-TV in Los Angeles, and later on CNN and MSNBC. I've heard from dozens of people from all over the country with the same last name, none of them directly related to our Press family. Yet every one with the same story: their ancestors were Russian Jews who emigrated to the United States from Latvia.

I was especially struck one night, attending a black-tie event at the Dorothy Chandler Pavilion in downtown Los Angeles, when a friend asked if I knew Jim Press, then head of Toyota Motors for California (later head of Toyota for the entire country). When I said I'd never met him, my friend disappeared across the ballroom, only to reappear with the more famous Mr. Press in tow. Jim walked up, stuck out his hand, and gave me a big smile. The first two words out of his mouth were "Russian Jew!"

How could it be otherwise? I have since, hit or miss, traced Pop-Pop's family back to the 1830s, all in the Salem or Pennsville, New Jersey, area. In immigration records, I've also discovered several Presses arriving in the Philadelphia area from Latvia in the early nineteenth century, long before Ellis Island. So I'm convinced there's a connection, even though not yet firmly established. Interestingly, even in Latvia in the 1800s, the name was already Press—although, much earlier, it must have been shortened from a longer family name.

So I have long considered myself the Catholic descendant of a Russian Jew—a prospect that did not go down well with Grandmom Press, a loyal Catholic of German descent, who made sure all of her grandchildren were baptized and raised Catholic and went to Mass every Sunday. On one visit from California, I told her I'd heard from a lot of people around the country named Press and, after doing a little research on my own, concluded that Pop-Pop's family were originally Russian Jews. "No!" she snapped. "Pop-Pop weren't no Jew!"

I thought afterward that maybe Grandmom Press's attitude toward Jewish people said a lot about why Pop-Pop hid his lineage. At any rate, I never met a (self-admitted) Jew the entire time I grew up in Delaware City. Of course, I never met a Native American, either.

For Grandmom, that was the end of the story. But not for me. In 1998, after mentioning on CNN that I believed my ancestors had immigrated here from Latvia, I was invited to a reception at the Capitol for Her Excellency Vaira Vike-Freiberga, president of Latvia, on her state visit to the United States. When I was presented to her, she greeted me as "America's most famous Latvian American"—this was well before current NBA Latvian sensation Kristaps Porzingis—and invited me to Riga for an official ceremony honoring my success in the New World. I begged off, telling her I wanted to verify and confirm my Latvian roots before publicly celebrating them. And the search continues.

Back in Delaware City, Pop-Pop was a big fish in a small pond. He owned and operated a gas station on Fifth Street, the main road into town from Highway 13. For years, my grandmother Marie operated a small grocery store on one corner of Pop-Pop's gas station property.

Pop-Pop was also a commercial crabber and fisherman. For several summers, he ran three party boats—the *Wave*, the *Aunt Kass*, and the *Happy Days*—out of Indian River Inlet, just north of Bethany Beach, in southern Delaware. During my entire childhood, he also served as Delaware City's mayor.

To my grandfather I owe my first taste of politics. I remember riding with him one day in his green pickup when he was flagged down by a resident complaining about a pothole in front of his house. At that time, most of Delaware City's streets were still unpaved. Pop-Pop listened politely and promised he'd take care of it promptly. I was probably only eight or nine at the time, but I never forgot the respect and attention Pop-Pop received as mayor and the power he was able to exercise. Simply by giving the word, he could fill a pothole—more than the United States Congress can get down in an entire year!

And that's where it began, my lifelong connection with politics. As we will see, it grew under my association with Peter Behr, Jerry Brown, Eugene McCarthy, Bill Clinton, Bernie Sanders, and others, but my love for politics started right there, over my grandfather and a pothole, and it continues to this day. I still consider politics "the noblest profession." To me, it's about much more than winning elections or fixing potholes. It's about how we shape and define our democracy, a challenge every citizen should be engaged in at some level. It's about how we fulfill our civic duty. It's about how we build a better America. I've been involved in politics for over six decades. I've seen some of the best of it and some of the worst of it—notably on November 8, 2016, when Donald Trump of all people was elected president of these United States. But I'm still a believer in the political process and the ability of the American people to make the right decisions, over time, and most of the time.

The apple didn't fall far from the tree. Growing up, my father, William H. "Billy" Press Jr., worked in the family gas station. Then, after returning from serving with occupation forces in Japan at the end of World War II, he built and operated his own gas station—Press' Esso Servicenter—on a piece of land his father gave him, across the street from his own former business. Later, Dad also took his turn as Delaware City's mayor.

And he worked his ass off. To this day, I've never seen anyone work a more demanding schedule. Dad opened up his gas station at 8:00 a.m. every morning except Sunday, when he opened at 10:00, following 8:00 Mass. He went home, two blocks away, every day for lunch, then back to work. He joined us for dinner at 4:30 or 5:00, before going back to man the pumps until closing time of 9:00 p.m. The only break he had was on Wednesday evenings after 6:00, when his assistant, Francis Walker, would take over and our family would celebrate his one free evening by climbing into the car for an outing to nearby Saint Georges or Augustine Beach. My mother and father never took a vacation until I was fourteen or fifteen, old enough to oversee the garage myself for a couple of days.

One important gas station rubric: Because we operated a small business in a small town and couldn't afford to alienate anyone, we never talked politics or religion. Never. Nowhere. Neither at work, nor at home. Which, you must admit, is most ironic. I left Delaware City to spend the rest of my life immersed—first, in religion; then, in politics—and built my career talking about religion and politics on national radio and television. I even wrote a book about it: *How the Republicans Stole Religion*. Maybe I've been making up for lost time.

My mother, Isabelle, was also very much part of the family business. She grew up on a farm just outside Delaware City and used to accompany her father, delivering milk door to door, before going to school every morning. She and Dad were married on April 6, 1939. I came along two days short of a year later. In addition to raising us three kids, preparing all meals, and managing the house, Mom also handled the books for the gas station, paid the bills, and sent out monthly statements to regular customers, who were allowed to buy on credit. This, of course, was long before credit cards.

Mom and Dad started out married life in a small apartment on Hamilton Street, where I spent the first couple of years. For $1,100, they then bought a house at 105 Washington Street, big enough to hold two more children: my brother David, born in 1944; and my sister Margie, who came along in 1949. For me, those were very formative years. Next-door neighbor Harry James taught me to swim in the Delaware River at our town beach, the Y, at the foot of Washington Street. His father-in-law, retired river captain Jack "Pee-Pop" Tugend, taught me to fish and introduced me to his favorite fishing spots out the old railroad tracks in the marshes north of town.

Pee-Pop was also a yellow-dog Democrat. He schooled me on the difference between Republicans, who only cared about wealthy people like Delaware's ruling Du Pont family, and Democrats, who stood up for working-class families like those of us who lived in Delaware City. I sat with him for hours in his living room, watching broadcasts of the 1952 Democratic convention—and I cried when Adlai Stevenson conceded the election to Dwight Eisenhower by quoting Abraham Lincoln: "It hurts too much to laugh, but I'm too proud to cry."

We were far from rich, but we never knew we were poor. Mom once told me that Dad never made more than $10,000 a year at the gas station. But we were better off than many of our cousins. And, besides, we had everything we needed. Indeed, the highlight of our days on Washington Street was our first television set, a twelve-inch black-and-white Philco. We were the first family in town to have a TV in our own home, and our living room became, in effect, the local movie theater, with friends and neighbors crowding in on Saturday afternoons to watch cowboy-and-Indian movies.

In 1951, we moved "uptown," four blocks away, to 301 Clinton Street and a big, three-bedroom Victorian, for which my father paid $10,000. In our new home, television remained a big part of our family life. We never missed *Dragnet* with Jack Webb, *The Honeymooners* with Jackie Gleason, *Texaco Star Theatre* with Milton Berle, *Your Show of Shows* with Sid Caesar, *The Red Skelton Show*, or *Amos and Andy*. Before going out on Saturday nights, my mother and father would dance in our living room to the bubbly sounds of Lawrence Welk.

Years later, when I was working at KABC-TV in Los Angeles, I was thrilled to run into Lawrence Welk one day, walking to his car in the ABC parking lot. I stopped and thanked him for all the happiness and good music he'd brought to my parents for so many years.

While living in Los Angeles, I also got to know Milton Berle through his wife, Ruth, who was active in Democratic politics. Milton, who loved talking politics, kind of adopted me. He once took me to a Friars Club luncheon to meet his fellow comedians. On July 4, 1988, he appeared on my radio show to plug his book *B.S. I Love You*. I still have my copy, inscribed: "To my good friend, Bill. A future Prez!" And when I ran for California insurance commissioner, Milton agreed to provide the evening's entertainment—for no fee—at my fund-raising dinner at the Beverly Wilshire Hotel. "I was so offended, walking into the hotel tonight," Milton began. "There were two men on the street corner, speaking Farsi. I couldn't help myself. I went up to them and said, 'Don't you realize where you are? This is the United States of America. Speak Spanish!'"

COUSINS CLUB

Mark Twain once said, "I spent $25 researching my family tree—and then spent $50 trying to cover it up." Not me. I'm proud of my family.

We were all part of the extended Cook Cousins clan, the biggest family in Delaware City, which numbered about a hundred people. My great-uncle John and great-aunt Peggy Cook had three children: Patsy, John, and Michael. John Cook had three sisters: Marie, Katherine, and Zita. Marie Cook, my grandmother, married Pop-Pop Press. They had five kids: John, Sis, Billy (my father), Georgina, and Harry. And they in turn produced fourteen cousins: Uncle Johnny and Aunt Toots Press, parents of Ruthie and Vicky (killed in Vietnam); Aunt Virginia, or Sis, and Uncle Wally Stephens, parents of Bobbie and Billy (my best friend, who died in July 2011); Aunt Georgina, or Georgie, and Uncle Leon, parents of Bootsie and Marie; and Uncle Harry and Aunt Louise Press, with their sons, Gene and Bobby.

My mother and father were the most prolific, with five kids: me, David, Margie, Mary Anne, and Joseph. In a sense, we were three families in one. Until I went away to college, we were only three kids. I was the oldest, born in April 1940. David came along four years later, March 1944, followed by Margie in October 1949. But our tight little family suddenly expanded in 1959, when Mom gave birth to Mary Anne. Two years later, my parents decided she needed a playmate, so Joseph came along. Now we were two distinct families in one.

But our family was still to grow. A year after our mother, Isabelle—or Izzy, who was already fighting a fatal case of breast cancer—died of a blood clot in December 1967, Dad married Dorothy Miller, a close family friend from Delaware City. He and Dot raised Mary and Joe. Then, in 1970, Dot gave birth to Patrick, just seven and a half months before my wife, Carol, and I welcomed our first son, Mark. Even though David, Margie, Mary, Joe, Patrick, and I grew up as three separate families, we've grown closer and closer over the years. Today, it's like we all grew up in the same house at the same time.

It's hard to believe any gang of cousins could be closer than we young Cook cousins. We were all about the same age. We lived in the same small town, within a few blocks of each other. We went to the same Catholic church. We gathered at our grandparents' house every Sunday after Mass. We spent summer weekends together at the beach in Fenwick Island. We even had our own Cousins Club.

Cousin Billy Stephens and I were best buds. He and I explored the entire Delaware City area on our bicycles. We'd ride out Wrangle Hill road to the railroad crossing and wait for hours for a freight train to roar past and flatten the pennies we'd placed on the tracks. Or out to the old Reedy Point drawbridge to watch the big freighters make their way in and out of the canal. Our greatest adventure was biking to the little town of Saint Georges, two miles away, walking our bikes up to the top of the Saint Georges bridge over the Chesapeake and Delaware Canal, then roaring like a bat out of hell down the other side.

Like any fraternity, we cousins even had our own secret sign and official song, both of which were inspired by my father's 1955 hemorrhoids operation. The Cousins Sign consists of linking index finger to thumb and holding up three fingers, as in making the sign for A-OK. Except, in our case, it was meant to signify *asshole*. Not as in accusing anybody of being an asshole, but just as in *asshole fixed*.

The Cousins Song, which some cousins still insist on singing at the top of their lungs at the most embarrassing times and places—like our son David's wedding reception, or at Osteria al Doge restaurant in mid-Manhattan—also celebrates my father's successful hemorrhoid surgery.

There was a little bird, no bigger than a turd,
Sitting on a telegraph pole.
He stuck out his neck, and shit about a peck,
And puckered up his little asshole.
(Chorus)
Asshole, asshole, asshole, asshole . . .
He puckered up his little asshole.

Actually, singing, not usually so vulgar, was a big part of our family life. Several of my aunts and uncles had wonderful voices. Aunt Kass was the top soprano soloist in our church choir. And we cousins never got together without breaking out in song. We sang all the old favorites: "When You

Wore a Tulip," "You Are My Sunshine," "Down by the Riverside," "I've Been Workin' on the Railroad," "Wait till the Sun Shines, Nellie," "Show Me the Way to Go Home," "How Dry I Am," and many others.

David, Margie, and I grew up learning the old songs from our mother while she was giving us our baths at night. At the age of five, I made my musical debut singing "I've Been Workin' on the Railroad" in a Delaware City minstrel show. (Yes, there was blackface, but not on me. More on that in a bit.) The following year, I sang a duet with cousin Sally Jordan.

More music. I was only eleven or twelve when Mom and Dad signed me up for accordion lessons; once a week, I took the local bus to Wilmington, then a city bus to Larry Laravella's home studio. He taught classic accordion, but all my mother wanted me to learn were her favorites, like "Roll Out the Barrel." In Delaware City grade school, I sang in the chorus of two Gilbert and Sullivan operettas: *HMS Pinafore* and *The Mikado*. I also sang the male lead in *Come Out Swinging*, our senior musical at Salesianum High School. Mercifully, that was the end of my musical career.

During the summer months, our family life in Delaware City moved one hundred miles south—to Fenwick Island. At that time, Fenwick straddled the Delaware-Maryland state line, half on one side, half on the other. Today, only Fenwick Island, Delaware, remains. Everything south of the state line is now part of an expanded Ocean City, Maryland.

In the 1950s, Fenwick was but a collection of small, rustic summer cottages built right on the beach, either on top of the dunes or right in front of them. Among them, three Cook cousin cottages: Pop-Pop and Grandmom Press, in Delaware; our own family's cottage, about one hundred yards south, in Maryland; and cousin Eddie Jordan's, next door. And we were all squatters. Nobody knew or cared who owned the land our cottages were built on.

When I say *rustic*, by the way, I mean really roughing it. We had no electricity, no running water, and no indoor plumbing. We used kerosene lamps, dug a well for drinking water, and built an outhouse behind each cottage. After dinner every night, we'd dig a hole in the dunes behind our cottage to bury the day's garbage.

For my first few years, we spent almost the entire summer in Fenwick, while my father commuted north for work. And if life was rough, we never knew it. For us, life was paradise. Our house sat right on the beautiful ocean beach. The Atlantic was right out our front door. For weeks at a time, we seldom wore anything but a bathing suit. The only time we put on clothes or shoes was on Sunday morning, before driving ten miles to Mass at Our Lady Star of the Sea Catholic Church in what was then the small hamlet of Ocean City. After Mass, each of us kids was given twenty-five cents to spend playing games or buying candy on the boardwalk. And, if we were really lucky, we were treated to Thrasher's french fries.

The rest of the time at Fenwick, we were in the ocean. All day long. We learned to bodysurf. We lay in the sun. We went fishing with our father. We went crabbing or clamming at favorite surefire spots. We took long walks on the beach, collecting seashells. We built bonfires on the beach at night, roasted hot dogs, toasted marshmallows. And sang, sang, sang.

Best of all, we ate what we caught. Fish fresh from the surf. Crabs from a nearby creek. Clams from an estuary behind Bethany Beach. Fresh corn, tomatoes, and peaches from the neighboring, plentiful farms of lower Delaware. Without knowing it, we were the first of the locavores.

Two big events changed Fenwick Island forever. The first, in the late '50s, was an edict from the State of Maryland requiring all Fenwick residents to acquire titles to their land by purchasing the properties their cottages were built on from the rightful owners, which state surveyors and title officials had somehow dutifully identified. For two oceanfront lots, our cottage, and that of cousin Eddie Jordan next door, we paid $1,400.

At about the same time, electricity and indoor plumbing arrived, making Fenwick more comfortable but much less colorful. Goodbye, kerosene lanterns and outhouses. Hello, electric lights, flush toilets, and showers. Somehow, it wasn't as much fun.

The second big event was a nor'easter in 1962 that ravaged the Eastern Seaboard. In Fenwick, the entire oceanfront row of cottages—including the three belonging to our family—were all swept out to sea. We lost our cottage. We lost our property. And we lost the fun experience of living on the beach at Fenwick forever. Because so much of the beach was lost, it was impossible for us to rebuild.

For a few years, our family decamped to a trailer (not fancy enough to be called a mobile home) in a Delaware City residents' trailer park next to the Fenwick Island lighthouse. Later, my father and his second wife, Dorothy, bought a bay-front home in Fenwick Island, Delaware, at 1407 Bora Bora Street, which became his retirement home and where he lived until he died in 2006.

My mother's side of the family, though smaller, was equally close. Her mother, Bessie K. Bendler, or Mom-Mom, was a real character, one of my favorite people, and a wonderful cook. I can still taste her vegetable soup, lemon butter, chicken and dumplings, and chocolate fudge.

My mother was one of three Bendler children: Aunt Marty, married to Uncle Mac McCoy, lived in Smyrna with their two sons: cousins Ronnie and Burris, or Bo. Cousin Ronnie McCoy is still a football legend at the University of Delaware. Uncle George, or GI, married Aunt Ruth and moved his family to Salisbury, Maryland, where they had four children: cousins Randy, Marie, Lisa, and Jimmy. I never met my grandfather Bendler, the black sheep of the family. He ran off with another woman, leaving my grandmother with three small children to raise as a single mom. And while serving as postmaster of Delaware City, he was caught embezzling money and served time in federal prison.

Only eleven years older, my uncle GI was like a big brother to me. On July 19, 1951, he took me to my very first concert, a string quartet, at the University of Delaware's Mitchell Hall. He taught me how to build a duck blind, which we did in Dragon Run at the beginning of every season—and took me duck hunting and rabbit hunting. Later, he taught me to play golf at Green Hill Country Club in Salisbury, Maryland.

Except for Mom-Mom Bendler, I must admit that our food experience growing up in Delaware City, living on a very limited budget, was not exactly haute cuisine. We ate a lot of boiled cabbage and hamburger gravy. My favorite snack was a slice of buttered white bread (was there any other kind of bread?) covered with sugar. Or a slice of white bread buried in ketchup. Mom often made hamburger gravy, served on toast. Our favorite dessert was Mom's cinnamon "war cake" (no eggs, milk, or butter). A favored seasonal treat was wild duck, shot by my father. We learned to chew our duck carefully, because of bird shot still in the meat. And nothing was more exciting than when one of the locals would show up with a snapping turtle caught in nearby Dragon's Run—out of which Mom made a great snapper soup.

We ate a lot of two other favorites, locally caught or captured. Surrounded by marshland, Delaware City's specialty was muskrat. In fact, my uncle Johnny made his living trapping muskrat. The exterior walls of his garage were lined with muskrat pelts, drying in the sun, which he later sold to clothiers to make popular muskrat coats. The meat he sold to locals for food. Fried muskrat was a big favorite in our home. We ate it often. It's still a delicacy in Delaware City and on the Eastern Shore of Maryland, where there's an annual muskrat festival.

As mentioned, during the summer months at Fenwick Island, the big treat was blue crabs. Our family would drive to our favorite crabbing spot, a bridge over a nearby creek, where we could easily catch a bushel of crabs in a couple of hours. Until the day he died, my father made the best steamed crabs west of the Mississippi, and my mother made the best crab cakes—a tradition continued after her death by our stepmother, Dot.

For us kids, the biggest event of the year came at Christmastime, when Mom-Mom Bendler would take us on the train—the slow, slow local train—from Wilmington to Philadelphia to see the Christmas decorations at Wanamaker's (meet at the Eagle if you get lost!), do our Christmas shopping, and have lunch at the famous Bookbinder's. She even insisted we have a touch of sherry in our turtle soup, just like grown-ups.

Mom-Mom was also famously outspoken. One day I came home from Salesianum, my Catholic boys' high school in Wilmington, to find Mom-Mom in our kitchen. Somehow we got around to talking about religion. She reminded me that she was a Presbyterian, but then assured me, "But I don't have anything against Catholics. They don't know any better."

Mom-Mom Bendler intrigued us kids for another reason, too. She worked as a nurse's aide at Fort DuPont, a stone's throw across the canal from Delaware City proper, where, among other things, she cooked and did laundry for German prisoners of war. I remember her telling us about those young German soldiers and how friendly they were, and showing us paintings they'd given her.

The military, in fact, was very much a part of our young lives in Delaware City. As mentioned above, most of the men in our family served in the army. Some, starting with my grandfather Press, first came to Delaware City as army recruits assigned to Fort DuPont. Others, like my father and several uncles, were drafted in World War II. Uncle Leon was career army. My father served with postwar occupation forces in Japan.

The war also made its mark on Fenwick Island, where my parents, grandparents, and several cousins had summer cottages. Oceanfront cottages were issued blackout shades for all windows facing the ocean. Army units patrolled the beach. The National Guard manned antiaircraft towers just north of Bethany Beach and did occasional target practice out over the ocean.

During these days, the beach was home to women and children only. All the men were off to war. I have vague memories of marching up and down the beach as a five-year-old with other kids and banging on pots and pans when word came that the war was over, gathering with other families around a big bonfire on the beach that night to celebrate.

Later, during the Cold War, we were again on military alert in Delaware City. As a teenager, I volunteered as a plane spotter. From a National Guard tower built on the river at the end of town, which we manned 24-7, we'd calculate the size, description, and direction of every aircraft passing overhead, enter that information in the daily log, and phone it in to civil defense headquarters. I'm not sure what we accomplished, but at the time, we believed we were playing a key role in keeping our country safe.

GROWING UP CATHOLIC

If family was our primary focus growing up in Delaware City, church was a close number two. Our lives centered around events at Saint Paul's Catholic Church: baptism, First Communion, confession every Saturday afternoon, Mass every Sunday morning, Benediction on Sunday evenings, novenas, feast days, and funerals. For us boys, that meant becoming altar boys as soon as we were old enough to memorize and mumble the Latin responses. Many were the mornings I rolled out of bed, walked the two blocks to Saint Paul's, and donned cassock and surplice to serve the 7:00 a.m. Mass.

For most of my childhood, our parish priest was Reverend Lawrence Ward, a member of the order of Oblates of Saint Francis de Sales. Father Ward was a jovial, friendly soul. He loved socializing with parishioners and taking us altar boys to major-league baseball games in Philadelphia. But he was also a strict conservative on social issues. I remember his trumpeting from the pulpit that, before marriage, young women should never let any man get close "by touch or by sex" (which made me run home to the encyclopedia to find out what *sex* meant).

He also insisted that, as Catholics, we should not socialize with non-Catholics. We weren't even supposed to talk to them. Which might have worked in Philadelphia, where he grew up, but was, of course, difficult in a small town of 1,200, of whom maybe only 300 were Catholic, and where there were Methodist, Episcopal, Presbyterian, and Baptist churches within two blocks of Saint Paul's.

If difficult for others, it was impossible for our family. Because while we kids were at Mass with our father, our mother—then still a Protestant; she later converted to Catholicism—was home preparing breakfast for us. We weren't allowed to talk to her when we got home?

So, on this issue, as on several others, I learned at an early age the most important lesson I ever learned about organized religion: listen to and respect what church leaders say, but don't assume they always get it right—and don't necessarily obey everything they say. God gave us the gift of reason, and he intends for us to use it, not just swallow whole everything we're told—not even by priests, bishops, or the pope himself—without thinking it through and asking tough questions. On the issue of birth control, for example, the male-dominant Catholic officialdom is simply dead wrong. Most Catholics realize that and simply ignore the Vatican on that issue. Same with demanding celibacy for priests and refusing to accept women priests. Someday soon, all that will change.

And, of course, that same healthy skepticism about dictates from above is not limited to the church. For me, it applies to all authority figures, especially politicians. Yes, even the president. We listen to what they have to say, but we don't have to blindly follow. Because, as often as not, they're just plain wrong. I think a good rule to follow is: Don't take anything as the Bible. Question everything and everyone. The more universal or popular an opinion is, the more you should suspect it, the more questions you should ask.

As welcome as I was at Saint Paul's as an altar boy, that changed dramatically years later, once I popped up as a liberal commentator on national television, taking the exact opposite positions on contraception, abortion, or same-sex marriage than those dictated by the church—as I discovered when cousins Bootsie and Marie invited me to give the eulogy for their mother, my favorite aunt, Georgie.

The night before the service, Marie called me in tears. Saint Paul's rector, Father Phil Siry, had been out of town when she made the arrangements. When he saw my name on the program upon his return, he asked Marie, "Is this the same Bill Press I see on television?" Enemy of the Vatican thus confirmed, he laid down the law: "That man will never be allowed to speak in my church!"

No worries, I assured Marie. Of course, Carol and I would still attend the service, even if I wasn't allowed to speak. Besides, it was all about Aunt Georgie, not me.

Not everybody accepted the news so calmly. When we arrived at Spicer's funeral home the next morning for Aunt Georgie's wake, my cousins were up in arms. Cousin Billy Stephens had already personally called Bishop Saltarelli in Wilmington and warned him he had a revolt on his hands in Delaware City. Billy suggested family members stage some kind of protest. Again, I urged them to calm down and think about Aunt Georgie and her family, not me.

From the funeral home, we walked a block through the snow to Saint Paul's. We hadn't been there long when we became aware of some commotion outside. After another ten minutes or so, the lay deacon showed up to announce that Father Siry had slipped, fallen on the ice, and broken his leg on his way into church—and had just been taken away in an ambulance. A substitute priest had been summoned from Wilmington, he told us; but it would take an hour for him to get there. He asked us to wait patiently for the service to start, then walked over to my pew, and with a big smile leaned over and whispered, "Looks like you'll be giving that eulogy, after all."

There was little surprise and no doubt in the minds of my cousins: God had punished Father Siry for messing with Aunt Georgie. Cousin Billy even received a letter of apology from Bishop Saltarelli. Later, I learned that Father Siry never did return to Saint Paul's. When he got out of the hospital, he resigned as parish priest and moved in with his housekeeper, with whom he'd apparently been having an affair for years.

It was also at Saint Paul's that I met an extraordinary woman who had a profound influence on my life. Rosalie Reybold was the heart and soul of Saint Paul's. She lived nearby, with her husband, Bill, and children, Billy, Patty, and Walter, in one of the biggest and most beautiful homes in Delaware City. The classic church lady, she attended daily Mass, scrubbed floors, prepared the altar, arranged flowers, and looked out over each and every member of the congregation. She took particular interest in young people of the parish, often inviting us over to her home for cookies and iced tea.

And she took special care of me. One Saturday, Rosalie took me on the bus to nearby Wilmington and helped me sign up for my very first library card—at the Wilmington Public Library on Rodney Square.

Getting that library card was one of the most important events in my life. It introduced me to a whole wide world I might never have discovered otherwise, and, as Philip Roth wrote about his own similar experience at the Newark, New Jersey, public library, it helped "to enlarge the sense of where I lived." It also made me an insatiable reader and awakened in me a love of books that is still my great passion today. Thank you, Rosalie.

Thanks to my mother, too. On weekends, she loved going out to auctions and estate sales with her friends. And, recognizing my nascent love for books, she'd often bring back for me a big box of used books, for which she'd paid twenty-five cents and which I would excitedly sort through, hoping to find at least one that I wanted to keep and read.

And then there was the Delaware City Volunteer Fire Department.

For any boy growing up in Delaware City in the 1950s, there was only one goal in life: reaching his sixteenth birthday so he could join the fire company. At the old Delaware City School, we grade school kids would watch in envy whenever the fire siren blew and high school boys bolted out the door to the firehouse. We couldn't wait to join them. Like all my buddies, I joined at sixteen and put in two excitement-filled years before I went away to college.

Unfortunately, at the time, the fire company was made up of only white men. No blacks or women were allowed. Fortunately, that's now changed, and all for the better.

Every evening, we young bucks loved just hanging out at the firehouse, listening to old-timers tell stories about big fires they'd fought in the past, reliving every minute of every last fire call, laughing at the same old dirty jokes—and waiting, waiting, waiting for the phone to ring. I remember feeling guilty about wanting somebody's house or car to catch fire so we could spring into action. But of course, I counseled myself, we only wanted fires with no loss of life or serious property damage, and impacting no friends or family.

Firefighters enjoyed their own brand of humor. Old-timers Harry Bright and Jukie Pasquino, for example, used to brag, "We haven't lost a foundation yet!" This was also the time the big Tidewater refinery was being built two miles north of town. Thus instructions were duly given: "If a call comes in for a fire at the refinery, roll up Clinton to the traffic light at Fifth Street—and turn south [away from the refinery]!"

Nighttime fires were especially exciting. We lived at Third and Clinton Streets, two blocks from the firehouse. Every night before going to bed, I carefully laid out jeans, shirt, and work shoes alongside my bed so I could jump into them just in case the siren went off in the middle of the night. Then I'd run out to the street corner. As the fire truck came up Clinton Street, the driver would slow down just enough for anyone waiting to leap onto the back running board and then race off to the scene of the fire, with those of us on the back of the truck holding on for dear life, usually arguing about whose turn it was to man the nozzle once we got there. That position, while clearly the most dangerous, was also considered an honor: to be first in line, closest to the flames, manning the nozzle.

As with everything else in Delaware City, firefighting was a family affair. My grandfather and father were both volunteer firefighters. And my family often followed the fire trucks to see what was happening. At one middle-of-the night call, I jumped on the truck while my father followed in our car accompanied by my sister Margie, then nine or ten years old. Mom stayed home, sitting on the porch, waiting for us to return. A couple of hours later, she was surprised to see the fire truck, returning from the fire, stop in front of our house. She was even more surprised to see little sister Margie, still in her nightgown, climb out of the truck. Dad's car had broken down, so firefighters gave Margie a ride home.

Speaking of a family affair, one Saturday around noon, my father and I were working at the gas station when the siren went off. Usually, I couldn't answer calls on the weekend because I was needed at the garage. But this time, the siren kept blowing and blowing. Clearly, this was a serious call. So, instead of going to lunch, I convinced Dad to go to the firehouse, where our dispatcher, Pop Cavalier, told us there was a big house fire over by the canal. They badly needed one more truck, he informed us, and couldn't find a driver.

Immediately, Team Press swung into action. Dad drove; I rode on the back. Arriving at the scene, we were ordered to hook up to a hydrant. Dad operated the truck while I unloaded the hose, grabbed the nozzle, and joined the fight. For years, we bragged about how Team Press had saved the day!

Another call did not have such a happy ending. One night, we were summoned to the fire hall in nearby New Castle to cover while their volunteers fought a hellish fire at a local factory. We'd sat around the fire hall for a couple of hours when a few New Castle firefighters returned, carrying the hat, fire coat, and boots of one of their young members. He'd been killed when a barrel of chemicals exploded as he entered the burning building. He was only sixteen. I fought back tears, realizing that kid could easily have been me, and thinking about my parents getting the grim news.

One Christmas, Mom and Dad gave me a book called *The Romance of Firefighting*. But that tragic incident made me realize that, yes, there is a "romance" to firefighting. But there's a real danger to it, too.

Firefighters, both professional and volunteer, men and women, are among our most outstanding public servants, putting their lives on the line every day to keep our communities safe and protect their fellow citizens. I have great admiration for them, and we all owe them a debt of gratitude.

My decision to enter the seminary and study for the priesthood after graduating from high school—more on that in a bit—meant not only going away to college but leaving Delaware City for good. So, before leaving town, my fellow firefighters surprised me by making me an honorary member of Delaware City Fire Company. It's one of the greatest honors of my life—and one I cherish to this day. In 2017, the Delaware City Fire Company celebrated its 130th anniversary.

Looking back, there's one other event during my high school years that had a profound impact on me, even if I wasn't aware of it at the time: construction of the mammoth Tidewater oil refinery, just north of town. Actually, it wasn't the construction of the refinery that made a difference. It was the destruction of the beautiful countryside where the refinery now stands.

At the time, Delaware City was surrounded by unspoiled marshland, cornfields, and peach orchards. It was the classic bucolic setting, with our little town nestled in on the banks of the river. And we loved it. We lived off the bounty of the local farms. We hiked, fished, trapped, hunted ducks in the marshes, and swam in the Delaware.

Then came rumors that King's College, a small evangelical school located two miles out of town, had been sold to Tidewater Oil Company, which planned to build on that property and surrounding farmland the largest refinery on the East Coast. At first, reaction was mixed. We were sorry to see the farmland disappear, but we were assured that the new refinery would create hundreds of jobs, we'd all get rich, and Tidewater would put Delaware City on the map.

None of that turned out to be true. The refinery, which Tidewater immediately dubbed "the world's most fabulous refinery," began operations in 1957. Yes, some locals got jobs there, including two of my brothers, David and Joseph, and my brother-in-law Herb Netsch. But more jobs initially went to experienced workers who moved into the area from out of state. Nobody got rich out of the deal, except maybe a couple of farmers who'd sold their land. And Delaware City today is no bigger or wealthier than it was before the refinery was built.

And the price paid was high: the loss of our town beach, replaced by Tidewater's oil tanker pier; loss of access to the great marshes north of town; and loss of the bountiful croplands and orchards. All replaced by a giant refinery and acres of storage tanks, surrounded by several satellite chemical companies located nearby for easy access to refinery by-products. Not to mention the foul smell of rotten eggs whenever the wind is blowing in the wrong direction, several major fires, and occasional accidental releases of toxic chemicals.

Commuting to high school in Wilmington every day, I watched them knock down the buildings of King's College, level the hills, mow down the orchards, fill in the marsh, and bulldoze the cornfields. In its place rose a virtual ugly city of industrial towers, smokestacks, holding tanks, pipelines, and service roads, all enclosed by chain-link fence. It's the image that popped into my head the first time I read Gerard Manley Hopkins's magnificent lament, "God's Grandeur."

> *Generations have trod, have trod, have trod;*
> *And all is seared with trade; bleared, smeared with toil;*
> *And wears man's smudge and shares man's smell.*

Later, after I had relocated to California and become active in environmental politics, I knew where my conservation ethic was born: in Delaware

City, watching God's creation destroyed to build a man-made monster. In those days, nobody ever talked *conservation* or *environment*, but we loved the land that sustained us. I soon came to realize that our corner of paradise had been sacrificed to corporate greed and gain, with little local benefit.

That experience planted deeply in me a powerful lesson: We have a moral obligation to care for and protect our planet. As God tells us in the book of Genesis, we are meant to be wise stewards of the land. And, as parents, part of our responsibility is, in the great tradition of the Native Americans who came before us, to enjoy our brief time on this land—but to leave it cleaner and healthier for our children and grandchildren. Everybody who lives on this fragile planet Earth should be an environmentalist. Indeed, we have no choice. As Adlai Stevenson said in 1964, when he was U.S. ambassador to the United Nations, "We travel together, passengers on a little spaceship, dependent upon its vulnerable reserves of air and soil, all committed for our safety to its security and peace; preserved from annihilation only by the care, the work, and, I will say, the love we give our fragile craft." I've never understood why Democrats and Republicans can't all agree on that.

SOUTHERN TOWN

Yes, Delaware City was a great place to grow up. What I didn't realize until much later was that Delaware City was a great place to grow up—as long as you were white. Not for African Americans. Even though we didn't live in the Deep South, Delaware was still a border state, and Delaware City was a segregated town. There were black churches and white churches, black neighborhoods and white neighborhoods, black markets and white markets. There was even a separate black section of town, across the canal, called Polktown. We white kids, grades 1–12, walked a couple of blocks to Delaware City School. Black kids walked a mile out of town to the "colored" school. We didn't call them *blacks* or *coloreds* then, of course. Like everybody else in the South or border states, we routinely and thoughtlessly used the N-word.

Cousin Billy Stephens once told me, though I was never able to confirm it, that Delaware City even had its own chapter of the KKK, led by two local businessmen, Harry Kirk, who was Grand Wizard, and his brother, Ray, both of whom we knew well. I once asked Aunt Georgie if the KKK were active in Delaware City. She told me she never saw them in action but remembered as a little girl being warned that "the Klan was on the march," whereupon she and her siblings would huddle together in a bedroom, afraid the Klan would burst into their house.

In their book about Fort Delaware, *Unlikely Allies*, Bruce Mowday and Dale Fetzer report that Delaware City was also the beginning of a reverse-direction Underground Railroad that took Southern sympathizers to Dixie to join the Confederate army.

It seems strange, looking back, not only to have experienced segregation but to have practiced it. Which we did, as kids, I'm ashamed to say, without even thinking about it. Why? Because that's just the way things were. That's how we were brought up. That's what we accepted.

One of the big events of the year, for example, was the annual minstrel show, performed by an all-white cast before an all-white audience. My father and several of my uncles sang in the chorus, all in blackface. Aunt Kass was the star of the show. Aunt Louise and Aunt Toots also sang solo numbers. As I noted above, I made my stage debut in a minstrel as a five-year-old, singing "I've Been Workin' on the Railroad" (thankfully not in blackface). And—talk about a sign of the times—the minstrel was a fund-raiser for our parish, Saint Paul's Catholic Church! Further evidence that, at the time, nobody thought of the minstrel show as a racist statement. But of course it was.

I'm also proud that, in their own way, my parents dared to buck the prevailing culture. My father welcomed "colored" customers at the station, hired several black employees, and extended credit to black customers, as well as white. He didn't preach about it, he didn't brag about it—he just did it. And his example made a powerful and lasting impression on me. I'll never forget how he'd make a point of inviting his black employees, as well as Bootie Carter, a black friend and customer, to the annual Christmas party at our home on Clinton Street. Bootie would show up, but, despite Dad's trying to talk him out of it, Bootie would always insist on coming in the back door. Because, he said, he didn't want to get my father in any trouble with our neighbors.

There was one other time that Dad bucked the segregationist trend. As one of the founders of the Delaware City Lions Club, he convinced members to move their weekly meetings from the Recreation Club, which banned black customers, to the Pea Patch Inn downtown—where the club soon became embroiled over whether or not to evict a white member who had adopted two black children.

Dad's response was to challenge the Lions Club by nominating Jim Mitchell, the head of the local NAACP, as the club's first African American member. Of course, that caused an even bigger uproar and prompted a long, bitter debate—which Dad ultimately lost. But he'd made his point, and I'm still proud of him for fighting the good fight.

It wasn't until high school that I fully understood what a segregated environment I was living in and how wrong it was. Following *Brown v. Board of Education* in 1954, and thanks to the courage of Principal Father Thomas Lawless, Salesianum became the first high school in Delaware, public or private, to accept African Americans as students. Yet in my freshman year, there were only three black students at Sallies. And all three of them commuted to Wilmington an hour on the train every day from Baltimore—because that was the closest integrated school they could get into.

Another life lesson learned the hard way: Discrimination in any form is just plain wrong. I still can't believe I once routinely used the N-word, called gays queers and faggots, and believed women inferior to men. Yes, I can hide behind the excuse that "that's just the way things were back then" and "I was never taught any differently," but I still feel guilty—and thus strive even harder to be open and tolerant today. In fact, because of my background, I'm even more intolerant of those who discriminate, especially those hypocrites who try to hide behind religion or politics to justify their prejudice against people of color, women, LGBTQ Americans, Muslims, or Jews.

There's no excuse for treating any group of people differently or denying them their full and equal rights under the Constitution. It is fundamentally un-American. Nor is there anything in the Bible to justify discrimination. So-called Christians used to cite the Bible to defend slavery, just as so-called Christians today cite the Bible to defend discrimination against gays. They're woefully ignorant, or they haven't read the New Testament. Either way, they're not true Christians—and they're not true Americans.

SALESIANUM

Ironically, my first break out of the small world of Delaware City came thanks to football, a sport I have never played, followed, or even liked. In the sacristy one morning after Mass, when I was in seventh grade, Father Ward showed me headlines in the morning paper about Salesianum High School's football championship. He asked if I might be interested in attending a big school like that, with such a winning football team.

Of course, I was too nervous to say anything but yes. I talked to my parents about it. They talked to Father Ward. He talked to his fellow Oblates of Saint Francis de Sales who taught at Salesianum. And the following September, I entered eighth grade at Sallies as one of twenty "gremlins," the designation then given to seventh and eighth graders.

I was the first boy from Delaware City to go to what everybody called *Sallies*. It was a big deal. But it was also a big sacrifice for my parents. Students had to wear a jacket and tie every day, which represented a big, new clothing bill. I had to commute fifteen miles to Wilmington, which meant bus or carpool money, on top of money for lunch and school books. And tuition in 1953 was eighty dollars per year, which my parents paid in four installments. Mom and Dad made that sacrifice because they wanted me to have the best possible education. Later, my brothers, David, Joseph, and Patrick, all attended Sallies.

Salesianum is a great school. Still today, I value my time there. It changed my life and shaped my life, more than any other experience before or since. All for the better. At Salesianum, for starters, I joined the staff of the school newspaper, proudly saw my first byline in print, wrote my first column, and became the paper's editor. I've been writing and publishing ever since. At Salesianum, I ran for student council and in my senior year was elected president. I've been involved in politics ever since. Perhaps most important, at Salesianum I joined the debate team, learned to see and understand both sides of every issue, and was trained to make my arguments succinctly, clearly, and convincingly. And I've since made a career of debating the issues on radio and television. Even though I didn't realize it at the time (who could?), the arc of my career in politics and journalism was set there. In a sense, I've never left Sallies.

Along the way, I made great friends at Salesianum, some of whom I'm still in touch with over fifty years later: Joe Stiller, Bill Taylor, Ted Burke, Pete Feeney, Dennis Reardon, Jack Hurley, Joe Mealey, and Stan Kisielewski, among others.

My love for Sallies remains strong, even though I agree with little of what we were taught there about Catholic morality. Sex, we were incessantly told, was acceptable only between man and wife—never before marriage, and certainly never, never, never between a same-sex couple. And even inside marriage, sex was okay only for the purpose of procreation—never for pleasure. None of which any of us believed or practiced. The obsession with sex even extended to school dances, where Father James Donovan warned us about slow dances, which he called "dry fornication."

As for masturbation: Don't even think about it. You'll go blind or grow hair on the palms of your hands, or run out of semen and never be able to have children. Wrong on all counts, Father!

Abortion, of course, was the ultimate wrong. Never acceptable under any circumstances or for any reason. And pornography was the evil influence that led to all the above. I'm embarrassed to admit that I joined a group of student council leaders from Sallies who met with the owner of the Warner Theatre in 1956 to protest his plans to screen the movie *Baby Doll*, a dark comedy written by Tennessee Williams, and threaten him with a Catholic boycott if he didn't cancel the film. It was my only involvement with the Catholic Legion of Decency, and I still regret it.

Sallies also had a great school spirit, which I enjoyed, even though I did not play sports in high school. Statewide, we were number one in basketball and football. Wildly enthusiastic rallies were held before each game. First at the old school at Eighth and West Street, and later, at the new school at Eighteenth and Broom, where we moved during Easter break of my junior year, we were all proud to be boys from Sallies, as reflected in our school fight song:

We're the boys from Eighth and West,
Not afraid to face the best,
We're the boys with the grim determination.
Oh, they say we are not tough,
That's because we are not rough,
But we're out for your complete extermination!

Salesianum was the first high school in America founded by the Oblates of Saint Francis de Sales, and we had a very colorful and talented faculty made up of Oblate priests, brothers, scholastics, and seminarians. Our principal, Father Thomas A. Lawless, all of five feet tall and already a legend for his bold anti-segregation stand, stalked the halls, smoking his pipe. His deputy, equally diminutive redhead Father Francis D. Dougherty, ran the school with an iron fist. Others who left a lasting impression on me: Father J. V. O'Neill, football coach; Father John Birkenheuer, basketball coach and religion teacher; Father Robert D. Kenney, baseball coach and math teacher; social studies teacher Father Thomas L. McNamara; English teacher Father James B. Donovan; and religion teacher Joseph A. Connolly.

Of all the Oblates, Father Joe Connolly became my best friend. We joked around a lot. He called me *Kingfish*, after the character in *Amos and Andy*. We played golf together. We often went to New Jersey for dinner with his sister and her family. He became such a regular visitor to Delaware City that the entire Cook cousin clan adopted him as our chaplain. He even converted my grandfather from basically no religion and baptized him a Catholic on his deathbed.

A proud Democrat, Father Connolly also loved politics. And in his role as faculty adviser to the school newspaper, where I served as editor, he introduced me to my first big-name Democrats. The paper was printed by the McClafferty Printing Company, whose owner, Bill McClafferty, was Democratic chairman of Wilmington. In my junior year, McClafferty set up an interview for me with the Democratic state chair of Delaware, Garrett Lyons. And in my senior year, he arranged an exclusive interview with a young senator from Massachusetts, John F. Kennedy.

I was a huge JFK fan, having watched him bow out of the contest for the vice presidential nomination at the 1956 convention with charm and grace. By showing such class at the convention, Kennedy was already a national star and considered a front-runner for the presidential nomination in 1960. He came to Wilmington to keynote the annual Jefferson-Jackson Dinner. Classmate Peter Feeney and I were waiting for him at Penn Station.

When Kennedy's train pulled into the station, we looked up and down the platform with no sign of the entourage we expected surrounding a national politician. Then I noticed a tall, thin man, toting a brown, leather briefcase step out of one of the forward cars and start walking, all by himself, down the platform. It was JFK. McClafferty introduced Father Connolly and the two of us, and Kennedy very generously and politely welcomed our questions.

I still have my notes for that interview, where I had prepared two questions. First: What advice did he have for young people like us, who wanted to get involved in politics but didn't know how to get started? Find a candidate you like, Kennedy advised, and volunteer for his political campaign. Get involved, gain some experience, meet some people, see whether you like it—and who knows what might happen. Good advice, which I was to follow several years later in San Francisco.

I also asked Kennedy how he, a busy U.S. senator, could find the time to write a book like his 1957 Pulitzer Prize–winning *Profiles in Courage*. Kennedy noted that while recuperating from back surgery, he ended up with a lot of time on his hands and devoted that time to putting his book together. Most presidential historians now agree that while Kennedy may have devoted a lot of attention to the book during that time, the book was largely written by speechwriter Ted Sorenson—in part because JFK's back injuries were more serious than anyone ever knew.

Frankly, I don't care who actually wrote the book. That interview with John F. Kennedy remains one of the highlights of my life. And, like Bill Clinton's famous 1963 handshake with JFK in the Rose Garden, it helped catapult me into a life in politics—even though the seeds of my political activity lay dormant until ten years later, after my seminary years, when I arrived in San Francisco.

As mentioned above, my experience on the Salesianum debate team also helped shape my career path. I loved the opportunity to debate the issues of the day, from the death penalty to the Cold War. One favorite challenge in those days was the classic debate question: "Better Red than Dead, or Dead than Red?" And it was out of that debate experience that I learned an important skill.

Because, depending on the luck of the draw, we could be asked to debate either side of an issue, I learned to anticipate what objections my opponent would make to my arguments—and be prepared to demolish them. Thus prepared, I never went into a debate without knowing the con side as well as the pro side. It was a valuable lesson that came in handy later on *Crossfire*.

Upon graduating from Salesianum, I had several great choices in front of me, having been accepted for admission as a freshman at Boston College, La Salle College, Notre Dame, and Georgetown University. But by that time, after months of inner turmoil, I had decided on a different path.

On the night I graduated from high school, Mom and Dad threw a party for me at our home in Delaware City. After everybody had had a couple of drinks, I stood up on a chair in our dining room and announced to family and friends what only my parents knew until then: that I would not be going to college that fall. Instead, I'd be joining the Oblates of Saint Francis de Sales in order to study for the priesthood.

And so I closed the door on Delaware City and opened the door to the rest of my life. While I wasn't yet a full-fledged progressive, there were already stirrings of the true progressive inside me ready to burst forth—but only after going underground for the next ten years.

2

JOINING GOD'S ARMY

It seems I've been asked a million times why I decided to join the seminary—and why I decided to leave. As if there's an easy answer. There's not. In fact, I'm still not sure I know the answer to either question myself. Both decisions were complicated. And neither was as pure or high-minded as one might expect.

One thing for sure: My decision to study for the priesthood was not because God spoke to me and said, "I want you to become a priest." Nor was it because I felt so religious or loyal to the Catholic Church. And it was certainly not because that's what my mother wanted me to do. Indeed, knowing my mother was so eager for me to join the seminary almost made me change my mind.

But there's no doubt about this: Of all other possibilities, the reason I joined the order of the Oblates of Saint Francis de Sales is because they were the only priests I knew, both from my home parish and from high school.

On the broader question, as near as I can figure it out, I decided to study for the priesthood because I wanted to do some kind of public service as lawyer, doctor, or priest. Of those three options, why a priest? One reason was because we didn't have enough money for me to go to law school or medical school. Another was because the priests I knew seemed to have a pretty good life; they didn't work that hard, they played a lot of golf, they had all their economic needs taken care of—and, most of all, they were admired, looked up to, even worshiped as minor celebrities. I decided to study for the priesthood, in other words, for a lot of the same reasons other people decide to go into politics. And for the same reasons a lot of former priests and nuns, such as the late congressman Robert Drinan, end up in politics.

When I tell people I spent ten years studying for the priesthood—indeed, when I think of it myself—it seems like an eternity. But those ten years actually flew by. Both because they were times of such personal growth and because they encapsulated such vastly different and colorful experiences: two years of religious training at the Oblate novitiate in Childs, Maryland; two years of teaching at Father Judge High School in Philadelphia; three years of college at Niagara University in upstate New York; summers as a camp counselor at Camp Brisson in North East, Maryland; two years of graduate school at the University of Fribourg, Switzerland; and one year of "sabbatical" while teaching at what was then Sacred Heart High School in San Francisco.

So, yes, the seminary took a big slice out of my life. But I have no regrets, because those ten years in themselves constituted an invaluable educational experience. I came out of them older, wiser, surer of what direction I wanted to take in my life, with far greater opportunities than I would ever have known otherwise, and better prepared to take advantage of them.

Not only that, which is itself a minor miracle, I left the seminary even more of a progressive than when I entered—despite the concerted efforts of some to make me a doctrinaire conservative Catholic.

The principal work of the Oblates of Saint Francis de Sales, the order I joined, is teaching high school. Founded in Troyes, France, in 1875 by Father Louis Brisson, recognized by Pope Benedict XVI in September 2012 as "Blessed" Louis Brisson and now a candidate for sainthood, Oblates today are active in Europe, Africa, and the United States, mainly in the northeastern and midwestern states.

My first stop on the Oblate train was a beautiful, idyllic, working farm on Soyhieres Hill in Childs, Maryland, outside of Elkton, which served as the order's novitiate. When I arrived, the novitiate consisted of one big, old, white farmhouse, attached to which was a relatively new annex containing classrooms, a chapel, a dining room, and dormitories. Nearby were the barn, garage, and one smaller farm building, which served as the laundry and general utilities area.

New Oblate recruits like me were sent to Childs for two years. Our first year, where we were called *postulants*, was our freshman year of college. Childs was officially an annex of Catholic University in Washington, D.C. That was followed by one year of training in the religious life and the teachings of Saint Francis de Sales, during which time we were called *novices*.

Even though we got college credit for our first year at Childs, life at Childs was as different from life on any other campus as you can imagine. For starters, it was for men only. We also observed silence all day long, which means we weren't allowed to talk at all, except for a half-hour recess after lunch and dinner. We took turns reading out loud during meals, usually from lives of the saints. We all followed the same rigid, fixed schedule: up at 5:00 a.m. and lights out at 9:00 p.m. And there was no alcohol, drugs, or sex.

As we were constantly reminded, this was a long-established regime, carefully designed to help us grow in wisdom and in grace. But even within those constraints, we hundred or so young Oblates had a good time under the direction of novice master Father John Conmy, as close to a saint as I've ever encountered. We studied hard, prayed hard, and played hard. Weather permitting, we'd squeeze in a quick softball game after lunch. On free Thursday afternoons, we took long hikes around the property or walked up the road to the nearby crossroad of Childs—one house, one post office, and one general store—for an ice cream treat. On feast days, we put on elaborate pageants and were even allowed to talk at mealtime.

Childs was also a working farm—and we were the farmhands. As novices, we had classes in the morning and work assignments every afternoon: housekeeping, weeding the garden, feeding the pigs, mowing the lawn, or killing chickens for dinner. We also had a herd of beef cattle, one of which would be selected to make the ultimate sacrifice whenever an American Oblate died and was brought to Childs for burial. I remember watching with shock from my classroom window the first time I saw Brother Tom lead a cow out of the pasture to a spot near the kitchen, just outside our classroom, tie it to a fence, pick up a shotgun, shoot it in the head, and dress it right on the spot. Even growing up in rural Delaware City, I'd never witnessed anything like that.

I admit it. One of the reasons I survived those two years so well was the pigs. For my work assignment as a novice, I was assigned the best job of all for a gregarious, nonmonastic person like me: the community shopper. Every afternoon, I'd jump in the Chevy station wagon and head to nearby Elkton to pick up supplies: produce from the supermarket for our cook, Sister Jane; materials from the hardware store; cough medicine from the pharmacy; or dressed pork chops, bacon, and scrapple from the slaughterhouse where Brother Tom had delivered one of our pigs. Once again, bacon makes everything better.

It was also at Childs that I met the most famous and colorful Oblate ever: J. Francis Tucker. Father Tucker's claim to fame was as a matchmaker. While serving as chaplain to the royal family of Monaco, he introduced Prince Rainier to the glamorous American movie star Grace Kelly, daughter of Philadelphia tycoon John Kelly. The match took. Father Tucker officiated at their wedding, and his photo was splashed in newspapers and magazines worldwide. Frank Langella played Tucker in the 2014 movie *Grace of Monaco*.

Father Tucker came to Childs for a visit in 1960—sans prince and princess, unfortunately—but he made a great impression on all of us, especially after one sermon in which he lamented that we Americans sometimes took things too seriously. If only we were more like the French, Tucker sighed. *Tant pis!* To illustrate his point, he told the story of a visit to the shrine of Our Lady of Lourdes, where he was asked to hear confessions in French and English.

First up, he said, was an American boy, who hung his head in shame and muttered, "Bless me, Father, for I have sinned. I abused myself ten times." Father Tucker told him to say five Our Fathers and his sins would be forgiven. Next up, a French boy about the same age, who looked Father Tucker right in the eye, big smile on his face, head held high, and exclaimed, "Bless me, Father, for I have sinned. I amused myself ten times!" *Vive la différence!* We pious young seminarians were both shocked and embarrassed, but couldn't stop laughing. Point made.

In the summer of 1965, before leaving to study in Europe, I also attended a retreat led by Father Tucker at De Sales Hall in Hyattsville, Maryland, where he returned to the same theme. In his homily on the sacrament of confession, Tucker advised, "Don't say, 'Father, I jerked off nine times. You know how it is!'" After the laughter subsided, he added, "He's right, but he shouldn't say it."

At Childs, I was greatly influenced by our patron saint, Francis de Sales. We studied his writings and teachings assiduously, especially his masterwork, *Introduction to the Devout Life*, and I came to greatly admire his approach to life and the world we live in. Bishop of Geneva in the early seventeenth century, De Sales became known as the "gentleman saint" for his patience and gentleness, virtues we were expected to emulate as young Oblates. No religious extremist, he preached moderation in all things. His best-known words of advice may be: "Nothing is so strong as gentleness. Nothing so gentle as real strength."

While far, far from perfect, I do know that some of De Sales's gentleness rubbed off on me during those seminary years and stuck with me after. Even in political debate, I've tried to live up to his admonition: "You can attract more bees with a spoonful of sugar than a cupful of vinegar." And I find "moderation in all things" an eminently practical rule of life, even if I don't always practice it.

Another big discovery for me at Childs was the great English philosopher, essayist, poet, and novelist G. K. Chesterton. One of the greatest and most bombastic writers of the twentieth century, Chesterton wrote everything from plays to mystery novels, with a great deal of Christian apologetics in between. Called the "Prince of the Paradox," he made brilliant use of contradictions and paradox to destroy commonly held falsehoods and set forth the truth as he saw it. As a seminarian, I was especially impressed by *The Everlasting Man*, his history of humanity leading up to the acceptance of Jesus Christ, as well as by *Orthodoxy*, the story of his own faith and conversion to Catholicism. Chesterton remains one of the most quoted writers of all time. One truism that sticks with me: "Christianity has not been tried and found wanting, it's been found difficult and not tried."

At the end of our novitiate, two big events loomed: the taking of religious vows and our first assignment as Oblates. Taking the vows of "poverty, chastity, and obedience" and promising to remain poor, celibate, and obedient for the rest of our years should have been a life-changing decision, but it wasn't. At least, not for me. Still feeling good about my initial decision to join the Oblates and still looking forward to a life of public service as a priest, I didn't give it a lot of thought. I walked up to the altar with my confreres at Saint Anthony's Church in Wilmington, Delaware, prostrated myself before the altar, and took my vows—to which I would remain faithful, more or less, until I left the Oblates eight years later.

Believe it or not, the whole chastity thing was not a big deal. Especially in the beginning. Not because I didn't have a raging set of hormones but because, as seminarians, we were kept so busy and focused on other things. And also because, as a merry band of aspiring priests, my classmates and I were all in the same boat: afraid of entertaining any impure thoughts, let alone acting out on them. For almost ten years, I lived surrounded by other smart, fun, vibrant, handsome young men. Yet, in all that time, I never heard of one case of inappropriate sexual activity, with a woman or another man, among our colleagues.

For me, chastity didn't become a problem until I was struggling with my decision to leave the Oblates. Again, that decision was multidimensional. But as we will see, it wasn't because I was so eager to jump over the wall and jump into bed with a secret girlfriend or boyfriend. I was still happy with the prospect of becoming a priest. I left the Oblates mainly because I wasn't ready to commit to the idea of being a high school teacher for the rest of my life. As much as I loved teaching, I wanted to be able to choose from more options and not be limited to spending my life in a high school classroom—which, I was later told, was the only choice available to me as a member of the Oblates of Saint Francis de Sales.

ROOKIE TEACHER

After the novitiate at Childs, there were two paths forward: either continuing our college education or teaching two years in an Oblate high school. We didn't get to choose. Like members of the military, we were told where to go. And, of course, having just taken a solemn vow of obedience, we followed orders. But I was lucky. Even though I had only one year of college under my belt, I was assigned to join the faculty of Father Judge High School in northeast Philadelphia.

Was I ready to teach high school? Hell, no! How much teacher training had I received? None. But did I hold my own? I think so, but it wasn't easy. At least, not in the beginning. I was assigned to teach five classes a day: three classes of world history to freshmen and two classes of French to seniors. The challenge I faced as a new recruit hit me in the face early on, when one of the seniors started acting up. I told him to sit down and shut up and then asked how old he was. "Nineteen," he said. I didn't dare tell him I was only twenty. The difference was I was wearing a cassock and Roman collar—and he wasn't.

There were four thousand students at Father Judge in 1960, all boys, and fifty-five students in every one of my classes. This was a big world for a kid who grew up in a town of twelve hundred and graduated from a high school with only eight hundred students. At first, it was tough finding my way. I felt like I had to pretend to be older, wiser, and tougher than I was, or else the students would run all over me. That lasted about a month, until Father Thomas Carlin, the debonair superior of the Oblate community at Father Judge, told me his secret of being a good teacher. It was just the opposite of what I had imagined. "Be yourself," he advised. "Don't try to fake it, or kids will see right through you. Just be yourself. You'll enjoy it more, and so will they."

He was right. I started to relax more in front of the students and ended up loving the two years I spent in the classroom at Father Judge. I also loved helping out with the school marching band and, especially, coaching the debate team, where we competed against some of the biggest and best high schools in Philadelphia and Wilmington. More practice for *Crossfire*!

My most memorable experience at Judge occurred when I flunked the star of Father Judge's top-rated football team. His F in French meant he'd be on the bench for the next few weeks, which, I was warned, could end up costing Judge the city title. First, our principal, Father Edward O'Neill, called me into his office and asked if it was even a close call. I told him it wasn't. He then asked me to meet with the football coach, who made an impassioned plea for me to show a little mercy (and loyalty to the football team). I lost a lot of sleep over it but in the end decided it was important to make the case that getting a passing grade counted more than scoring the winning touchdown. I didn't win any friends among the school jocks, but the good Father O'Neill backed me up 100 percent.

Another window on the outside world from my time at Judge: With just about every priest and seminarian on the faculty, I rejoiced in the election of John F. Kennedy, the first American Catholic president, whom, as recounted in the last chapter, I had met and interviewed as a senior at Salesianum High School. Even though I was still too young to vote, I joined in the celebration.

Which raises an important question: What the hell happened? Catholics used to be a reliable bloc of Democratic votes. Indeed, sinner that he was, John F. Kennedy was the overwhelming political favorite of priests, bishops, nuns, and Catholic laypersons nationwide. Yet, today, the institutional Catholic Church is a conservative, Republican institution, whose leaders actually denounced Catholic candidates Geraldine Ferraro, Tim Kaine, Nancy Pelosi, Rosa DeLauro, John Kerry, and many others.

Part of the answer, of course, lay in the Kennedy magic. He was so young, so attractive, and the first Catholic, with apologies to Al Smith, to have a serious shot at the presidency. Plus, this was a time before tabloid journalism, when a candidate's private life was not public fodder. And also a time before abortion was a much-talked-about issue.

Things changed with the Supreme Court's ruling on *Roe v. Wade*. They also changed with a host of conservative bishops appointed by Popes John Paul II and Benedict XVI who turned away from the message of the social gospel and instead made opposition to abortion and same-sex marriage the two defining issues of the Catholic faith, demanding that lifelong Catholics who were Democratic politicians make loyalty to the Catholic Church, not loyalty to the United States Constitution, their guiding star. They turned the status of the Catholic Church upside down, from a force of liberalism to a citadel of conservatism.

Thankfully, that appears to be changing back under Pope Francis, who has told American bishops to stop being so narrow-minded, stop focusing so much on abortion and homosexuality, and get back to the church's central mission of helping the poor and dispossessed as taught and lived by Jesus in the Gospels. Francis has also appointed many progressive bishops, like Chicago's Archbishop Blase Cupich, to deliver that message.

The Catholic Church has always encouraged its faithful to be supportive members of their community, active in civic affairs, schools, sports, and yes, even politics. In everything they do, they carry their Catholic faith with them. But that doesn't mean the church should tell Catholics how they must vote. Faithful Catholics can vote for Democratic or Republican candidates, depending on which candidate they believe will best serve the needs of their community or nation, not the Vatican. I accept that fully, although I also believe that the Democratic Party, with its core mission of helping the underprivileged and middle class, is much more in keeping with the essence of Catholicism than a party that pampers the wealthy.

After two years of practice teaching, it was time to complete my college education. Again, there were two options, and again, it was all decided by our superiors: We would be assigned either to Catholic University in Washington, D.C., or Niagara University in Niagara Falls, New York. And again, I got the lucky break: on to Niagara!

Among Oblate scholastics, Niagara was the preferred choice. Catholic University was known as a big, impersonal, highly rated institution of higher education, attended by many priests, seminarians, and nuns, which inspired little loyalty or love. And nearby De Sales House, where student Oblates resided, was considered one step up from federal prison, presided over by the notoriously tightly strung Father Ed Carney, who demanded that every scholastic engage in strenuous physical exercise every day, lest he be tempted to seek release in some other less salutary way. The scourge of masturbation raises its ugly head again.

By contrast, De Chantal Hall, where Niagara University Oblates lived, was as close to a country club as seminaries could get. It was located in nearby Lewiston, about ten miles downhill from the famous falls, high up on the banks of the wild Niagara River. And it was presided over by the fun, colorful Father Joseph Woods. Woodsie, a true character and a leader in both prayer and play, ran a tight ship and insisted on strict observance of the rules, but he also enjoyed treating us to unplanned celebrations, group excursions, evenings watching television, or ice cream parties. There was lots of time for serious study but also for sports and recreation. Field trips to Niagara Falls, nearby Buffalo, or even Toronto were part of the program.

Five mornings a week, robed in cassock and collar, we Oblates climbed into our big, blue bus and headed to campus, where we attended classes with Niagara's undergraduate men and women. Classes were demanding. I continued to major in French but took enough required philosophy courses to declare a joint major. English literature, Spanish, history, and biology rounded out the curriculum. Although we seminarians made up only a small percentage of the student body, we were welcomed as fellow Purple Eagles and treated with equal disrespect by professors, two of whom I remember best.

Marvin La Hood taught Modern Poetry. To my utter confusion, he began the year with the great English poet—and Jesuit priest!—Gerard Manley Hopkins and one of his most famous poems, "The Windhover": "I caught this morning morning's minion." At first reading, I couldn't understand a word of what Hopkins was saying, but an Oblate colleague who'd taken the same course the year before urged me to persevere. "Keep reading it," he said. "Eventually you'll understand it."

I'm glad I did. To this day, Hopkins remains my favorite poet, and, if you catch me at a particularly romantic or reflective moment, I may even recite one of his poems by heart. In dark times, I still receive comfort from Hopkins's lament based on the book of Jerome, chapter 12, first verse:

> Thou art indeed just, Lord, if I contend
> With thee; but, sir, so what I plead is just.
> Why do sinners' ways prosper? And why must
> Disappointment all I endeavour end?
> . . . .
> birds build—but not I build; no, but strain,
> Time's eunuch, and not breed one work that wakes.
> Mine, O thou lord of life, send my roots rain.

Which, I guess, could simply be translated: "Hey, Lord. What did I do wrong? Why are you picking on me? Give me a break!"

Professor La Hood had an especially wry sense of humor, which I was one of the few students to appreciate. Locals, of course, were proud of Niagara Falls, the international tourist attraction and preferred honeymoon destination. So it was almost scandalous, one day, when La Hood cynically dismissed the falls as "a young bride's second big disappointment." Roman collar and all, I was the only one in class who got it—and laughed out loud. "Thank God for Bill Press," said La Hood.

Same thing happened in Biology 101, taught by Richard Keiley. For the mostly Catholic students at a liberal arts Catholic college, this was the first time any of us had been told the full facts of life. Keiley described the male and female sex organs and all you could do with them in the most explicit language, illustrated with big color charts, and always with his irreverent sense of humor. "Ninety-five percent of men masturbate," he declared one day, to the shock of his coed class. And then, after a pregnant pause: "The other five percent are liars!" Again, I was the only one who laughed out loud.

One other major impact on my days at Niagara came from a book that became required reading at De Chantal Hall: *The Intellectual Life*, by French philosopher and Dominican priest A. D. Sertillanges. I'm still kind of embarrassed by embracing a book with such a snooty title, but its basic premise is very down to earth. God has blessed us with strong bodies and strong minds, and we have an obligation to take care of both. It's important to live well, eat well, and exercise to keep our bodies in good shape. Most people recognize that. But it's equally important, says Sertillanges, especially after leaving a structured academic setting like the university, to set time aside to exercise and grow the brain, through continued reading, studying, research, and writing. As I said, pretty basic, but also very wise advice that I've tried to take seriously.

This was also the time that Catholics, and indeed much of the academic universe, discovered the great French philosopher Pierre Teilhard de Chardin. As seminarians, we all read *The Phenomenon of Man* and struggled to understand his complex theory of evolution in which the entire universe was evolving, through the noosphere, toward the Omega Point. I'm still not sure I understand, or buy, it all. Chardin's theory has since fallen out of favor, but it was exciting stuff at the time and the subject of many late-night conversations at De Chantal Hall.

It was at De Chantal Hall that I learned another important lesson. Fellow Oblate Jim Shannon was the most studious, and probably the smartest, member of his class. But he was also a very good basketball and football player, a bridge addict, and first in line to take advantage of any fun extracurricular opportunity. When I expressed my worries about juggling all the school work and fun stuff at the same time, Jim told me his secret: "Don't let your studies interfere with your education." His sage advice not only got me through college, I've applied his wisdom to my professional and personal life.

Of course, college is as important for the friendships you make as the lessons you learn. Niagara was no exception, other than the reality that for me, after five years at an all-boys high school and four years in the seminary, it was my first opportunity to make friends with a girl! Her name was Ginny Howe, a very attractive, vivacious, wicked smart, and fun classmate who shared my passions for the French language and poetry. Given my limited availability, we never saw each other outside of class, but we did develop a close friendship that would someday develop into my very first serious relationship. But that's getting ahead of the story.

Everyone alive in 1963 knows the answer to that horrible question: "Where were you when you learned that President John F. Kennedy was shot?" I remember where I was: in the pool at the University of Niagara, where I swam laps at lunchtime with fellow Oblate Jack Costigan. Suddenly, classmate Michael Moore rushed in with the horrific news: "Did you hear? The president's been shot!"

At first, we thought he was talking about the president of the university. Then the full impact of the news hit us. We got dressed, ran out of the gym, and, like most other Americans, parked ourselves in front of a television set, where we remained for the next few days through that unforgettable sequence of events: the swearing in of President Johnson, the return of JFK's body to Washington, the murder of Lee Oswald, JFK's majestic state funeral, the burial Mass at Saint Matthew's Cathedral, little John John saluting his father's casket, the burial at Arlington, the eternal flame, the agony, the agony, the agony.

You had to have lived through it to know what a profound impact the assassination of the popular, young, handsome president had on his country, particularly for Catholics, who had seen one of their own ascend to the nation's highest office for the very first time. And, of course, I remembered his own kindness to me, six years earlier, on the train platform in Wilmington, Delaware.

We Oblates watched coverage of the Kennedy funeral and opening days of the Johnson administration not as Democrats or Republicans but as Americans. Indeed, politics was almost as frowned on in the seminary as pornography. But if we couldn't engage in political activity, at least we could vote. And I got my first chance to vote in 1964. A proud Democrat, there was no doubt I was going to vote for Lyndon Johnson over Barry Goldwater. But the contest for U.S. senator from New York presented a more difficult choice.

Nine months after his brother's assassination, Attorney General Robert F. Kennedy left the Johnson administration, moved to New York, and announced his candidacy for U.S. Senate. As a Democrat and a big Kennedy fan, at first I leaned toward voting for him automatically. But I learned that the Republican candidate, incumbent Senator Kenneth Keating, was also a good man. A moderate Republican in the old Nelson Rockefeller mode and an effective voice for New York State, Keating had even refused to endorse Barry Goldwater, the nominee of his party for president, because the Arizonan was too conservative! The more I thought about it, the more I was also bothered by Kennedy's sudden parachuting into New York just to snag a Senate seat, which made him a real carpetbagger.

So, in the end, I made a tough choice and voted for Keating over Kennedy. It's the only time I can remember voting for a Republican. In many ways, I regret that vote today, because I admire so much what Bobby Kennedy did and stood for and became friends with at least three of his children: Joe, Kathleen, and Bobby Jr. And, of course, I voted against a fellow Catholic. God, forgive me!

Many years later, at the 2012 Democratic National Convention in Charlotte, I appeared on a panel of liberal Catholics with Kathleen Kennedy Townsend, who was asked about problems her father had with the conservative Catholic hierarchy. She related riding in the car with Bobby one day and asking why priests were so mean to him. "Always remember, Kathleen," he told her. "The priests and bishops are Republicans. The nuns are Democrats."

EUROPEAN EDUCATION

My graduation from Niagara University in June 1965—the first of our extended Press family ever to graduate from college—marked the end of the college phase of my seminary training. Since I had already put in two years of practice teaching, it was now on to the main course: four more years of theology, ending with ordination to the priesthood.

Again, there were two options. And again, the student gods were with me. For theology, most Oblate seminarians were automatically assigned to Catholic University in Washington, D.C.—back to the institutional prison known as De Sales House. A few scholastics—those whom the order had destined to return to the United States and teach theology at the university level—were chosen to study in Europe instead at the Pontifical University of Saint Thomas Aquinas, or Angelicum, in Rome; at the University of Paderborn, in Paderborn, Germany; or at the University of Fribourg, in Fribourg, Switzerland.

According to reviews from Oblates who had previously studied in Europe, Germany was considered the least desirable assignment, because Paderborn was not a first-class university and the city of Paderborn itself was a remote outpost, far from the action. Rome, while the most prestigious and historically significant post, was also considered too stifling and too close to the Vatican to allow any real freedom of thought. Fribourg was everybody's number-one choice because the university had a great reputation for scholarship; because the Oblate house in Fribourg was headed by Father Robert McNally, a popular American bon vivant; and because Fribourg was, well, in Switzerland!

Yet again, lucky me. I was not only assigned to study in Europe, I was sent to Fribourg! And so, after a summer of intensive French classes at Georgetown University in Washington, I found myself with two fellow Oblates in New York City one September 1965 afternoon, on board the SS *United States*, ready to sail to Europe. Classmate Jim Marks was headed to Paderborn; an older colleague, Brother John, had been assigned to Rome. The three of us shared a small, second-class cabin.

For such a joyous occasion, my parents and a dozen or so family members had come up to New York from Delaware City, together with our Oblate pastor, Father Lawrence Ward. Jim and John also had several family members present. We were all enjoying a glass of champagne in one of the ship's lounges when I suddenly noticed, standing at the edge of the crowd, another person I'd invited but totally forgotten about: my friend and classmate from Niagara University Ginny Howe. I was glad to see her and, somewhat awkwardly, introduced her to my family. In all the crowd and confusion, Ginny and I never really had a chance to talk, but any doubt about why she was there—and why I had invited her—dissolved an hour or so later.

It was that exciting moment just before we pushed back from the dock, when only passengers remained on board, all lined up at the railing, while friends and family crowded the dock, glasses of champagne in hand, cheering and wildly waving their last goodbyes. That's when I looked off to the side and spotted Ginny, standing by herself away from the crowd, openly sobbing. *Oh my God*, I thought. *Something's going on here!* And it was. But that seed, thereupon planted, wouldn't sprout until two years later.

Even though our crossing was uneventful—no "man overboard," no shipboard romance, no norovirus—looking back on it today, I realize how hugely symbolic that voyage was in representing a dramatic change in my life. Five days at sea did more than take me from one shore to another. It took me from one world to another, and from one person to another. From a relatively sheltered small-town boy to a man of the world. From an orthodox disciple of tradition and authority to a radical challenger of authority. From believer to nonbeliever. From conformist to rebel. Upon returning to the United States in August 1967, after two action-packed, life-changing years in Europe, I was not the same person who'd boarded that ship in New York.

Our first stop was Paris, where, like millions of young Americans before and since, I fell in love with the City of Light and still return as often as I can. But we three Oblates got off to a rocky start. We checked into a Left Bank hostel for visiting priests and seminarians without realizing that it operated under quasi-monastic rules, which included an early curfew.

Returning from our first night on the town, sometime after midnight, we discovered that the gate to the property was locked tight, and nobody answered the bell. At which point—and, needless to add, somewhat drunk— we decided to scale the wall. As I was standing on Jim Marks's shoulders, trying to scramble up to the top of the wall, a couple of tourists from Australia wandered by. After convincing us we would never make it over that wall, they invited us to join them in their nearby hotel room. Which we did—all three of us spending our first night in Paris sleeping on the floor in a room occupied by two total strangers. *La vie parisienne!*

After a brief stop in Troyes, mother house of the Oblates, I went to Fribourg, Switzerland, and the Oblate house at 37 chemin de Bellevue, launching pad for the exciting two years to follow.

Fribourg is a medieval university town. Of its population of thirty-four thousand, ten thousand are students at the University of Fribourg, created in 1580, and best known today for its schools of law and theology. The city itself, nestled on both sides of the Sarine River, is a beautiful, clean, bustling commercial center, with a quaint, old city core surrounding the beautiful Cathedral of Saint Nicholas. Located on the border of Swiss Romand and

Swiss Allemand, Fribourg is bilingual, French and German. As are, by necessity, most of its residents—many of whom also speak the local dialect, Schweizerdeutsch. I was always amazed to hear the kids in our neighborhood playing outside and, without even thinking about it, switching back and forth from French to German to Schweizerdeutsch, fluent in all three languages.

The Oblate residence was located in the Schoenberg neighborhood of Fribourg, across the river from the city center. It actually belonged to the French province of the Oblates, so we were a French-speaking house in a German neighborhood of a bilingual city. There were five Americans in residence: myself, Tom Moore, Jerry Bartko, Adam Radomski, and Father Robert McNally, the superior. We were joined by seven French confreres: Jean-Paul, Jean-Mark, Denis, Maurice, Laurent, François, and Father Joseph Goumaz. Housekeeping chores were handled by two young Swiss German interns, Pius and Walter.

Switzerland, I soon discovered, lived up to its reputation: a country of breathtaking beauty, startling cleanliness, and unbelievable efficiency—their trains really do run on time! No graffiti, no litter, streets scrubbed. Even dirt paths looked like they'd been recently vacuumed. Stores of firewood outside of farms were neatly, if anal-retentively, separated and stacked from the smallest twigs up to the biggest logs. But for a so-called pacifist country, the Swiss are also strangely militaristic.

At that time, every Swiss man between the ages of nineteen and fifty belonged to the Swiss Army, kept an assault weapon in his home, and spent a couple of weeks a year in military training and one weekend a month practicing on the target range. Every day, we'd see caravans of heavily armed Swiss Army "volunteers" making their way through Fribourg on military maneuvers. The Swiss still brag that the strength of their army is what dissuaded the Nazis from invading Switzerland during World War II. But of course, we know now that Hitler didn't have to invade Switzerland. He just bought it.

As wound tight as the Swiss were, the French were just the opposite, which made living in our French house so much fun. Our French colleagues mocked the Swiss, especially the Swiss Army, mercilessly. Indeed, the French didn't take anything seriously, including their religion. A couple of years earlier, the Vatican had relaxed its rules, allowing Mass to be celebrated in the vernacular instead of Latin. The pope then reversed himself, demanding a return to Latin, which, of course, American Catholics readily obeyed.

Arriving in Fribourg, then, and surprised to discover Mass still being celebrated in French, I asked how they were able to get away with it. "Because the pope's just wrong," they said, shrugging. No guilt, no problem.

It was the first open defiance of religious authority I experienced and embraced.

We were a fun, stimulating community of young Oblates, all ostensibly destined for the priesthood, though most of us would never make it. And, as in the United States, we were all assigned tasks to help run the house. By some strange twist of fate, I was designated as the official house *caviste*, the man in charge of the wine cellar—even though I had only enjoyed my very first glass of wine a couple of weeks earlier, on board the SS *United States*.

My job was to stock the dinner table with the appropriate wine, with advice from my more wine-knowledgeable French confreres. What wine, for example, do you serve with horsemeat, which was often the only steak we could afford?

On weekdays, we would enjoy red or white table wine, usually diluted with water. On weekends, we stepped it up a notch. And on feast days, we went all out, as I learned the hard way only a couple of days after arriving in Fribourg. Dinner was preceeded in the community room with an aperitif: wine, whiskey, port, martini, or cocktail. We then moved to the dining room and a selection of fine wines: white with the first course; red with the entrée; a second round of red with the cheese course; and, of course, a dessert wine with dessert. Followed by coffee, with a dash of liqueur—*seulement deux doigts*—in each cup. After which, it was back to the community room for an after-dinner drink, or digestif. By that time, I was barely able to crawl back to my room on the second floor, where I slept for the next four hours.

Of course, we'd been sent to Fribourg not to party but to study. Each morning, we'd walk down to the river, cross the bridge over the Sarine, and climb up the hill, through the old city and around the cathedral, to the university. Home for lunch, then back up the hill for afternoon classes. The University of Fribourg probably had more students of theology than any other university outside of Rome, all male, most of whom—like us Oblates—dressed in cassock and roman collar. Coming from the States, it was strange to see so many people in the streets, on public transit, in restaurants, or riding bicycles, dressed in clerical garb.

Almost every morning while walking to the university, rain or shine, we'd encounter an older priest in black cassock and cape, stooped over with age, slowly making his way up the hill to pray at a little shrine to the Virgin Mary. Months later, I learned that this unassuming priest was the famous Swiss theologian Cardinal Charles Journet, a major player in the Second Vatican Council of 1965, who had resigned from the Fribourg faculty but whose writings were must reading for theology students.

In keeping with its geographic location, the University of Fribourg was bilingual. All classes were offered in French or German, except for the basic theology classes, which were taught in Latin! Classes were held in an amphitheater, holding some two hundred students. The Dominican professors lectured, in Latin, for an hour; and we took notes, in Latin. There were no textbooks. No translation. No visual aids. No exams. And no opportunity to ask questions.

Unable to express themselves verbally, students did so physically. Seats in the amphitheater were actually rows of attached wooden desks, arranged in a semicircle, with a front wooden wall separating them from the row of desks below. When the professor said something especially interesting or amusing, students would tap or bang on their desks in approval. When he said something they didn't like or agree with, they would kick the front wall of their desks in a deafening clamor. It was like being back in the sixteenth century.

We had a good life in Fribourg. Classes were challenging. It was exciting, living in an international, bilingual city. My French improved, and I made enough progress in German to get by around town. One added benefit: The countryside around Fribourg was storybook, enchantingly beautiful Switzerland. We made frequent pilgrimages to nearby Gruyères to visit the castle and sample the world-famous cheese. On weekends, my friend Laurent Peltier and I often bicycled to nearby villages. A couple of times, a gang of us piled into the car for a long day trip through the Great Saint Bernard Tunnel into Italy. During winter break, we rented a chalet in Les Contamines, a low-budget ski resort in the French Alps, where I learned to ski—and where I learned to make cheese fondue. Our "chalet" was hardly fancy. There were cracks in the walls and roof. We'd wake up in the morning with snow covering our sleeping bags.

While most of our skiing was at Les Contamines, late in the spring of 1967, we went skiing on the Kaiseregg, a mountain just outside Fribourg—which didn't turn out so well for this novice. On my very first run, near the top of the mountain, I fell and broke my left leg. The ski patrol took me on a harrowing toboggan ride down the mountain, put some kind of temporary cast on my leg, and hustled me into the backseat of our car, which confrere Maurice Riguet drove back to Fribourg—first stopping by our house so I could enjoy a of glass of wine and break the news to our community before continuing on to the hospital. I was operated on the next day and still, as a souvenir, walk around with three metal screws in my left tibia.

Switzerland was also my first exposure to Europe's system of universal health care. I was operated on for my broken leg and spent almost a week in the hospital in Fribourg. It didn't cost me a dime. I had a similar experience a few months later in France, when I lost control of a motorbike and crashed into a field, injuring the same leg. Other than being chewed out by the doctor for being so stupid as to ride a motorbike with a still-healing left leg, the hospital care in France was also free. Universal health care, or single-payer health care, has been a hugely successful program in every European country for decades. It's embarrassing it took us Americans so long just to get to Obamacare—which is a far cry from universal health care, but which Trump-inspired Republicans are still so eager to repeal. It was a sign of Obama's overcautious political nature—see my book *Buyer's Remorse* on this!—that he rejected single payer, which works effectively and efficiently in so many countries, as a possible option to be considered, even before debate on Obamacare began.

If, instead of the complicated, half-ass, public/private system called Obamacare, President Obama had simply enacted "Medicare for All," it would have proven so widely popular and successful, Trump and Republicans would never have dared try to replace it.

My skiing accident wasn't the only memorable mountain event. In early October 1966, the day before classes resumed, four of us decided to climb Vanil Noir, the highest local peak around Fribourg. We set out early the next morning and started up the trail in total darkness—so dark, in fact, we did not see signs warning that the mountain was closed that day so the mighty Swiss Army could hold target practice.

Having reached the summit just about dawn, we sat down to enjoy the breakfast snack we'd brought along when suddenly, off to our right, we heard a strange whistling sound, followed by a loud explosion. Then another, even closer. And another, closer still. And suddenly we realized they were real, live mortar shells lobbed at the mountain—by the Swiss Army. The pacifists were at it again!

We started frantically shouting and waving our arms until the shelling stopped, and then we began making our way down the face of the mountain, rather than down the trail, so we could easily be spotted. Sure enough, about halfway down, a couple of angry army officers roared up in a jeep, chewed us out for making them lose a couple of hours of valuable bombing time, and drove us back to our car. At the same time, they were probably relieved to avoid the headline: SWISS ARMY BOMBS THREE FRENCH AND ONE AMERICAN. We came close to becoming the Swiss Army's first and only casualties of war!

The best part about Fribourg was that the university was in session only six months a year. That left a lot of time for new adventures and activities, and I took full advantage of it. My first summer in Europe, I packed as much in as possible: three weeks studying German in Salzburg, Austria; three weeks as camp counselor for a group of teenagers from Marseille touring Germany; and a month working at the Oblate parish in the vibrant city of Marseille. With what little money I'd earned, I then set off hitchhiking across France: across the Massif Central; back to Paris; out to the hamlet of Ploudalmézeau at the tip of Brittany; and then on to Normandy's Saint-Michel and Saint-Malo before ending up in Reims, where I looked forward to visiting the famous cathedral and catching up with a couple of student friends I'd met along the way.

Little did I realize the evening I spent with them turned out to be one of the most meaningful of my life.

Over dinner, someone raised the subject of America's ongoing war in Vietnam. And, like any loyal American, I took the bait. As a student at Niagara, I'd actually written a letter to President Lyndon Johnson supporting the Vietnam War. So I seized the opportunity to staunchly defend the war, using all the establishment talking points about Communist threat, dominoes falling, superiority of airpower, certainty of success as long as we held the course, and so on.

My French friends listened politely, then asked, "Have you ever heard of Dien Bien Phu?" Sadly, like most Americans, I hadn't. So they proceeded to educate me about the French Army's five-year war in Vietnam: the precursor to and mirror image of America's war in Vietnam, conducted with the same hubris, the same belief in superior firepower, the same underestimation of the potency of Vietnamese nationalism, and the same level of denial—all leading up to their ignominious defeat at Dien Bien Phu in May 1954 and the end of French colonial influence in Indochina.

Why didn't we Americans learn from history, they wanted to know. We were repeating all the same mistakes and heading for the same results. Proving once again Santayana's old adage that "those who don't know their history are doomed to repeat it"—and its sad corollary: "Those who *do* know their history are doomed to watch others repeat it."

We talked all night. The power of their arguments and the weight of history finally convinced me I was wrong. I left Reims not only having changed my mind about the Vietnam War but shaken about my initial naïveté and with a new understanding of what it meant to be an American—and, from then on, forever skeptical, as citizens everywhere should be, about their government's stated reasons for declaring war on another country.

On that night in Reims, at least on the important issue of war and peace, a new progressive was born.

I am a true American. I love my country as much as anybody else. I'm proud, and feel blessed, to have been born in the United States. But here's a lesson I first learned in France and have seen reinforced many times since. You can love your country and still disagree with the policies of your president and other elected officials—and say so openly. You can love your country and still oppose certain actions your country takes today or has taken in the past. You can love your country and still admit that, in some areas, other countries do better than we do, that we could actually learn from them. They don't always have to take lessons from us. That's what's wrong with the silly philosophy called American Exceptionalism, which some conservatives consider a saliva test. Yes, America is an exceptional country. But that doesn't make us right about everything. Far from it. On universal health care, for example, Canada puts us to shame. On gun safety, Australia's number one. On universal preschool, Norway and Sweden are far out in front. As loyal Americans, we would do well to stop bragging about America's superiority in all things and start examining how we could become an even greater country by learning from others.

Returning to Fribourg, I couldn't wait to meet our new neighbors. Earlier that year, I'd been translating correspondence between Madame Dietrich, who owned the big house next door, and Seth and Margery Warner from Malibu, California, who were looking for an apartment in Switzerland to spend Seth's sabbatical from Santa Monica City College.

After dinner my first day back, I walked next door and banged on Seth and Margery's door—without giving any thought about what I was wearing. You can imagine their surprise, never having seen anyone in a cassock and roman collar up close before, discovering a fully dressed cleric on their doorstep. Recognizing their shock, I quickly identified myself as their go-between translator and apologized for my clerical garb. They invited me in for a glass of wine, became instant friends and, as we will soon see, were instrumental in easing my way out of the seminary and into a new life in California.

My second year of classes at Fribourg got off to a good start, but, at the same time, my personal life began falling apart: I started having serious doubts about my vocation. Again, the issue wasn't chastity; it was what work I'd be doing after ordination. As much as I had enjoyed practice teaching at Father Judge, did I really want to spend the rest of my life teaching high school? Was there some more meaningful contribution I could make?

After consulting a psychiatrist, I decided to make a stand. And here's where the newborn rebel surfaced. While in Paris the previous summer, I'd explored the "worker priest" movement founded by Father Jacques Loew, a radical departure from tradition where priests—instead of running a parish or teaching school—got a job in a factory or office building, lived in an apartment, and ministered to their coworkers and neighbors. Some even ran for political office. Why not me? Becoming a worker priest was one way to have my cake and eat it, too.

Fortuitously, right about that time, our Oblate superior general, Father William F. Buckley, visited Fribourg. I met with him and laid out my plans: I'd remain as an Oblate, but only if I could become a worker priest. Otherwise, I planned to leave.

Father Buckley would have no part of it. As an Oblate priest, he said, only one line of work was cut out for me. I would be a high school teacher or theology professor for the rest of my life. There was no other option. Take it or leave it. I left it—sort of.

Actually, following weeks of negotiations worthy of the Vatican, I agreed, rather than leave immediately, to take a year's leave of absence before making a final, final decision. I also agreed to his demand that, rather than stay in France, my choice, I would return to the United States—at which point I immediately vowed to go anywhere but back to Delaware, where I would face pressure from my fellow Oblates and my family.

But where to go? Reenter Seth and Margery Warner, my new friends and neighbors from Malibu. For the very first time, they agreed to help someone relocate to California, instead of, like most Californians, trying to keep interlopers out. Not only that, they gave me a list of private schools in California that might be looking for a young French teacher right off the boat from France. Hugh Coughlin, an American Dominican priest I'd also become close friends with, provided a list of Catholic high schools in the San Francisco Bay Area.

I sent off scores of letters, offering myself as a fluent French speaker available for the next school year, with no mention of my closeted seminarian status. And, to my utter surprise, I received two job offers: from Danville Academy, in the East Bay, near San Ramon, California; and Sacred Heart High School, in the heart of San Francisco. Danville was a more prestigious school but, due to its remote location, more difficult for a single man without a car. So I accepted a job with the Christian Brothers, teaching French and religion at Sacred Heart High School.

At this point, confessing to growing up a Catholic, attending four years of Catholic high school, and spending nine, soon to be ten years, in the seminary, it's fair to ask: Are you still a Catholic? And, more fundamentally, what do you believe?

Am I still a Catholic? Well, I suppose so. At least, even though I've received many angry letters from Catholics in response to some of my columns, I've never received a letter from the pope or any bishop telling me I'm no longer a Catholic. So, on that level at least, I'm still a Catholic.

At the same time, if being a Catholic means attending Mass every Sunday and believing everything the church teaches and everything some priests spout from the pulpit, I'm definitely not a Catholic any longer. In fact, I find it harder and harder to justify belonging to any "organized religion"—which is, when you think of it, a real contradiction in terms.

As for what I believe, it's easier to say what I don't believe. I don't believe in the Virgin Birth. I don't believe in the Immaculate Conception. I don't believe God created the world and all its creatures in six days so he could take a nap on the seventh. I don't believe in heaven or hell, and I certainly don't believe that God makes little babies sit in limbo forever just because, through no fault of their own, they were never baptized. I don't believe the pope, even Pope Francis, is infallible. I do believe Jesus was a historical figure and a great role model who left a remarkable set of teachings we would all be wise to follow, most notably in his Sermon on the Mount (Matthew 5:1–12).

In fact, the nicest thing anyone ever said about me was said by the great Tim Russert, longtime host of *Meet the Press*. Tim also hosted a weekend interview show on MSNBC, where Pat Buchanan and I, both former seminarians, appeared together in 2005 to promote our recently published books. Pat's latest was *Where the Right Went Wrong*; mine was *How the Republicans Stole Religion*. Not surprisingly, we three Catholics, following Tim's lead, ended up discussing Catholic doctrine and whether Catholics were ever allowed to question it. Pat took the strict, every-word-of-the-Bible-is-sacred approach. I argued for sticking to the core of Christ's message, which was helping the poor and disadvantaged.

At which point, Tim Russert said to me, "In other words, you're a 'Sermon on the Mount' Catholic." I'd never heard that phrase before, so I paused for a moment before responding, "Yes, I'm a 'Sermon on the Mount' Catholic—and proud of it!"

Go back and read it again. As a person of any faith, it's not a bad place to hang your hat.

> *Blessed are the poor in spirit,*
> *for theirs is the kingdom of heaven. . . .*
> *Blessed are the meek,*
> *for they will inherit the earth. . . .*
> *Blessed are the merciful,*
> *for they will be shown mercy. . . .*
> *Blessed are the peacemakers,*
> *for they will be called sons of God.*

I would argue that you can appreciate and practice the wisdom of the beatitudes without having to buy the fact that Jesus was also the Son of God. In fact, I'm not sure I swallow the whole God thing anymore. Why do we have to? Isn't the world a fabulous place, full of marvelous plants and animals? Isn't the human body itself a wonderful, beautiful thing to hold and behold? And isn't the human mind an unfathomable, inexhaustible treasure with unlimited potential? Why do we have to muck it up by dragging religion into it? Or by giving some remote, unforgiving, inaccessible deity all the credit?

I guess you could call me a Christian humanist, but only in the sense that Jesus is an exemplary historical personage, and not divine. Otherwise, like Thomas Jefferson, who compiled his own New Testament by leaving Jesus in, but taking all references to the divinity of Jesus out, I am a secular humanist. And I believe our mission during our brief sojourn on this planet is threefold: to achieve our full potential as man or woman; to do good works; and to practice the Golden Rule, treating others as we would want them to treat us.

For me, religion does not have to be so complicated. It doesn't require a lot of ritual and ceremony, guilt or fear. Perhaps the revered Rabbi Hillel, a contemporary of Jesus, summed it up best in a quote I put on the first page of *How the Republicans Stole Religion*: "What is hateful to you, do not do to your neighbor. That is the Torah. All the rest is commentary."

In that sense, I do believe in the afterlife. I do believe we live on after death, but not in some eternal picnic in the sky or flames beneath the earth. We live in on in the good works we have performed. We live on in the memories of friends we have made, fellow citizens we have helped, and those very special people we have loved.

That is what I took most from my decade with the Oblates—not the religious teachings, definitely not the proscriptions, but the values I learned, the appreciation of life I adopted, and the many friends I made.

Meanwhile, briefly, back to Fribourg. Liberated by my decision to leave the Oblates, at least temporarily, I finished my classes and passed my oral exams—the only exams we faced in two years of studies—to obtain a bachelor's degree in theology from the University of Fribourg.

I was ready to travel back to the United States, except for one small problem. I was still recovering from my broken leg and walking with crutches. My best friend in the seminary, Laurent Peltier, came up with the perfect solution: arranging for me to spend a month recuperating at his home in the fabled French Alps ski resort of Megève, where his father was a prominent architect.

The widower Pierre Peltier, a handsome, debonair, popular bon vivant, adopted me as his American son. During the day, I walked the streets and surrounding hills of Megève until I got my strength back. In the evening, I accompanied Pierre to all the dinner parties and soirées he was invited to. We made a great team. It was a glorious way to wrap up two years of studies in Europe.

Early one July morning, I took the bus from Megève to Annecy and hopped on a train from there to Brussels, where I caught an Icelandic Airlines flight, known as "The Hippie Airline," back to the United States. After spending a couple of weeks with my family in Delaware City and Fenwick, I made a beeline to San Francisco in late August 1967 to begin yet another exciting chapter of my life.

Little did I imagine that California would be my home for the next thirty years. Nor did I have any idea what I was getting into by arriving in San Francisco at the height of the Summer of Love. There was no better place to come out of my shell as a true progressive.

3

CALIFORNIA DREAMIN'

I didn't think about it at the time, but I realize now that I didn't choose California. California chose me—in the same way it's chosen millions of Americans before and since—and catapulted me into all kinds of new directions I never would have dreamed possible. That's what California's all about.

More than anyplace else, California, with its face turned toward the Pacific and the future, represents a new beginning. In fact, for me, California's not so much a place as it is a state of mind. It was as far as I could get from my past and as close as I get to the future. After leaving the seminary, I was both uprooted and rootless, which is a good thing to be when you're in your twenties. And California was the perfect place to land. It offered a whole new life filled with exciting new opportunities I would never have enjoyed anywhere else.

Of course, as I prepared to head to California, there were a lot of unknowns: Outside of teaching school, what was I going to do once I got there? Where would I live? How would I find my way around? How would I make new friends?

In 1967, the population of California was nineteen million. But I only knew six of them, three of whom—Seth and Margery Warner, and Hugh Coughlin—were still in Fribourg. That left Ben and Emily Gershinoff, and their daughter, Rochelle.

Ben and Emily, close friends of my parents, lived across the street from us on Washington Street in Delaware City. I grew up playing with Rochelle and her brother, Richard. Like several of my uncles, Ben had arrived in Delaware City as a young soldier at Fort DuPont, married a local girl, and decided to stay—until he was assigned to occupation forces in the Philippines. He and his family returned to the States and settled in Daly City, just south of San Francisco.

Now married, Rochelle lived with her husband, Jerry Sullivan, and their four kids in nearby Pacifica, where I shared a bunk bed with one of their twins for my first month in California.

Sacred Heart High School proved to be a perfect landing pad for my new start in California. Located at Franklin and Ellis Streets, in the heart of San Francisco, it was known—unlike rival Saint Ignatius, favored by sons of doctors and lawyers—as the school of choice for blue-collar Catholics, sons of police, firefighters, and working-class families. The school was run by the Christian Brothers, where nobody but the principal, Brother Francis, knew that I was actually a seminarian on a leave of absence.

I was paid $600 a month and assigned to teach five classes a day: two freshman French, and three senior religion. I also coached the debate team and took my turn as faculty adviser or chaperone at football games, basketball games, and school dances.

I hadn't been at Sacred Heart long before the budding radical inside me was put to the test—this time, helping lead a campaign against the bishop! At one of our first faculty meetings, several lay teachers complained they could no longer raise their families on the dirt wages they were paid. So we agreed to press for a pay raise. Our first step was to meet with the priest in charge of Catholic schools for the Diocese of San Francisco. He listened politely but insisted the diocese could not afford to pay its teachers more.

Thus rebuffed by the diocese, the lay teachers convened to decide their next move. It was an emotional meeting. Several teachers described the hardship of trying to support their families. Some talked about taking second jobs. Others admitted they were between a rock and a hard place, because they knew the bishop wouldn't budge and they didn't have the necessary state credentials required to get a job in a public school. At which point one teacher raised the stakes and suggested the only way to put enough pressure on the bishop was for us Catholic high school teachers to go on strike.

Many of us immediately endorsed a strike (even though, as a closet seminarian, with neither "chick nor child," I had the least to lose). Others, already stretched to their limit financially, feared the consequences. Without a Catholic school teachers' union, some pointed out, we'd be on our own, with no resources to support teachers while on strike. In the end, we agreed to meet again a week later with lay teachers from other Catholic high schools to make a final decision.

Unfortunately, when that moment came, we couldn't round up enough votes to authorize a strike. I was disappointed, but, a couple of years later, in Sacramento, I rejoiced when I turned on the news and learned that Catholic high school teachers in San Francisco were out on strike against the bishop, walking the picket line. The seeds we'd planted had finally sprouted. My fellow teachers went out on strike—and they won a big pay raise!

The best part of teaching at Sacred Heart was the excitement of living in San Francisco. I soon left Rochelle and Jerry's home for my own furnished apartment on Clay Street on Nob Hill (the downhill, shabby side of Nob Hill) and began exploring that beautiful city—which, after Paris, is still my favorite city on the planet. I loved walking along the bay, the atmosphere and smells of North Beach, the color and fun of the Mission, the wild scene in Haight-Ashbury, the mysteries of Golden Gate Park. I couldn't wait to read *The San Francisco Chronicle* every morning, with its great columnists Herb Caen, Charles McCabe, and Art Hoppe.

San Francisco's a city with an outsized personality, and in the late 1960s it was on full display, embodied by colorful San Francisco mayor Joe Alioto. Alioto was the perfect mayor for San Francisco: outspoken, flamboyant, in love with life, upbeat, and scary smart. One of his most colorful moves was turning the sixty-third anniversary of the 1906 earthquake into a celebration of San Francisco's rebirth and renewal. At midnight on April 18, 1969, I joined thousands gathered on the east side of city hall to hear Alioto and other notables memorialize the occasion. As the San Francisco

Symphony played the score, the silent classic *1906* was projected on a giant screen over the speakers' platform. The renowned poet Brother Antoninus, a.k.a. William Everson, read a long, original poem he had written for the occasion, "The City Does Not Die." And, true to the spirit of the City by the Bay, the crowd rose to the occasion.

At that time, one of the big controversies in San Francisco, every step of which was breathlessly reported in *The Chronicle*, was whether local bakeries should be allowed to sell presplit English muffins. Public fever ran hot, those supporting the tradition of intact muffins opposing those arguing for the convenience of having them presplit. And, sure enough, in the middle of the earthquake crowd that night stood a lone protestor, dressed in black, holding a black sign with bold white lettering: SPLIT THE EARTH, NOT THE MUFFINS!

In 1967, San Francisco was ground zero for the Summer of Love, centered in the wild hippie scene of the Haight-Ashbury. Walking through the Panhandle, or walking up Haight Street and into Golden Gate Park was, indeed, like walking in a different country, if not a different planet: with flowered shirts, jeans, and beads, the ubiquitous smell of pot, many people of all ages stoned out of their minds, music and dancing in the streets. Mellow, mellow, mellow. But also dangerous for a lot of young people who'd run away from home and headed to the Haight, lured by the promise of free drugs and free love, only to find neither. Nor any free food.

While teaching at Sacred Heart, I became a regular visitor to the Haight as a volunteer, two or three nights a week, in an intervention center called the Off Ramp, located in the basement of a local church. We served coffee and day-old doughnuts to anybody who walked in. As staffers, our job was to welcome our guests, chat with them, and see if they needed any help. Many were teenagers who'd run away from home and were looking for a way, or "off-ramp," to get back home. We connected many of them by phone with their parents and bought bus tickets for some of them.

As if teaching full-time and volunteering in the Haight were not enough to keep me busy, I also decided to continue my studies and pursue a doctorate in theology. Serendipitously, I applied and was accepted for graduate studies at Berkeley's Graduate Theological Union—affiliated with, and located just north of, the UC–Berkeley campus—where I signed up for GTU's program of study in Religion and Society and discovered a whole new world of purpose and meaning.

At GTU, fortune smiled on me once again when I was assigned Dr. Bob Lee as course adviser. A professor at Marin County's San Francisco Theological Seminary, Bob had authored fifteen books about faith in the real world, or what was loosely called *applied theology*. He was a committed and very down-to-earth Christian and good family man who stressed the application of faith to real-life events. He taught us the power of the faith community in leading the civil rights movement—whose public face was a Baptist minister, the Reverend Martin Luther King Jr.—as well as other historic causes, ranging from the abolition of slavery to women's suffrage to the prohibition of alcohol. He also introduced us to the great work of Reinhold Niebuhr and his epic book *Moral Man and Immoral Society*.

Niebuhr's central premise in that landmark work is that we are called upon to operate within and try to improve an imperfect world—a purpose that soon became one of the driving forces of my life. More than anything else, Niebuhr injected a healthy dose of realism into both theology and politics. In *The Children of Light and the Children of Darkness*, for example, he wrote: "Man's capacity for justice makes democracy possible; but man's inclination to injustice makes democracy necessary."

I'm in good company as one of Niebuhr's disciples. He was the leading influence on the work of Dr. King. Other leading figures who cite Niebuhr as an influence on their life's work include Hillary Clinton, Madeleine Albright, John McCain, and President Barack Obama. He was awarded the Medal of Freedom by President Lyndon Johnson in September 1964.

To me, Reinhold Niebuhr's work is what Christianity—or, indeed, any organized religion—is all about. It's also the focus of the great Jewish tradition Tikkun Olam, or "healing the world." And, I believe, that's what God taught us in the words of the Lord's Prayer: "Thy kingdom come, thy will be done, on earth as it is in heaven." We may get to heaven someday, but for now, we are citizens of this planet, this country, this city or town, and that's where our work must be focused—applying the lessons of Christianity in our everyday lives, striving for justice for all, and helping build a better world. And we should reach out especially to the poor and disadvantaged. It's not enough to go to church on Sunday or accept the world as it is. Our responsibility as Christian realists is to get involved, to transform the world in the cause of justice, and to speak out on the issues of the day. Niebuhr acknowledged "a tremendous urge to express myself." In that respect, I am his disciple. And in that spirit, I don't see how you can be pro-war, anti–gay rights, anti–women's rights, anti-environment, anti–programs to help the poor, or pro–discrimination of any kind—and still call yourself a Christian. Jesus Christ was a liberal. All Christians should be liberals, too.

I also took advantage of my new freedom from the seminary to try dating, which got off to an awkward start. At first, I went barhopping with another bachelor teacher from Sacred Heart, who promised to teach me how to "pick up chicks," but never did. Totally turned off by that scene, I joined a single dating club at Grace Cathedral. Nice people, wrong church. It was while walking out of Catholic Mass at the Church of Notre Dame on Bush Street one Sunday morning that I met Gisele Favre, a young Frenchwoman in San Francisco on a work permit. Years of teaching and speaking French paid off; we spent the rest of that day together, as well as the next few months. We both loved to dance. Our favorite hangout was a dance club named Sergeant Pepper's, on Bush Street near Van Ness Avenue, where we danced to the exciting, new sound of the Beatles.

Soon after my arrival in San Francisco, I heard from my good friends Seth and Margery Warner, now back from Switzerland and resettled in Malibu, who invited me down for Thanksgiving. My first visit to Southern California! Seth picked me up at LAX, and we spent most of the weekend at their modest but comfortable ranch house on Point Dume, walking down to the beach every day for a swim and picnic. Even then, Malibu was home to many movie stars and writers. The great novelist and screenwriter John Fante, one of the major influences on Charles Bukowski, lived on Point Dume, as did prolific police thriller writer Ross Thomas, whom I met at one of the Warners' lively dinner parties. Years later, Johnny Carson built a mansion on the bluff overlooking the little private beach at Point Dume. I ran into him one day, walking back from his tennis court.

There are not enough superlatives to describe what an important role Seth and Margery Warner played in my life. First in Fribourg, then in California, they adopted me as a best friend. I adopted them as my older brother and sister. Living such a wonderful, fun, meaningful life together, they were my role models as a couple. I loved spending time with them, both in Malibu and at their charming getaway in Carmel, and learned so much from both of them. I still think of them as California's version of Gerald and Sara Murphy, the beautiful young American couple who graced the gathering of ex-patriots on the French Riviera in the '20s, as chronicled by Calvin Tomkins in his wonderful little book, *Living Well Is the Best Revenge*.

Margery was the artist, the gardener, a great chef, an avid reader, author of children's books, and lively conversationalist. Seth was the professor, the intellectual, the connoisseur of bargain California wines from Trader Joe's, and a colorful raconteur. He introduced me to several of his favorite books, including *The Uses of the Past* by Herbert J. Muller, which reminds us that we are not the first society to face many of the problems we're struggling with and that we would do well to look back on, and learn from, earlier civilizations. Seth was also a great fan of *The Nation* magazine and loved reading out loud favorite passages from Alexander Cockburn's great, acerbic Beat the Devil column. With great gusto, he enjoyed dismissing most politicians with his favorite word: *feckless*.

Later, after I moved to LA, I was able to spend more time with Seth and Margery. But in those first couple of years, even while living in San Francisco, they served a very important purpose: the filter through which every one of my girlfriends had to pass. Whenever I felt I was getting serious about someone, I would arrange for us to drive to Malibu and spend a weekend with the Warners. I needed to see how she would relate to them and what they would think of her. As we will see, after several near misses, they helped me make a damned good choice.

One Friday night in early December 1967, I had just left a party at Gisele's apartment on Nob Hill when I heard her calling after me. There was an urgent phone call for me, she said. Knowing that none of my friends or family knew where I was that evening, I knew it had to be bad news—and it was. Rochelle, not finding me at home, guessed correctly that I must have been at Gisele's. "I just got a call from Delaware City," she said. "Your mother died." I immediately called home. Cousin Billy Stephens answered the phone and confirmed. "Chip, I hate to tell you this, but she's dead."

There's no way to soften the blow of losing your mother. Mom and I had our differences, especially as I became a rebellious teenager, often too aggressively asserting my independence. And I knew I had broken her heart by leaving the seminary. But I loved her. And I knew she loved me. She supported me in, and was proud of, everything I did. And I was proud to have such a young, beautiful, vivacious, life-of-the party woman for my mother. She dropped dead of a blood clot, only 47 years old. But if the thrombosis hadn't claimed her first, the cancer would have. While I was a senior at Niagara, she'd been operated on for breast cancer and never fully recovered from the same cancer that had already taken her mother and sister.

I flew home for the funeral, surrounded by the Cook cousin clan and several of my Oblate colleagues. Mom was buried in Delaware City's Catholic cemetery, under a tombstone that read simply: ISABELLE F. PRESS. WIFE-MOTHER. During the reception at our house after the burial, I noticed that Dad was missing. I found him upstairs in his bedroom sitting alone, looking out the window, lost in grief. At that point, he and I finally both broke down and cried.

I stayed around for a couple of days, helping Dad make arrangements for someone to help take care of Mary Anne, age eight, and Joe, age six. Then I headed back to the West Coast—but not without a detour to New York to see what was really going on with me and Ginny Howe. She met me at Penn Station, we went immediately to her apartment, and I returned to San Francisco and broke up with Gisele. For the next few months, Ginny and I enjoyed a wonderful, fun relationship, meeting up as often as we could in New York, San Francisco, Malibu, Chicago, and Neenah, Wisconsin, where her parents lived.

Back in San Francisco, I was flipping through my address book one evening, wondering whom I might call or get together with, when I made a great discovery: Just three blocks from my new, second apartment on Clay Street, this one in lower Pacific Heights, lived Vincent, Fred, and John Siciliano—three former campers from Camp Brisson, an Oblate summer camp on the Elk River in North East, Maryland, where I'd served as counselor before going to Europe.

I got to know the Siciliano boys well. They were the only ones who signed up, three years in a row, for the entire six weeks of camp. But I'd never met their parents, because they never came to visit. All we knew was that their father was some big shot in the White House. And, indeed, he was. Appointed by President Dwight Eisenhower, Rocco Siciliano is still the youngest person ever to serve as assistant secretary of labor. He then moved to the White House as special assistant to the president for personnel management, where he arranged the historic June 1958 meeting between President

Eisenhower, Martin Luther King Jr., and other prominent civil rights leaders. Rocco later served as undersecretary of commerce in the Nixon administration.

After school the next day, I walked up the street and knocked on their door. Marion Siciliano answered, I identified myself, she invited me in, we talked, she invited me to stay for dinner, I accepted—and never left!

From that day on, I've been part of the wonderful Siciliano family—Rocco and Marion, Loretta, Vincent, Fred, John, and Maria—and have benefited greatly from their love and support. Rocco and Marion, in fact, soon started calling me their "fourth son." We spent a lot of time together in San Francisco and at their vacation home in Alpine Meadows, near Lake Tahoe.

At the time, Rocco was head of Pacific Maritime, a West Coast–based trade association representing shipping companies. His wife, Marion, on the other hand, was a liberal Democrat and a force of nature. She clearly ruled the roost, somehow successfully balancing the raising of five children with remaining active in community affairs. Later, after they'd moved to Beverly Hills, where Rocco took over the helm of the title insurance firm TICOR, Marion became an accomplished painter, whose bold panels are still displayed in several Los Angeles public buildings and museums.

I'm grateful to Rocco and Marion for many things, not just for the good meals but especially for renewing my faith in Catholicism. For a while, in my role as seminarian in exile, I still went to Mass on Sunday mornings, but with less interest every week, because I was so turned off by the pabulum most priests offered as homilies or sermons. In my view, at a time of great, shuddering change across the nation and all over the world, priests never talked about anything of real consequence to the real lives of the real people before them. When I complained about this one day to Rocco and Marion, they invited me to join them the following Sunday in a private worship circle they'd helped organize.

Thus my introduction to San Francisco's wonderful Underground Eucharist. Once a month, we'd convene in someone's home for a very special worship service. We'd begin with reading of a passage selected by that day's host—from scripture, from a favorite book, or from the morning newspaper—followed by a lively discussion about what it meant, what lessons we should take away from it, or what actions it should trigger. For the Eucharist, we then shared a real loaf of bread and a real bottle of wine, blessed by one of two or three priest friends, organized by Jesuit Jim Strau-kamp. We ended with a potluck lunch or dinner.

And, like the early Christians of Rome, who were forced to meet secretly in the catacombs, we also met in secret to avoid the wrath of the bishop—who, had he found out about it, would have fired the priests involved and somehow penalized those of us who attended.

Even counting all my years in the seminary, those underground "masses" were the most meaningful religious experiences of my life. We were with close friends. We were living our faith. We were talking about real issues and applying them to our lives. To me, that's what the faith experience is all about. I was sad when a couple of families moved away and our group fell apart. I've never experienced anything like it since.

For me, it was back to the institutional church. But oh, what a difference. Having heard of Glide Memorial Church as a real force in community affairs, I decided to give it a try. Actually, I was disappointed in my first visit to Glide because it was so traditional. The ministers all clean-cut, garbed in flowing robes. Members of the choir, in their own colorful robes, arrayed behind the pulpit. The whole ceremony was decidedly old-world for a church with a reputation as a mover and shaker.

But that soon changed dramatically when the pastor resigned and the assistant pastor, Cecil Williams, took his place. Cecil took off his robes and let his hair grow. The choir disappeared, replaced by a live band and a light show. Cecil came out from behind the pulpit, sporting an Afro and a dashiki, and paced up and down the aisles preaching the most powerful sermons I've heard anywhere. Soon it was standing room only every Sunday, and Glide became my new home.

Sunday worship was only part of the Glide experience. A social hour was held in the church hall after services, with one of the most economically and socially diverse crowds you'd find anywhere. Williams was far ahead of most pastors in embracing members of the LGBTQ community, and there I had my first encounters with cross-dressers and transsexuals. Many Sundays, I joined a group from Glide that served free meals in Haight-Ashbury's Panhandle. I also volunteered several evenings in the Black Man's Free Clinic, founded by Glide in the Western Addition. Glide was where things were happening. It's the finest example I know of the vital role black churches have played and still play today in the life of American cities.

So it was only natural that, on the evening of April 4, 1968, when I learned of the assassination of Martin Luther King Jr., I immediately headed for Glide. So did hundreds of others. The church was packed with people seeking the comfort of friends in their grief. There was no organized service. Instead, spontaneously, people just stood up and started talking about what King had meant to them. It was a very powerful and genuine religious experience and a reflection of the true community that was Glide.

MY START IN POLITICS

At the same time, I was still drawn to politics, encouraged by my friend Rocco Siciliano, who—even though I was a registered Democrat—introduced me to then New York governor Nelson Rockefeller, who was gearing up for a possible presidential run in 1968. At Rockefeller's suggestion, I contacted his staff about a position in the campaign, but no job offer ever followed.

Eager to get back into politics after being forced to the sidelines during my seminary years, I looked for another opportunity—and found it. Or, maybe, it found me.

In the spring of 1968, nearing the end of my first year of teaching at Sacred Heart, I had a big run-in with the principal, Brother Francis. At a meeting in his office, he pointed to the peace button on my jacket and accused me of being a bad influence on students by taking a public stand against the Vietnam War.

I actually found this amusing. As I pointed out to Brother Francis, in my religion class, we had debated the war in Vietnam for six weeks, after which we had taken a vote. The class was well aware of my own anti-war position, yet the final vote was 15–1 in favor of the war. Obviously, my peace button hadn't poisoned the minds of too many students. Brother Francis nevertheless ordered me to remove the pin and informed me that Sacred Heart would not welcome me back for the fall '68 term. In other words, I was fired.

As they say, when one door closes, another opens. About the same time, I heard about an anti-war senator who had dared stand up against President Lyndon Johnson in the 1968 Democratic primary over the war in

Vietnam. Not only that, Eugene McCarthy was a Catholic and a former seminarian, a man I could identify with.

McCarthy's remembered today as one of America's most colorful and beloved politicians, respected by members of both parties for his courage, honesty, wisdom, and wit. When he retired from the Senate, even Lyndon Johnson sang his praises: "He's one of those uncommon men who puts his courage in the service of his country, and whose eloquence and energy are at the side of what is right and good."

I was thrilled, on March 12, when McCarthy racked up 42 percent of the vote in the New Hampshire primary, coming in a close second to LBJ's 49 percent, and demonstrating that there was, indeed, deep anti-war sentiment inside the Democratic Party. But I still remained on the sidelines, doing nothing other than following news of the primary—until four days later, March 16, when Bobby Kennedy announced he was jumping into the race.

To me, Bobby came across, as he had in his New York Senate race, as an interloper late to the feast. This time, he was trying to steal the challenger spotlight from Gene McCarthy, who'd earned that title by getting in first. Bobby's attempt to steal the anti-war torch from McCarthy pissed me off so much that the very next day I walked into the San Francisco McCarthy headquarters at Fox Plaza, Ninth and Market, and signed up as a volunteer.

You may remember: When I met and interviewed Senator John F. Kennedy in 1957, he told me the best way to find out if I liked the nitty-gritty of politics was to volunteer for a campaign. Now here I was, eleven years later, finally following his advice—and campaigning against his younger brother, no less. Little did I realize how much volunteering for the McCarthy campaign would determine the course of the rest of my life.

A word about politics. As the grandson and son of a small-town mayor, and as a high school student council president who interviewed a future president of the United States, it may not seem so unusual that I got involved in politics. Indeed, I turned to politics after leaving the religious life for the same reasons many former priests, nuns, and seminarians—Jerry Brown and Gene McCarthy, being prime examples—did so: because it was another form of public service and because if offered a similar opportunity to improve the human condition, without all the trappings or limits of organized religion.

What may be unusual is that forty years later—after my experience as a campaign manager, legislative chief of staff, press secretary, lobbyist, fundraiser, candidate, state party chair, and political commentator on radio and television—I'm still a believer. Yes, I've seen the best of politics and the worst of politics. And I'm still a believer.

For me, politics is about a lot more than winning or losing elections, even though I've fought like hell to win every election I've ever been involved in. For me, politics is how we make a contribution. It's how we build a better city, state, or country. It's all those decisions, big and small, that make this a better world for our children and grandchildren. It's one of the ways we exercise our responsibility as citizens of this great country. It's how we create democracy.

Democracy, after all, is not something invented once and for all in 1776 and put on the shelf to collect dust for the next 250 years. Democracy is always in the process of creation. Each generation in turn gets to create its own version of democracy, the kind of democracy it wants to live in. And now's our turn: to expand opportunities, to break down barriers, and to make sure all Americans enjoy the same basic freedoms in pursuit of the American dream. We do that through the political system. That's why politics is so important. And that's why we can never walk away from it.

For my baptism in politics, I spent two or three evenings a week and weekends doing grunt work: answering the phone; addressing, stuffing, and licking envelopes; and handing out flyers. When the end of the school year arrived, I told campaign manager Frank Moran I could put in even more time. Whereupon Frank named me office manager. Who says you need experience to get ahead in politics?

Spring of 1968 was a hot time in California politics, which became even hotter with LBJ's surprise March 31 announcement that he would not seek reelection. That made it a real rat race between Gene McCarthy and Bobby Kennedy on who would challenge Vice President Hubert Humphrey for the Democratic nomination.

In San Francisco, whichever challenger won, McCarthy or Kennedy, the well-connected Burton brothers were in the catbird seat. California State assemblyman John Burton was chair of the McCarthy campaign. Two blocks up Market Street, his older brother, Congressman Phil Burton, chaired the Kennedy campaign.

In effect, because he was the leader of opposition to the war, the McCarthy campaign was the anti–Vietnam War campaign. A strategic part of our campaign was organizing anti-war marches or rallies, most of them in front of San Francisco City Hall. John Burton was always a featured speaker. At one rally, I was assigned to accompany the legendary Jeannette Rankin from Montana, the first woman elected to Congress, a lifelong pacifist, one of fifty members of Congress to vote against U.S. entry in World War I, and the one and only member of Congress to oppose a declaration of war against Japan after Pearl Harbor.

Famed folk singer Pete Seeger performed at almost every rally. And anti-war activist Allard Lowenstein, who had persuaded McCarthy to challenge Johnson after Bobby Kennedy at first refused, would often fly in, totally unkempt, lugging books and papers under both arms, give a rousing speech, and then fly off to another rally in another city. Many of us, myself included, worshiped Lowenstein as a political hero.

It was an exciting time and, working at McCarthy headquarters, I was in the heart of the action. John Burton held frequent news conferences at Fox Plaza. State campaign leaders Jerry Hill, Mike Novelli, Joe Holsinger, and June Degnan held strategy sessions there. McCarthy himself stopped by on a couple of campaign swings through Northern California, always attracting huge crowds. McCarthy was the Bernie Sanders of his time. I never saw such genuine enthusiasm for any candidate, especially among young people, as I did for Gene McCarthy—until Bernie Sanders in 2016.

Morning, noon, and night, the San Francisco McCarthy office was always swamped with volunteers. The music of Carole King's *Tapestry* album filled the air. It was my job to hand out daily assignments to volunteers and keep them busy.

One day, Frank Moran's girlfriend, Joan, showed up with Carol Perry, a girlfriend of hers from Providence, Rhode Island, who was spending the summer in San Francisco in between her first and second years of graduate school at Boston's Simmons School of Social Work. Joan asked where the two of them might be most helpful that day. Without thinking about it, I dispatched them to Fisherman's Wharf to hand out flyers announcing an upcoming McCarthy rally.

As they walked out the door, I glanced at Carol again and quickly realized how strikingly attractive she was and what a dumb move I'd made.

Fortunately, she and Joan both returned to volunteer the next day, when I could find plenty of work for Carol right there in the office. By this time, my relationship with Ginny had ended—sadly, but on good terms. Carol and I soon struck up a friendship, started dating, and, thanks to Gene McCarthy, the rest is history. We were married less than a year later. And thirty-five years later, Carol and I hosted a birthday party in our home in Washington to celebrate Gene's eighty-seventh birthday.

As I write this, Carol and I have enjoyed forty-eight wonderful years together, and I can't believe how lucky I am. First, to have met her. Second, that she's put up with me all these years. For her, given my schedule, frequent career changes, often impatient and petulant nature, and zero interest in or aptitude for all those household chores husbands are supposed to take care of, but I don't, it hasn't been easy.

For me, it's been a dream. Carol is Audrey Hepburn beautiful. She's a talented artist and weaver. She's even more liberal than I am, politically. She's quiet where I am loud, graceful where I am clumsy. She may seem meek, but she has nerves of steel. She's a great cook. She's a devoted mother and grandmother. She's a loyal and warm travel companion, lover, and friend. Almost fifty years later, I still feel about Carol the way Abigail Adams felt about husband, John, at the same period in their marriage. When her sister asked her in February 1814 if she would still marry John if she had her life to live over again, Abigail wrote back: "Yet after half a century, I can say my first choice would be the same if I again had my youth and opportunity to make it."

But 1968, as anyone who lived it will remember, was also the worst of times. The glory of that primary season, sadly, ended in tragedy at the Ambassador Hotel in Los Angeles shortly after midnight on June 5. Just a week before, May 28, McCarthy had upset Kennedy in Oregon and moved into the California primary with a head of steam. We worked like hell that last week, confident we could carry California for McCarthy over of Kennedy—and then crush Hubert Humphrey at the Chicago convention. But our hopes were dashed as we gathered at McCarthy headquarters the evening of June 4 and saw the votes pile up for a narrow Kennedy win. I left the party as soon as McCarthy conceded, rather than wait for Kennedy's victory speech. As soon as I got home, shortly after midnight on June 5, I turned on the radio and heard the horrible news that Kennedy had been shot. He died the next day, twenty-six hours later, at Good Samaritan Hospital.

The assassination of Bobby Kennedy alone was a tremendous shock. I didn't dislike him. I admired him greatly. I just identified with Gene McCarthy more. But coming only two months after the assassination of Martin Luther King Jr., and only five years after the assassination of President John F. Kennedy, Bobby's murder seemed to take all the joy and meaning out of politics. We limped through the summer, still pretending we could make a difference in Chicago. Yet, deep down inside, we knew it was all over and didn't want anything more to do with politics as usual.

The night of August 28, we young McCarthyites joined the official gathering of San Francisco Democrats in a North Beach restaurant to watch the proceedings from Chicago—which meant, mostly, watching footage of Mayor Daley's goon squads beating up anti-war protestors in Grant Park. Then the voting started. As soon as the Pennsylvania delegation put Humphrey over the top, we stood up en masse, put on black armbands we'd brought along for the occasion, and paraded out of the restaurant.

One week later, we formed a new organization called VNP, Volunteers for New Politics, determined to support only those candidates, Democrat or Republican, who met our high ideals. Pro-war Hubert Humphrey was not one of them. In fact, I can't even remember whom I voted for that November. I simply may not have voted. I did not vote for Humphry.

Whatever option I took, I learned a powerful lesson about spite voting and refusing to vote: Don't do it! Clearly, Humphrey would have made a much better president, but thanks in part to a lot of people like me, we got stuck with Nixon.

I was reminded of that mistake again in 2000, when so many Democrats cast a vote for Ralph Nader for president, even though he couldn't possibly win, just to spite Al Gore. That's how we ended up with the Florida recount and the Supreme Court's decision to cancel the election and appoint George W. Bush president of the United States.

That was the end of the McCarthy campaign, in all respects but one. By this time, I was enjoying Carol's company so much that I didn't want to lose her. So, one night, while driving across the Golden Gate Bridge to join friends in Marin County for dinner, I suggested she might want to stay with me in San Francisco. Happily for me, she agreed, drove back to Boston to pick up her stuff, stopped in Providence to explain everything to her parents, then drove back to California.

For a while, Carol and I shared an apartment together in the Haight with a couple of roommates, then got our own place in the Upper Haight, on Buena Vista Terrace, with a magnificent view of downtown San Francisco and Mount Diablo—for which we paid the grand sum of $150 per month.

Carol comes from good, solid New England Quaker stock. You'd be hard-pressed to find two better people on the planet than her parents, Tom and Mackie Perry. Tom was a general surgeon at Rhode Island Hospital in Providence, an avid birder, and an accomplished bird photographer. Mackie supported Tom's career, shared his passion for birding, managed the family beach house in Weekapaug, and for many years served on the board of Laurelmead, the retirement home they helped establish off Blackstone Boulevard in Providence. Both were active members of Providence Friends Meeting, very active in Quaker affairs, and very well informed on local and national issues. And, of course, very devoted to their daughters, Carol, Margaret, and Phebe, and their grandchildren.

Back in San Francisco. I enjoyed my volunteer work for McCarthy so much, I asked John Burton for his help in finding a paid job in politics. A couple of days later, he told me he'd scoured the entire Bay Area and found only one politician with a job opening: Roger Boas, successful Pontiac dealer, running for reelection to the San Francisco board of supervisors. John's famous for never pulling his punches. He didn't this time, either. "He's a real asshole," he warned, "but at least it's a job."

It didn't take me long to discover that John was right. For my job interview, sitting on the patio of his weekend retreat in Stinson Beach, Roger read a list of prominent San Francisco political names, asking me which of them I knew personally. Answer: Zero. Roger concluded with typical bluntness: "When it comes to politics, you don't know shit from Shinola. But Johnny Burton says you're okay, so you've got the job."

At first, I served as Roger's administrative assistant, working out of his Pontiac dealership on Geary Street or his tiny office in San Francisco City Hall. Six months later, he named me manager of his reelection campaign, and we opened a campaign office at Eighth and Market Streets, just a couple of blocks from city hall. At the time, Roger also served as chairman of the California Democratic Party. Executive director Don Solem ran the party from his office next door.

In the middle of Roger's campaign, on April 6, 1969, Carol and I got married. We had to scuttle our original plan to be married in the Siciliano home on Clay Street once the family moved back to Washington. But fortunately, Carol and I were adopted by Jim and Mary Anna Colwell, good friends from the Underground Eucharist group, who lived with their five kids in a rambling old Victorian on California Street in the Western Addition.

The evening before—Saturday, April 5—we gathered with family and friends at the Alta Mira Hotel in Sausalito. Carol's father and Seth Warner each offered warm toasts and tributes. Early the next morning, Carol and I showed up, with our friend Jean-Max Guieu as witness, at the rectory of a nearby Catholic church, where we were secretly but officially married by Father Dominic, another Underground Eucharist regular. Jean-Max and I then hooked up with another friend, Mike Witte (who, after graduating from medical school, later founded the wonderful West Marin Clinic) and went out to Ocean Beach for a little bachelor party on Ocean Beach, smoking a couple of joints to celebrate.

Later that day, we gathered in Jim and Mary Anna's living room. Our priest friend Dominic presided over a nontraditional, combined Quaker/Catholic wedding ceremony: silence, followed by a couple of readings—including a passage from Kahlil Gibran's *The Prophet*, the hippie favorite of the time—and the sharing of bread and wine. Carol's parents, grandparents, and sisters, Margaret and Phebe, were there from Rhode Island. My father and Dot and Grandmom Press flew out from Delaware for their first ever visit to California. The wedding reception was held right there at the house, after which Carol and I drove down to Carmel for our honeymoon in Seth and Margery's vacation home.

As newlyweds, Carol resumed her graduate studies in social work at San Francisco State, and I continued managing Roger Boas's reelection campaign.

We also got involved in our first boycott—the nationwide grape boycott organized by César Chávez and Dolores Huerta to pressure growers to pay farmworkers a living wage and allow them to form a union. Carol and I joined the protest in front of the Safeway on upper Market Street. It was my very first picket line, the first of many. On the spot, I vowed never to cross a picket line. I never have, and never will.

While the grape boycott enjoyed great success in establishing better working conditions for farmworkers under the banner of the United Farm Workers Union (UFW), the struggle to achieve safe working conditions and a living wage for both permanent and seasonal farmworkers continues today.

Later, I worked very closely with leaders of the UFW in Jerry Brown's 1976 presidential campaign and often participated in meetings with the great César Chávez. He's one of the most impressive people I ever met but also one of the most humble. He seldom spoke up in meetings, and when he did so, he spoke softly, almost as if asking permission to speak. Yet there was no doubting his moral authority and power. He radiated goodness and inner strength.

In 1993, as Democratic state chair of California, I attended César's funeral in Keene and helped carry his casket for part of the procession from the church to his final resting place. The UFW now thrives under the leadership of Arturo Rodriguez, César's son-in-law.

Carol and I also became involved in events across the bay, where tensions left over from Vietnam War protests erupted in confrontation over plans by UC–Berkeley's Free Speech Movement to create a public space north of campus for open debate, called People's Park. At first, university officials recognized existence of the park, but they were soon overridden by Governor Ronald Reagan, who had previously called Berkeley "a haven for communist sympathizers, protesters and sex deviants" and who now ordered the California National Guard to clear the park, erect a chain-link fence around it, and take over downtown Berkeley and the university campus.

The next day, I called our Jesuit priest friend Jim Straukamp, who answered the phone: "Hello. Occupied Berkeley." I laughed and accused him of exaggerating. Whereupon he described how Berkeley had become an armed National Guard camp and insisted that we get off our liberal asses and join the movement. Which we did. On May 30, 1969, Carol and I joined a crowd of thirty thousand in the now-famous People's Park March, protesting Reagan's military occupation of Berkeley. It was a peaceful protest but eerily unnerving to march past row after row of California National

Guardsmen, rifles drawn, some of them sitting on tanks, their turrets pointed directly at us.

As for my paid job, I can best describe working for Roger Boas as a baptism by blood. Most of the time, he was a total asshole, probably the coldest, crudest, meanest, most heartless human being I ever met, and working for him was often a total humiliation. My daily assignments included picking up several newspapers for him every morning and dropping them at his door, then driving him to various meetings around town, where I was ordered never to speak to him, not even to say, "Good morning," unless he spoke to me first. And, of course, I was always to call him *Mr. Boas.*

That arrogance sometimes got in the way of my job as campaign manager. At one point, Roger complained that we had no young people volunteering for his campaign, and asked me to do something about it. So I got to work and invited a whole bunch of politically-active friends to my apartment for a 6 to 8 p.m. "meet and greet" with the candidate. Roger arrived 15 minutes early. At the stroke of 6, when only a few people had arrived, Roger demanded that I introduce him to speak. I suggested we should really wait till more people showed up. Fifteen minutes later, he insisted: "You introduce me now, or I'm walking out of here." I did. He spoke. He left. My apartment was soon jammed with friends and potential supporters, all of whom had a great time, few of whom had heard the candidate, and none of whom volunteered for the campaign.

But here's the contradiction. At the same time, Roger could be one of the most charming people alive: witty, engaging, caring, knowledgeable, great fun to be around, with a wicked sense of humor and infectious laugh. That's the side of him most people saw, and it explains why he was such a popular man about town: successful businessman, civic leader, sought-after tennis partner, and host of a highly regarded weekly show recapping world news on KQED-TV. True, no man is a hero to his valet, but Roger was more Jekyll and Hyde than anyone I ever met.

As difficult as it was working for Roger, some good things actually came out of it—like meeting John Monaghan. John was the quintessential seasoned San Francisco political pol. Recently retired from running his own Irish bar, he was hired by Roger as a campaign consultant and sidekick. Every evening, Roger, John, and I worked the campaign circuit, with John providing insightful campaign analysis while at the same time keeping us in stitches with his running commentary on all the other candidates.

It was also a joy working with Roger's publicist, Marion Conrad. Out of her home at 1948 Pacific Avenue, Marion ran the most successful public relations company in San Francisco. She was beautiful. She was smart as a whip. She was sharp-tongued and profane.

Two experiences with Marion, I'll never forget. One morning, Roger, Marion, and I met in his campaign office, reviewing names of possible contributors. As Roger's secretary, Rita O'Laughlin, read out each name, Roger would cite a dollar figure he thought they were good for—$500, $1,000, $5,000. Marion or I would then add our own comments, then Rita would write down the agreed-upon ask. When she came to the name *Joe Holsinger*, Roger exclaimed, "Cocksucker!" Shy Rita blushed royally. I held my breath. Marion couldn't hold back: "Roger, really! Couldn't you use a less profane term? Couldn't you call him a cunt-lapper?"

Months later, I made a special trip to Marion's office one morning to tell her the good news: Carol was pregnant. Without even looking up, Marion said, "You phony intellectuals. I knew you'd fuck!" God, I loved that woman, as well as her husband, Hunt, successful lobbyist, and brother of the great writer Barnaby Conrad.

Roger's election campaign was a free-for-all. There weren't just two candidates, there were ten or twelve—all running for one of three empty seats on the board of supervisors. A few, like Roger, were running for reelection; the rest were running for their first time—including a dynamic, charismatic young lawyer named Dianne Feinstein.

Whichever candidate received the most votes would automatically become chairman of the board, and that was Roger's primary goal. But even though successfully reelected, he lost the number one slot. Dianne Feinstein topped the field of candidates, became chair of the board, and began her historic political career.

During that campaign, I may have been working for Roger, but I became a big fan and friend of Dianne's. Unlike Roger, she was very relaxed on the campaign trail, very persuasive in her arguments, easy to approach, and great company. She and I have remained good friends ever since, and she and her husband, Dick Blum, have always been among my biggest supporters. Dianne and I haven't agreed on every political issue. No matter.

She's been there whenever I needed help, and, over the years, she and Dick have included Carol and me in many delightful social events in their home.

That campaign was also my introduction to Dianne's campaign manager, Sandy Weiner. Unlike me, Sandy was a seasoned pro, veteran of many successful campaigns, with a sardonic take on politics in general. He quickly became a good friend and mentor and, before long, my new boss.

Pat and Owen Martin, friends of Roger's, were another direct gift of the Boas campaign. One of San Francisco's most popular and colorful couples, they lived on Nob Hill's Sacramento Street, across from Grace Cathedral, where they entertained lavishly almost every night. Owen showed up one Saturday to walk precincts for Roger in the Sunset District. He and I hit it off, and Carol and I soon became regular guests in their home.

Owen was a real gadfly. A highly successful businessman, owner of a school-uniform company, Owen usually greeted his dinner guests wearing a bright green tracksuit. Pat was an incredible chef, who night after night turned out fabulous meals with ease. Joe Hughes was their live-in man-about-town, who came to dinner one night and, literally, never left. Their three Weimaraners had the run of the house and were invited to take any empty seat at, and eat off, the table. Needless to say, it made for interesting dinner parties.

I remember many wild evenings at Pat and Owen's, where it was not unusual to find the mayor, the police chief, TV anchors, top reporters, and other San Francisco luminaries all mixed together. One Sunday morning, Pat called with a last-minute invitation to brunch. When Carol and I showed up, there were only two other couples present: the top two columnists for *The San Francisco Chronicle*, Herb Caen and Art Hoppe, with their wives.

OMG. Caen and Hoppe were like movie stars to me. I was nervous just being in their company. But Pat immediately put us at ease, introducing us as good friends, and then noting that Carol was not only obviously pregnant but already past her due date. The baby could come at any minute. At which point Art Hoppe asked, "And when and where was the baby conceived?" Which I thought was not only an impertinent question but impossible to answer. When I told him we had no idea, he laughed and said, "That's because you're so young. At my age, you'd definitely remember!"

Roger Boas was indirectly responsible for one other high spot in my early political career. One night, I drove him to dinner at the Italian American Athletic Club in North Beach, where Governor Ronald Reagan was guest of honor. Excited to finally see Reagan in action, I was disappointed when Roger shook a few hands, then ordered me to drive him home. Which I did, only to turn around and beeline it back to North Beach, just in time to see Reagan take the podium.

The man known as "the Great Communicator" was every bit as impressive and entertaining as his reputation. He brought the house down with his famous story about the new father who didn't know how to change a diaper. His wife explained:

> For a baseball fan like you, it should be easy. Here's what you do: Spread the diaper in the position of the diamond, with you at bat. Then fold second base down to home and set the baby on the pitcher's mound. Put first base and third together, bring up home plate and pin the three together. Of course, in case of rain, you gotta call the game—and start all over again.

I learned an important lesson from the master that night: Audiences want to be entertained first and informed second—and never bored or lectured to. The perfect speech formula is: Start out by making them laugh; give them some good meat to chew on in the middle; and close with another good laugh, inspiring story, or uplifting message. Works every time.

Nearing the end of the campaign, I'd grown so sick and tired of being treated like shit by Roger that I told John Monaghan I couldn't take it anymore and was going to resign. Wise old John gave me some of the best advice of my life. "I understand," he said. "I couldn't take it, either. But look at it this way, kid: This is your first political job. You're going to win this campaign. But if you quit now, you'll have a reputation as a quitter, and you'll never get another job in politics. If you stay with it, you'll soon have a winning campaign on your résumé and you'll be able to get any political job you want."

Thus convinced, I put on my asbestos suit and hunkered down for the rest of the campaign. Roger easily won reelection, and when he walked into the office the next morning, I handed him my resignation.

IDEAL POLITICIAN

The big question was: What next? Despite winning my first campaign, the combination of my own unhappy experience with Roger Boas and the violence that scarred the political process in 1968 had soured me on politics. Yet, somehow, I still wanted to stay involved in public policy.

Which is why I was so excited to pick up a copy of the *Pacific Sun*, Marin County's popular, free weekly newspaper, and read about a man named Peter Behr.

Behr was a lawyer and member of the Marin County board of supervisors who had most recently led the successful Save Our Seashore campaign to create the Point Reyes National Seashore. Here was a man with a cause, a conservationist, and a man I could believe in. I made a cold call to Peter's office and introduced myself. He invited me to lunch two days later at San Francisco's Stock Exchange Club (now the City Club).

Peter and I immediately hit it off. But I was thrown when he told me the reason he'd wanted to get together: He was planning to run for the California State Senate—and wanted me to run his campaign. Here I was, trying to get out of partisan politics. Yet, here he was, trying to lure me back in—working for a Republican, no less! Nothing decided, we agreed to stay in touch.

Meanwhile, Sandy Weiner, Dianne Feinstein's former campaign manager, offered me a job in Weiner & Co., his new campaign management/advertising firm. Not having heard from Peter Behr, I accepted Sandy's offer, whereupon he informed me he'd already signed up one new client on condition that I be assigned to run his campaign.

You guessed it. That candidate was none other than Peter Behr—who still wanted me to run his day-to-day campaign but also wanted the experienced hand of Sandy Weiner overseeing the operation.

Sandy put together an exciting team of young professionals, including Regina Forbis, Greg Lipscomb, and Rob Coughlin. Peter Behr was not our only candidate. We also managed the successful campaigns of Arlen Gregorio for state senate and Wilson Riles for state superintendent of education, and the losing campaigns of Sam King for governor of Hawaii and California millionaire Norton Simon for U.S. Senate. I traveled a couple of times with

Riles, a wonderful, charismatic candidate, but was assigned full-time to the Behr for Senate campaign.

To this day, the Peter Behr campaign of 1970 is the best campaign I've ever been part of. For one thing, Peter had a devoted army of followers left over from the Save Our Seashore campaign, led by the formidable Bunny Lucheta. Carroll Joynes, a friend of Peter's daughter Trudy, left Stanford to volunteer full-time for the campaign—and went on to become one of my closest, lifelong friends. But the best part was Peter himself. He was a phenomenal candidate. He had boundless energy, was quick on his feet, smart as a whip, loved meeting people, knew the issues inside and out, and was very thoughtful and caring toward his staff and volunteers.

Behr was running for the district vacated by the retirement of Senator Jack McCarthy: Marin, Napa, and Solano Counties. As a moderate, or "Rockefeller," Republican, Peter had wide bipartisan support. Our real challenge was in the Republican primary against right-winger Ray Schoen, who accused Peter of being a Marxist and Socialist. Sound familiar? I was so impressed by Peter I decided to reregister as a Republican—until I saw the grief he took from his own party in the primary and came to realize that for too many in the Republican Party there was no room for a moderate like him, let alone a liberal like me. Which, of course, is even truer today.

On Sandy's advice, we first commissioned a poll, which showed that Peter's name recognition was sky-high in Marin County but practically nonexistent in Napa and Solano counties. It also showed strong public support for environmental protection, Peter's long suit. We then put together a campaign budget.

One Sunday morning, I drove to Mill Valley to deliver the bad news to the candidate. Peter and I sat out by the family swimming pool, where I nervously presented our recommended budget for the state senate race: $80,000! To my relief, Peter took one look at it and said, "I think that's reasonable. I just wanted to be sure that, if worse came to worst, I could pay for the entire campaign out of my own pocket."

Again, Peter was a joy as a candidate. He loved campaigning, and it showed. He had the strong support of his wonderful wife, Sally, who worked alongside volunteers at the campaign office. Peter and I were on the road almost every day in a Chevy Camaro he'd had retrofitted to drive on propane—on top of which was a specially made sign: PROPANE-FUELED CAR.

Remember, this was in 1970, long before anybody was talking about alternative fuels.

No matter the audience, no matter the issue, Peter never trimmed his sails. One night, at the Marin Rod and Gun Club, Peter himself raised the issue of gun control. After admitting that he supported tougher gun control measures, Peter told them, "That's the difference between me and my opponent. Agree or disagree with me, you'll always know where I stand on every issue."

The greatest coup of our campaign was the brainchild of press secretary Charlotte Riznik, an intrepid reporter recently retired from *The Marin Independent Journal*. Even though the Save the Seashore campaign had created the Point Reyes National Seashore on paper, the park would never become a reality until sufficient funds were appropriated by a bill then moving through Congress and headed for the president's desk.

Charlotte swung into action. Through the intermediary of attorney Lew Reid, who had served on the staff of the FCC, Peter was invited to the signing ceremony in the Oval Office, and Charlotte persuaded the Associated Press to post a photo of the signing on the wires. Result: That very afternoon, *The Marin Independent Journal* featured a front-page photo of Peter Behr standing behind President Richard Nixon as he signed the Point Reyes National Seashore legislation.

With that million dollars' worth of free publicity, Peter won the Republican primary and, six months later, defeated Democrat Mike Peevey to become California's newest state senator. Then things happened fast.

Ten days later, Carol and I welcomed the birth of our first son, Mark Thomas Press. One week after that, Peter offered me a job in Sacramento as his chief of staff, which wasn't as easy a decision as it might appear. I had a great job with Sandy Weiner. Carol and I had a fabulous apartment and a lot of friends in San Francisco. And I was well along in my graduate studies at Graduate Theological Union.

Before making a decision, Carol and I did a little homework. First, we spent a weekend with friends Phil and Marilyn Isenberg, former neighbors from Buena Vista Terrace, now living in Sacramento, where Phil worked for Assemblyman Willie Brown. They convinced us that Sacramento was an okay place to live, at least for a while. They also suggested we drive up to their favorite art gallery, the Candy Store in Folsom, run by the one and only Adeliza McHugh, who represented such great California artists as Bob Arneson, David Gilhooly, and Roy de Forest. Adeliza persuaded us to purchase our very first original piece of art, a small ceramic Gilhooly sculpture, for fifty dollars—for which we agreed to pay her five dollars a week!

Next, I sought the advice of Bob Lee, my course adviser at Graduate Theological Union. I explained my dilemma: I had this great job offer, but I was also really committed to finishing my doctorate in theology. What should I do? It may have seemed difficult for me, but it wasn't for Bob. He responded immediately, "I don't think that's a hard decision at all. In fact, I'll tell you what: If you don't take that job with Peter Behr, I'll resign from GTU and I'll take it!"

One thing for sure. Three active years in San Francisco—challenging the Catholic bishop, protesting the war in Vietnam, counseling runaways in the Haight-Ashbury, volunteering for Glide Methodist's community outreach programs, joining the grape boycott, and working for Gene McCarthy—had turned me into a full-fledged progressive. In effect, I got my degree in progressive politics from San Francisco and was ready for graduate studies in the state capitol.

Indeed, I was ready for a new challenge, and in Sacramento I found it big-time: a new job, a new baby, a new city, a new home, a new decade. So began some of the best and most eventful years of my life.

4

LOWER YOUR EXPECTATIONS

When it comes to American legislative politics, outside of working in the United States Capitol, working in the California Legislature is as big-time as it gets. And there, this newly hatched progressive took to Sacramento like a fish to water.

Freshman senator Peter Behr and I put together a first-rate team, combining a veteran secretary who knew where the bodies were buried with eager young staffers, including former campaign aide Carroll Joynes.

Carol and I rented a little bungalow on Sacramento's Fifth Avenue, about a mile and a half south of the capitol, with our two-month-old son, Mark. I rode my bike to work every day, except when I visited one of our district offices: in San Rafael, Marin County; Yountville, Napa County; or Vallejo, Solano County.

Visits to Napa were especially welcome, since not only was our office located in the heart of the world-famous wine country, but Napa director Astrid Edington and her husband, Lowell, owned a vineyard and sold their grapes to Charles Krug Winery—which, in turn, offered me the growers' discount of premium wines at one dollar per bottle. Every week, I'd return to Sacramento with the car stuffed with cases of wine ordered by friends in the state capitol.

Then, as now, Sacramento was a one-industry town. And that industry is state government. In 1971, Ronald Reagan was governor and Republican Bob Monaghan had succeeded the legendary Jesse Unruh as speaker of the state assembly.

There'll never be another Speaker like Jesse Unruh, or Big Daddy. He was both a visionary and a down-to-earth politician. Acknowledging the reality of how things got done in politics, he once famously observed, "Money is the mother's milk of politics." And he counseled freshmen legislators unsure of how to deal with lobbyists: "If you can't eat their food, drink their booze, screw their women, and then vote against them, you have no business being up here."

Serving as senate president pro tempore was the enigmatic James Mills of San Diego, an unlikely politician and well-known scholar of California history with a bizarre sense of humor. On those rare occasions when both the governor and lieutenant governor traveled out of state, leaving him in charge, Mills would set up a tiny cannon on the front lawn of the capitol and fire several shots into the air. The Bear Flag Republic rises again!

But what surprised Carol and me most was discovering that, even in that hotbed of California politics, it was still possible to escape the political scene. We made friends with many young couples—some of whom, like Vic Fazio, who later was part of the Democratic leadership of Congress, and attorney John Moulds and his wife, Betty, administrator at Sacramento State University, remained friends for life.

Sam Farr, son of the great state senator Fred Farr, also worked in the legislature as administrative assistant to Assemblyman Alex Garcia. Sam and his wife, Shary, threw wonderful, wild parties at their house on Curtis Park. They soon numbered among our best friends, and still are today. Sam's tour de force was organizing an annual ski trip for capitol staffers to Yosemite.

Sam began his own career of public service when Governor Jerry Brown appointed him supervisor of Monterey County. He then served in the state assembly until he was elected to take Leon Panetta's seat in the United

States Congress in 1993, when Panetta became President Bill Clinton's director of the office of management and budget. In 2016, Sam retired from Congress, after representing the California coastline from Santa Cruz to Big Sur, the most beautiful congressional district in the country, for twenty-three years.

The Farrs and Presses did a lot of fun things together. We were young. We were carefree. We got drunk and smoked a lot of pot. We had a lot of laughs. We traveled to Baja California together. We went camping in Big Sur. We went skinny-dipping whenever we could. In fact, we took our clothes off a lot. And we played pranks on each other. One morning, after a dinner party at our home on Fifth Avenue, we awoke to discover that someone had TP'ed the entire house. Having no doubt it was Sam and Shary, we retaliated in similar adolescent terms. We wrapped up a dirty diaper of Mark's and mailed it to their home, properly marked "Do Not Open Till Christmas!"

At the very first of Sam and Shary's parties we attended, we met Malcolm and Judith Weintraub, who also became best of friends and important role models for us. Malcolm, a prominent Sacramento attorney, and Judi, an inspired chef, were well-known art collectors. For a while, Judi had her own gallery. They and their six kids lived in south Sacramento in a fabulous contemporary home they had designed and built themselves, which was itself a remarkable piece of art. We spent many wonderful evenings there, surrounded by their incredible art collection, including original portraits of them by their friend and king of the Sacramento art world, Wayne Thiebaud. Through their friendship and contacts, we also met and purchased works by leaders of the burgeoning Davis-Sacramento art world, including Thiebaud, Bob Arneson, and David Gilhooly.

Judi and Malcolm helped and inspired us in many ways, personally and professionally. They also inadvertently handed down to us one lasting legacy. Having joined the Farrs at the Weintraubs' for dinner one evening, we were enjoying drinks in the living room when their young son Nicholas, maybe four or five at the time, appeared in his pajamas. When Judi gently told him to go back to bed, Nicholas shouted, "No! You're a fucker and a shit!" We could barely contain our laughter until Judi rushed Nicholas out of the room, but *fucker and a shit* instantly became our nicknames for each other. To this day, Sam and I call each other *fucker and a shit*—although in polite company we sometimes abbreviate it to *F&S*.

Which has created some embarrassing moments over the years. At a big conservation dinner at San Francisco's Palace Hotel, I once introduced Sam as the recent winner of the prestigious F&S Award of Monterey County. The audience, having no idea what *F&S* meant—"Field and stream?"—heartily applauded, while Sam just stood up and glared at me.

Worse yet, the morning after he was elected to Congress, Sam's secretary rushed in to tell him he had a call from the president of the United States. Immediately suspecting it was me, pulling his leg, Sam picked up the phone and was on the verge of blurting out, "You're a fucker and a shit!" when he heard a familiar voice on the line saying, "Hi, Sam. This is Bill Clinton."

Notwithstanding its political importance, we found the city of Sacramento itself not all that exciting. But we soon discovered that part of Sacramento's appeal was its proximity to beautiful country nearby. Lake Tahoe was only a couple of hours away, an easy escape for skiing in winter and hiking or swimming in summer. San Francisco was only an hour and a half in the other direction. Just south of the city lay the magical but underappreciated Sacramento Delta, great for biking along its levees and visiting quaint little towns like Rio Vista and Locke, home of Al the Wop's steak house. North of Sacramento lay the historic Gold Country—Placerville, Jackson, Angels Camp—and access to great white-water rafting. The Marin County coast was two hours away, and we'd often drive out to Inverness and Drake's Beach just for the day.

In the capitol, I soon discovered that I was a rare bird among legislative staffers. Many of them worked for men or women they were ashamed to admit working for. For me, it was just the opposite. Whenever anybody asked me for whom I worked, I was proud to say, "Peter Behr!"—whereupon many of them would tell me, secretly, how jealous they were. Gregarious and smart, Peter instantly made friends with several senators: Democrats Nick Petris, Tony Beilenson, Arlen Gregorio, Jim Mills, and George Moscone; and Republicans Howard Way, John Nejedly, Milton Marks, and Fred Marler.

Believe it or not, Peter also struck up a cordial relationship with Ronald Reagan. No matter that Peter was a much more moderate brand of Republican than Reagan. Actually, the governor, soul of congeniality, reached out to legislators of both parties. He fought like hell with Democrats like

George Moscone during the day, but he'd often invite them over to his home in West Sacramento for drinks that same evening.

Reagan didn't work that hard, either. In fact, I discovered you could set your watch by his arrivals and departures. His three-car motorcade would pull into the capitol garage at 9:00 a.m. sharp every morning—and depart at precisely 5:00 p.m., no matter what pressing business remained. What a contrast to the chaotic lack of schedule I would experience, four years later, under Jerry Brown.

Soon after arriving in Sacramento, Peter took me along for his first visit with the governor. I'd seen a few of his old movies and had observed that one speech in San Francisco, but I still didn't know what to expect in person. In advance of our meeting, Peter and I had prepared responses to all the issues the governor might ask about. Wasted time. We didn't discuss any policy matters at all. For Governor Reagan, it was nothing but a photo op. Like any professional movie director (or actor), he spent all his time arranging the right background and lighting for the perfect photo. There was zero discussion of issues. Hooray for Hollywood!

Actually, it would not have been possible for Peter to have a serious discussion on any issue with Ronald Reagan. Even then, the governor was lost without his cue cards. An eerie, early version of Donald Trump, Reagan never took the time to delve into any issue, nor did he seem intellectually capable of doing so. The difference was that Reagan had a top-notch staff and followed their advice. Trump is surrounded by people as ignorant as he is, and he listens to no one. God help us!

As state senator, Peter bit his tongue. It was only later, in 1980, when Reagan became the Republican candidate for president, that Peter offered his devastating quip to *Newsweek* about Reagan's intellectual capacity: "You could wade through his deepest thoughts and not get your ankles wet."

In Sacramento, it didn't take long for Peter to establish his reputation as the state senate's leading conservationist (the word *environmentalist* was not yet in anyone's vocabulary). In his first two years in office, he authored and secured passage of legislation banning the bounty hunting of mountain lions and the use of exploding devices to kill coyotes. He also persuaded the governor to agree to reintroduce a dozen tule elk, also known as the California or dwarf elk, once native to Marin County, into the Point Reyes National Seashore.

Ironically, the tule elk are now a challenge for our son David, who, in his position as wildlife manager for the seashore. now has to deal with hundreds of elk—they are prolific!—that have expanded their range in the seashore and now encroach on several ranchers' lands. I'm not sure David counts helping with passage of the tule elk legislation as one of his father's better accomplishments.

But Peter's signature achievement was Senate Bill 107, the Wild Rivers Bill. It all began during his senate campaign, when I spotted an article in *The San Francisco Chronicle* about the status of "wild" rivers in California. As reported, out of California's original fifty-eight rivers, only three remained free-flowing from the mountains to the sea: the Eel, the Trinity, and the Klamath. Dams had been built on all the rest. Peter loved the idea of saving those rivers. We got in touch with the colorful Joe Paul, founder of the California Committee of Two Million, representing California's two million licensed fishermen, which he had formed to protect the three rivers.

There was only one problem. None of the rivers were in Peter's district. All three rivers were located in Northern California's redwood country— Mendocino, Humboldt, and Trinity Counties—territory of Democratic senator Randy Collier, the Silver Fox of the Siskiyous, the most powerful member of the legislature and chair of the senate finance committee. Collier didn't like Behr's meddling in his district. And he certainly didn't like any bill opposed by his beloved timber companies, which owned him lock, stock, and barrel.

But Peter didn't care. He wasn't afraid of Collier. He introduced the Wild Rivers Bill on his first day as state senator, and the media loved it. After all, it was great theater, pure *Mr. Smith Goes to Sacramento*—a freshman state senator daring to take on the chairman of the senate finance committee, the entire timber industry, the mighty agribusiness of the Central Valley, Southern California developers, and Governor Reagan's Department of Water Resources, led by director Bill Giannelli. "He can't stand the sight of a free-flowing river," Peter once charged of Giannelli. "He has a bad case of beaver fever."

Supporting SB 107 were the California Committee of Two Million, the Sierra Club, and a new alliance of conservation organizations known as the Planning and Conservation League, or PCL. Peter traveled up and down the state promoting the legislation. "California was once blessed with fifty-eight rivers that flowed free from the mountains to the sea," he would explain. "All but three have been dammed and destroyed. We must save those three remaining rivers, the Eel, the Trinity, and the Klamath."

In Northern California, wild rivers country, we also had the help of savvy local leaders: Dan Frost, in Shasta County; Jim Eckman, Siskiyou County; Al Wilkins, Trinity County; and Rich Wilson, Mendocino County. Slowly, public support built for three rivers most Californians had never seen and never would.

One memorable experience from that first year of battle: a trip Peter and I made to Randy Collier's Humboldt County as guests of Pacific Lumber Company, California's number-one logging company and leading opponent of the Wild Rivers Bill. We flew to Eureka on Pacific Lumber's World War II–era plane, dipping low over the Eel, Trinity, and Klamath watersheds. Once on the ground, we were taken on a tour of logging operations.

That evening, Peter was honored guest at a timber industry dinner at the exclusive Ingomar Club in downtown Eureka. Toward the end of the meal, I was standing in the back of the banquet room, sporting the shoulder-length, hippie-style hair I had at the time, when Senator Collier spotted me while on his way to the men's room. The powerful senator walked right up to me and blurted out, "Your hair's too long—and your boss is a son of a bitch."

Whether in Washington or state capitols, most successful legislation is seldom achieved in one year. And so it was with the Wild Rivers Bill. After Peter and I spent months honing our arguments and building support, SB 107 passed the Natural Resources Committee—but died in the senate finance committee, where Chairman Collier simply stuffed the bill in a desk drawer and never brought it up for a hearing or vote.

We were better prepared the next year. By the time we reached the finance committee, Peter had lined up enough votes to force Collier to hold a hearing. Not only that, he'd lined up the support of Senator Howard Way, the powerful president pro tem of the senate and point man for California agribusiness. Howard Way was the last man Collier expected to vote for the Wild Rivers Bill, but Peter had convinced him it would not harm Central Valley farmers.

Peter and I had learned another lesson, too: Never walk into a committee hearing without knowing you have the votes. Which we did and Collier didn't.

Our star witness, again, was Joe Paul of the California Committee of Two Million. When he'd finished his prepared statement, Chairman Collier asked Paul, "What's the name of your organization mean, Committee of Two Million?"

Paul explained, "Mr. Chairman, we represent California's two million licensed fishermen."

Collier protested, "Well, I'm a fisherman. And you don't represent me."

And Paul immediately shot back, "No, Senator, and you don't represent us, either!"

Moments later, the cocky Collier called for a roll call vote. He was visibly shaken when Howard Way boomed, "Aye." Freshman Peter Behr had beat senate king Randy Collier in his own committee. The bill later sailed off the senate floor, easily passed the state assembly, and was soon on the governor's desk. That's where the real fun began.

For the last two years, the Reagan administration, under DWR director Bill Giannelli, had opposed the Wild Rivers Bill. But once the bill passed the Legislature, two more senior Reagan officials stepped in: policy director Don Livingston and resources director Norman "Ike" Livermore. And, here again, Peter had an ace up his sleeve. Livingston was a real pro, who maintained close ties with Republican legislators. He and Peter had developed a good working relationship on several issues. But the key was Livermore.

Ike Livermore was one of three Livermore brothers from Marin County, sons of the legendary Carolyn Livermore, cofounder of the Marin Conservation League and early leader of California's environmental movement. He and Peter had been friends for years. Ike had always secretly supported the Wild Rivers Bill, but waited until it was on the governor's desk before making a move.

More than the support of fishermen, kayakers, white water enthusiasts, or backpackers, Ike knew what would touch Ronald Reagan. One evening, he secretly arranged for a group of Native Americans from the Round Valley Indian Reservation, located on the Eel River in Mendocino County, to visit with the governor. As Ike related later, as the Native American leaders pleaded with the governor to save their ancestral homeland from being destroyed by a dam on the Eel River, tears rolled down Reagan's cheeks.

A week later, I stood in the governor's office with Peter Behr and state environmental leaders for the signing of SB 107. In very moving terms, Governor Reagan spoke—without cue cards!—about his lifelong love affair with rivers, growing up on the banks of the Rock River in Dixon, Illinois, his years as a young lifeguard in Lowell Park, and how proud he was to sign the Wild Rivers Bill. No shit. You'd think his administration had championed SB 107 all along, instead of fighting it all the way.

Peter Behr had beat the odds. He'd triumphed over the most powerful special interests in California. The Wild Rivers Bill was now the law of California. And Peter was now indisputably the leading and most effective environmentalist in the California Legislature.

SAVE THE COAST

Peter was also involved in a long-standing legislative battle to protect the California coastline, led by Assemblymen Alan Sieroty of Los Angeles, Ed Z'berg of Sacramento, and John Dunlap of Napa County. At that time, the magnificent California coastline was badly threatened. Developers were seeking to build a Berlin Wall of hotels, expensive homes, and condominiums from Eureka to San Diego, cutting off most of the coast from public access. The Sea Ranch development in Mendocino County had already locked up ten miles of the coastline. The state highway department released plans to widen the scenic coastal route Highway 1 to four lanes. And utilities planned nuclear power plants in Malibu, Moss Landing, Bodega Bay, and Point Arena.

Alarmed by this planned destruction of the California coastline, Democrats Sieroty, Z'berg, and Dunlap, with the strong support of Republican assemblymen Paul Priolo of Los Angeles and (later governor and U.S. senator) Pete Wilson of San Diego, tried for years to get legislation protecting the coast through the legislature to no avail. So in 1972, they agreed to sponsor a ballot initiative instead. The result was Proposition 20, on the California ballot in November 1972.

Enter Janet Adams. Much more than a citizen activist, Janet was a human dynamo. Working out of her home in Woodside, as head of the California Coastal Alliance, Janet organized the statewide Save Our Seashore campaign, whose army of volunteers gathered enough signatures in just thirty-four days to get Prop 20 on the ballot. She then led the initiative campaign to secure its approval by voters. With Peter Behr's blessing, I took a leave of absence to serve as the Prop 20 campaign press secretary. Peter Douglas, Alan Sieroty's chief of staff, who had written both the original legislation and the ballot initiative, joined as chief strategist.

The Prop 20 campaign was the most lopsided campaign I've ever been involved in. Our opponents—developers, realtors, and utilities—had all the money; we had none. And I mean none. In the meantime, the big boys saturated the airwaves with misleading commercials and lined the highways with billboards claiming that Prop 20 would actually deny public access to the coast—when, in fact, it was just the opposite. They outspent us, they cheated, and they lied. But in the end, we beat them, because we had a cadre of incredibly dedicated and creative people on our side.

People like Mel Lane, a leading Republican businessman and publisher of the popular *Sunset* magazine. He and his brother, Bill, were strong environmentalists. Mel loaned us his private plane for the campaign and actually became part of our Prop 20 team. A couple of days a week, he and I would fly a rotating cast of politicians of both parties into media markets large and small for news conferences, urging voters to "save our coast." State senator Jim Mills and Monterey County supervisor Sam Farr, that fucker and shit, led a bicycle caravan down the coast, from San Francisco to San Diego, generating tons of free publicity along the way. Actor Jack Lemmon and *Dennis the Menace* cartoonist Hank Ketcham added their voices of support.

With no funds to buy billboards, we made up for it by having Republican Paul Priolo stand in front of one of the opposition's billboards in Los Angeles and tell the cameras, "This billboard is a lie!" Meanwhile, a band of supporters went around Southern California at night, slapping a giant YES over billboards urging people to vote no. Developers woke up the next morning discovering billboards they'd paid for now urging a yes vote on Prop 20.

Also key were citizen activists up and down the coast who had long fought to save their own stretch of coastline. I remember especially Rachel Binah, Mendocino County; Bill Kortum, Sonoma County; Fred Farr of

Monterey; Naomi Schwartz, Santa Barbara; Dorothy Green and Ellen Stern Harris, Los Angeles; Faye Hove of Malibu; Judy Rosener, Orange County; and Roger Hedgecock, San Diego; and, of course, Peter Behr in Marin.

Our most successful gambit by far was getting free TV commercials. Because developers were flooding the airwaves with anti–Prop 20 spots and we had zero money to respond, we petitioned the Federal Communications Commission, arguing that under the Fairness Doctrine, stations had an obligation to give us free time to respond to the opposition spots. There was no way the FCC would rule before Election Day, but we still hoped to get a little publicity out of it.

But attorney E. Lewis Reid, a member of our steering committee, came up with a bold plan. Having once worked at the FCC, Lew called one of the commissioners and convinced him to write a letter stating that, while there was not time for the commission to rule before the election, there was no doubt that, were the FCC to hear our case, it would rule in favor of the Prop 20 campaign and against the TV stations.

Bingo! Armed with that ominous but meaningless letter, Lew and I started contacting TV stations in San Francisco and Los Angeles and demanding—demanding!—equal time under the Fairness Doctrine. It was all a bluff, and—to our total surprise—we actually succeeded. Several TV executives gladly offered us free airtime.

But that created another problem: We also didn't have any budget, or talent, to produce TV spots. Problem solved: Advertising executive Bud Arnold suggested we contact a friend of his from Los Angeles named Sidney Galanty, who turned out to be the perfect man for the job.

Sid had produced TV spots for a host of liberals, including Hubert Humphrey, Tom Bradley, César Chávez, Tom Hayden, Teddy Kennedy, and Harold Washington, first African American mayor of Chicago. He also later produced Jane Fonda's wildly successful workout videos, still among the bestselling videos of all time. Sid immediately hopped on a plane to San Francisco, met with campaign staff, and produced our winning TV spots without charging a dime.

Galanty was another extremely important person in my life. The Proposition 20 campaign was just the first of many fun collaborations between the two of us over the years. Later, when I got my first job in television at KABC-TV in Los Angeles, I never went to the studio without first rehearsing my daily commentary with Sid, in his office or over the phone. Sid and his wife, Joan, were wonderful, warm, and generous friends.

In the end, even though outspent a hundred to one, we won the Proposition 20 campaign by eleven points, fifty-five to forty-four. As written, Proposition 20 created a state coastal commission and six regional commissions to review, grant, or deny applications to build within the coastal zone, anywhere within a mile of the shoreline. But only for four years. Then the legislature would have to act to renew or terminate the commission and its new limits on coastal development.

I was there at the beginning and, four years later, as one of Governor Jerry Brown's environmental advisers, I was proud to assist in passage of the final coastal legislation and creation of the permanent coastal commission. Once the permanent commission was established in 1976, Peter Douglas left Sacramento to become its executive director in 1985, a post he held until his death in 2012.

PCL

The Wild Rivers Bill and Proposition 20 were hard acts to follow. But just as I was beginning to wonder what might come next, Jud Clark, board member of the Planning and Conservation League, approached me with an interesting offer. The founders of PCL had decided to turn a loose collection of conservation organizations into a new environmental lobby in Sacramento—and wanted me as its first executive director. With Peter Behr's blessing, I accepted.

Heading PCL for almost three years was a great experience and taught me a lot about building and leading a grassroots organization. I was fortunate to work with a very influential board of directors made up of representatives of local and regional environmental organizations, including Dwight Steele and Jim Bruner of the League to Save Lake Tahoe; the great Sylvia McLaughlin, founder of Save the Bay; Ralph Perry, Dave Hirsch, and Dorothy Green of Los Angeles; Dan Frost, from Redding; Bill Evers of San Francisco; Rich Wilson of Mendocino County; and Jud Clark, right there in Sacramento. We also worked closely with Huey Johnson, head of the Trust for Public Lands, as well as Mike McCloskey, executive director of the Sierra Club; Will Siri and Edgar Wayburn, Sierra Club trustees; and Sierra Club Sacramento lobbyist John Zierold.

We also shared office space with one of our most effective member organizations, Legislative Birdwatchers, founded by the dynamic Joan Reiss. At that time, there were no records kept of how members of the legislature voted in committee. In fact, most of the time, there were no roll call votes; bills were decided by voice vote. So Joan organized a group of volunteers who attended every committee hearing and took notes on how each committee member voted, which often involved lip-reading or analyzing nods of heads.

Legislative Birdwatchers then reported their observations to the media— which ended up driving legislators so crazy that both the senate and assembly eventually adopted new rules requiring a roll call on every vote in committee. That put the Legislative Birdwatchers out of a job, but not before performing a valuable public service.

Even back then, on environmental issues, it was easier to secure Democratic votes than Republican votes. But one important lesson I learned early on: Never give up on anybody and never take anybody for granted. You just never know where you might pick up a vote, or for whatever reason. Even the most conservative Republican might give us a vote on an environmental bill sometime, because he or she knew they couldn't be anti-environment all the time. They needed a couple of pro-environment votes in their quiver.

So we at PCL lobbied all members of the legislature, Republicans and Democrats alike. With one difference. Unlike lobbyists for the timber companies, developers, labor unions, or power companies, we had zero money for campaign contributions. All we could offer was good information and the facts behind any given piece of environmental legislation. Plus the gratitude, or outrage, of their constituents, once we informed them of how their state senator or assemblyman had voted on our legislative priorities.

And we had surprising success on many issues. In my second year on the job, *The California Journal* asked legislators to name their favorite lobbyists. I was ranked number ten, with this comment: "He knows how to disagree agreeably." I'm still proud of that.

Perhaps our greatest legislative achievement during my tenure at PCL was legislation creating the Los Angeles Air Quality Control Board, still the toughest air-quality enforcement agency in the country. It also provided a valuable lesson in political power.

Assembly speaker Bob Moretti himself agreed to carry the legislation, and it was my job to brief him before the first committee hearing. Two weeks in advance, I'd prepared talking points on the bill, which I assured Moretti's staff would take no more than an hour of the Speaker's time. But even though I checked in every day, the day before the hearing I still had not met with Moretti.

The next morning, I showed up in the Speaker's office an hour ahead of time, ready to brief the Speaker. I waited. And waited. Ten minutes after the hearing had already begun, Moretti finally walked out of his office and asked, "Do you know this bill?"

"Of course," I said.

He gestured toward the door. "Okay, let's go."

We walked to the committee room, where he was immediately recognized. Moretti read the title of the bill: "An Act to Create an Air Quality Control Board for the City and County of Los Angeles."

At which point a voice piped up: "I move the bill."

Another voice: "Second!"

The chairman: "All those in favor, say aye. . . . The ayes have it. The bill is approved." And Moretti and I walked out, two minutes later, with no discussion, no debate, no testimony, no witnesses, just a positive vote.

It was my first exposure to pure political power. But I don't feel guilty about it because I know how much good was achieved and how many lives were saved because Moretti was willing to put his name on that legislation. And if you have power like that, you might as well use it to accomplish good things.

Moretti's leadership on environmental issues paid off for him, as well. Since, due to term limits, Ronald Reagan could not run for reelection in 1974, the race to succeed him was wide open. In the Democratic primary, candidates included Bay Area congressman Jerome Waldie; San Francisco mayor Joe Alioto; shipping magnate William Roth; Secretary of State Jerry Brown; and Speaker Bob Moretti. I knew them all. I especially liked Jerry Brown. But Bob Moretti had supported us every time we called on him, so PCL decided to support him for governor—even though one of three issues

Brown campaigned on was the need for statewide land-use planning, PCL's signature issue.

That, in fact, led to a fateful encounter with Brown on a Pacific Southwest Airlines (PSA) flight to Los Angeles one day. I said hello, admitted I was supporting Bob Moretti, but told him I still wanted, in total confidence, to share something about land-use planning. As exciting as it was to hear him promise to create a new, statewide, land-use planning agency, I pointed out that such an office, with all the powers he envisioned, already existed—in the governor's office! It was called the California Office of Planning and Research (OPR), created years before but, since then, actually lying moribund. Jerry listened politely, thanked me—and I figured that was the end of that. Oh, no. One year later, I learned that Jerry had a mind like a steel trap.

Jerry Brown won the Democratic primary and went on to defeat state controller Houston Flournoy to become, at the age of thirty-six, California's youngest governor. In 2011, in one of the great comeback stories of American politics, Brown would also become California's oldest governor at the age of seventy-two. Who says there are no second acts in politics?

As Brown started assembling his cabinet, despite having supported his opponent in the primary, I decided to take a stab at becoming Brown's secretary of resources. I worked hard at it, updated my résumé, and lined up an impressive list of endorsements from leading conservation organizations and leaders of both parties in the legislature. And actually came close.

In the end, as I learned during my job interview over dinner at Fuji restaurant with chief of staff (and later governor himself) Gray Davis and legal affairs secretary Tony Kline, the search for resources secretary had boiled down to two candidates: me and Sierra Club director Claire Dedrick. Gray and Tony informed that, at the tender age of thirty-four, I was too young to lead such a big agency.

"What the fuck," I shot back. I was only two years younger than Jerry Brown—and he was governor! The next morning, I sent them a follow-up memo pointing out all the great things that people in their thirties, starting with Mozart, had accomplished. But in the end, the job went to Claire Dedrick, who was actually a good friend and environmental partner. I called to congratulate her and resumed my duties at PCL.

In the meantime, Carol and I had abandoned our rental home on Fifth Avenue and bought our first house, a magnificent English Tudor three-bedroom in Sacramento's Old Curtis Park neighborhood, built by legendary developer Squeaky Williams. We'd also doubled the size of our family, welcoming son David at Sacramento's Kaiser Hospital on March 2, 1974.

ON TO OPR

Jerry Brown was sworn in as governor in January 1975. At PCL, we continued pressuring the legislature, as well as the new governor, on environmental issues. We blasted Brown, for example, for refusing to support tough new regulations on clear-cutting of timber.

Nevertheless, about six months into his term, I received an unexpected call from Brown's legislative director Marc Poche, who told me Governor Brown wanted to know if I'd be interested in heading up that land-use planning office I'd told him about on PSA. Steel-trap mind at work! The plan was that I would join the Office of Planning and Research as deputy to interim director Preble Stolz, ready to step up as soon as he stepped down.

Of course, I was interested, so Marc said he'd set up a meeting with the governor. I told him I'd be available anytime, day or night, for the next three months, after which Carol and I would be leaving for a long vacation in the South of France.

Welcome to the early Jerry Brown style of governing. Three months dragged by, and I heard nothing. In fact, I'd given up on OPR. The night before our flight to France, Carol and I were busy packing when the phone rang at 10:00 p.m. It was Lucie Gikovich, the governor's executive assistant, inviting me to join Brown for a late dinner at Frank Fat's, a legendary lobbyists' hangout near the state capitol.

To Carol's dismay, I agreed—out of curiosity, more than anything else. Over a couple of beers and second-rate Chinese food, Jerry, Marc Poche, and I talked for an hour about everything but the Office of Planning and Research. Then, as we got up to leave, Jerry told me the job was mine if I still wanted it. I accepted, and the next morning, Carol and I took off with

Mark and David for France. Back home, a month later, I started out as deputy director of OPR.

In many respects, the Office of Planning and Research was a dream job. The office has two principal responsibilities. *Planning* means reviewing and acting as state liaison with city, county, and regional land-use plans. *Research* entails providing whatever research the governor needs in any policy area: energy, transportation, urban development, water, health care, immigration, jobs, prisons, business. In effect, the director of OPR serves as the governor's policy director. The best part of the job was working so closely with the youngest, smartest, brightest, and most exciting of all the nation's governors.

To support Brown's agenda, we recruited a great team at OPR. Peter Detwiler, Pike Oliver, Dean Misczynski, Chuck Brandes, Mike Bledsoe, Larry Hynson, Dennis Castrillo, and Bob Remen ran the planning side of the operation. The policy side was led by Terri Thomas on health care, Rich Hammond and Suzanne Reed on energy, and Jim Neff, legislative director. I recruited Mike Fischer from the San Francisco Bay Conservation and Development Commission as my deputy.

Working for Jerry Brown was at once exhilarating, challenging, frustrating, and an incredible learning experience. He has the quickest, most penetrating mind of anybody I know. In meetings, I would often just sit back and marvel at his laser-like focus, his capacity to grasp the weakness of any issue and move in for the kill, destroying within seconds the argument others had taken weeks to prepare. Or, alternatively (but more rarely), immediately grasp the wisdom of an idea, embrace it, and suggest how to make it even better and stronger. He was a progressive, but he was also a realist. His embrace of the phrase "Lower Your Expectations" became the watchword for his administration: Don't expect government to do too much.

Yes, meetings always started later and lasted longer than they should have. Yes, he explored issues that may have seemed like flights of fancy. But in his own way, he got things done. Which is why it's so unfair that he got branded as *Governor Moonbeam*. Still today, every time I hear that sneer, it pisses me off.

The moniker was actually created by legendary Chicago columnist Mike Royko in 1976, during Brown's first run for president when, Royko noted, he was attracting "young, idealistic, and non-traditional voters." For many, the term took on even more meaning when Brown proposed—not such a crazy idea—that, with the federal government failing to act, California launch its own weather satellite.

Today, in his second stint as governor, Brown is again similarly taking the lead on climate change—vowing to launch California's own weather satellite if Trump cancels NASA's eyes in the sky and scheduling an International Summit on Climate Change in San Francisco in September 2018 after Trump embarrassed the United States by withdrawing from the Paris accords. He is the world leader on climate change.

In 1980, Royko changed his tune. "I have to admit I gave him that unhappy label," he wrote. "Because the more I see of Brown, the more I am convinced that he has been the only Democrat in this year's politics who understands what this country will be up against." And by 1991, Royko was begging people not to use it: "Enough of this 'Moonbeam' stuff. I declare it null, void, and deceased."

But by then it was too late. The sobriquet still sticks. And, for his part, Governor Brown's not all that concerned. "Moonbeam also stands for not being the insider," he rightfully contends. "But standing apart and marching to my own drummer. And I've done that."

Check the record. Jerry Brown was a very effective governor the first time around. With the benefit of experience, and thanks in great part to his dynamic wife, Ann Gust Brown, he's been even more effective in his second tour of duty, bringing California back from fiscal ruin to a vibrant state economy, leading the nation in health care, and, as noted above, leading the world on climate change.

Serving under Jerry Brown was like being a graduate student again, complete with a required reading list. All of us in the governor's office, for example, were urged to read *Small Is Beautiful: Economics as if People Mattered*, a manifesto against the rush toward globalization and dominance of megacorporations by British economist E. F. Schumacher. At Jerry's invitation, Schumacher came to Sacramento and gave a lecture arguing that many goods could be produced more efficiently, with far better quality, at the local level. "Small is beautiful." That evening, Carol and I hosted a dinner party for Schumacher, with the governor presiding, at our home on Markham Way.

Schumacher wasn't the only big thinker or writer invited to the governor's office. The great Wendell Berry read from his poetry celebrating the American land and small farmers. Leading beat poet Gary Snyder often came down from his home in Nevada City. And presidential historian Page Smith, author of the eight-volume *A People's History of the United States*, became a Brownie regular. His wife, Eloise, was head of the California Arts Council.

One other must-read for us Brownies was Ernest Callenbach's prophetic little novel *Ecotopia*, a strong condemnation of the materialism and consumerism then represented especially by Southern California. In his novel, citizens of Northern California finally get so "sick of bad air, chemicalized food, and lunatic advertising" that they secede from California and join Oregon and Washington in forming a new, environmentally conscious state called Ecotopia.

It was also in Sacramento that I came across the best political book of all time: *Plunkitt of Tammany Hall*, William L. Riordan's profile of an actual Tammany chieftain named George Washington Plunkitt, who painfully explains the difference between "honest graft" and "dishonest graft." Plunkitt dictated the one sentence he wanted on his tombstone: "I seen my opportunities—and I took 'em." If you haven't read Plunkitt, you don't know politics.

With such a facile, fertile mind, Jerry Brown was ahead of his time on many issues, and at OPR, we were involved in all of them. Before he acted on proposals from cabinet secretaries, he'd send them to OPR for our review. He'd also routinely send his own ideas and initiatives over to OPR for a reality check. And he often summoned me to his office when outsiders showed up to pitch a new plan or project.

At one such encounter, I walked in to find him meeting with Stewart Brand, former member of Ken Kesey's "Merry Pranksters" and creator of the famous *Whole Earth Catalog*. Stewart's a man who spews out good ideas nonstop, and this one was particularly good: to create a series of atlases telling the story of California—its resources, its agricultural production, its energy production, its forests, its great cities, you name it. We agreed to start with water—which is, more than any other, the one issue that defines

California. And, of course, Jerry immediately handed the assignment to OPR. In 1979, under the direction of Bill Kahrl, we published the beautiful *California Water Atlas*, hailed by the California Historical Society at its publication as "an indispensable sourcebook for decades to come." In January 2010, the atlas was made available online as part of the David Rumsey Map Collection at the University of California.

Please bear with me as I salute the talented team I worked with in Jerry's office. They include legislative directors Marc Poche, Tony Dougherty, and Diana Dooley, succeeded by Terri Thomas and Jim Neff; legal affairs secretary Tony Kline; chief of staff Gray Davis; Tom Quinn, chair of the Air Resources Board, succeeded by Mary Nichols; Richard Maullin, head of the Energy Commission; Marty Morgenstern and Don Vial, labor liaisons; Robert Batinovich, chair of the Public Utilities Commission; business and transportation secretary Dick Silberman; Lynn Schenk, Silberman's deputy, before taking over as secretary; press secretaries Bill Stall and Elisabeth Coleman; astronaut Rusty Schweickart, science and technology adviser; and B. T. Collins, director of the Civilian Conservation Corps and, later, chief of staff.

Keeping it all together was executive assistant Lucie Gikovich, all of twenty-four years old, who deftly managed the impossible job of keeping Jerry's schedule and placing his phone calls while juggling cabinet secretaries, staffers, members of the legislature, hangers-on, and the countless media celebrities who paraded through Sacramento.

Somehow, I inherited another assignment at OPR: unofficial liaison to the governor's father, former governor Pat Brown, whose legacy includes building the state water project, the state highway system, and the great University of California.

Pat was a wonderful, warm, ebullient human being and a highly successful governor of California. Unfortunately, he also became known as *Mr. Malaprop*. Arriving in Eureka to survey damage from the 1964 floods, for example, Brown said it was the greatest disaster to strike California "since I was elected governor." In 1966, running for reelection against Ronald Reagan, he told grade school students, "I'm Governor Brown and I'm running for reelection. And do you know who's running against me? That actor! And, remember, it was an actor that shot Abraham Lincoln!"

Pat was one of the most popular politicians in California, but he still had a hard time getting his son on the phone. So he'd call me instead—often!—with ideas and advice he'd ask me to pass on to Jerry. Which I dutifully did, with one exception. That's when Pat told me to tell Jerry to marry Linda Ronstadt. "Bill, you know he's going to run for president someday. So don't you think he ought to marry that girl?" There's no way I was going to butt into Jerry's romantic life.

And then there was Jacques Barzaghi. Even today, whenever someone learns that I once worked for Jerry Brown, one of the first questions is usually "What was up with Jacques Barzaghi?" The truth is, I really don't know. All I know is that, for a while, Jerry had total confidence in Barzaghi as a close adviser.

In effect, Barzaghi was the Colonel House to Jerry Brown's Woodrow Wilson. He had his own office but no assigned responsibility. Instead, he was involved in everything going on, with authority to walk into and sit in on any meeting, any time, on any subject. But he wasn't just window dressing. Barzaghi also had a very quick, intuitive mind and often offered valuable suggestions. At the same time, he could be as enigmatic as the governor himself. In 1992, when Brown's third presidential campaign was floundering, Barzaghi told reporters, "We are not disorganized. Our campaign transcends understanding."

My very first assignment from Governor Brown was to find California a new state architect. Actually, Jerry had already found the man he wanted: Berkeley professor Sim Van der Ryn. There was only one problem: Sim was not a licensed architect. Actually, he was an architect, but in a dispute with the state architects board over its refusal to embrace new, energy-efficient design, Sim had let his license expire—and the board now refused to support his appointment.

On behalf of the governor, I worked out a compromise with the board whereby Sim would pay his past dues and get officially reinstated as a licensed architect. And in 1979, California got its first green state building designed by state architect Sim Van der Ryn: the beautiful, energy-efficient Gregory Bateson Building at 1600 Ninth Street in Sacramento.

Sim Van der Ryn not only presided as state architect, he also created a new government agency, the Office of Appropriate Technology, or OAT, which became part of OPR. Inspired by E. F. Schumacher's "small is beautiful" teachings, OAT's staff—led by Kirk Marckwald, Peter Calthorpe, Scott

Matthews, Bob Judd, and Wilson Clark—pursued alternative, smaller-scale approaches to almost every field of human endeavor, from agriculture to energy production.

Of all the issues we worked on at OPR, the California Urban Strategy was the most important and the most lasting. At the time, California had no land-use policy. As a result, urban development was happening helter-skelter around the state. The historic, older cores of many cities were being abandoned and allowed to run down. Urban sprawl gobbled up valuable cropland. New housing was being built far from jobs, with no public transportation to connect the two. California was killing the goose that laid the golden egg.

Convincing Jerry Brown to accept anything resembling a new statewide land-use plan wasn't easy. He once derided planning as the "squid process," whereby planners merely squirted ink at a problem, believing they'd thereby solved it. Nonetheless, we brought together business leaders, labor leaders, and local and state government officials in a twelve-month series of hearings—out of which came a set of recommendations for guiding future urban growth according to commonsense principles:

- First, urban areas, both cities and suburbs, should be renewed and maintained.
- Second, vacant and underutilized land within existing urban areas should be developed.
- Third, when urban development is necessary outside existing urban and suburban areas, land that is immediately adjacent should be used first.

By late 1977, our work was done. Everybody involved in the project had signed off on the final recommendations. All we needed was the governor's approval. But first, we needed his attention. And that was always hardest to get.

After hovering around the governor's office for days, hoping to grab him between meetings, with no luck, Gray Davis informed me the governor was leaving for Los Angeles, but I could ride to the airport with him and make my case. That seemed like a good plan, except that Jerry ignored me and talked on the phone the entire fifteen minutes.

Arriving on the tarmac, Jerry suggested I jump on PSA with him so we could talk on the way to LA. Another good plan, except that, this time, he read the newspaper the entire flight. When we landed in Burbank, Jerry and I climbed into the waiting blue Plymouth and headed off with Jerry again on the phone nonstop. Next thing I knew, we'd pulled up to a Mexican restaurant on Melrose Avenue in Hollywood, across the street from Paramount Studios. It was my first of hundreds of visits to Jerry's favorite hangout, the famous Lucy's El Adobe.

Owners Lucy and Frank Casado greeted Jerry and showed him to his favorite table, where we were quickly joined by several friends who just happened to be having dinner there that evening. By this time, I'd given up on making any progress on the urban strategy. I decided to just have a couple of margaritas, eat some good Mexican food, and enjoy watching Jerry in his element, relaxing with friends.

The restaurant had started to empty out, and Jerry and I were alone at our table when he summoned Frank and Lucy over and said, "Bill's got something he's been working on. Let him explain it, and tell me what you think." And that's how the California Urban Strategy came to be: over margaritas and arroz con pollo, in the back room of Lucy's El Adobe restaurant, on Melrose Avenue in Los Angeles, as seen through the eyes of Frank and Lucy Casado. Jerry figured that if it made sense to them, it made sense to him.

I explained the problem with urban sprawl and how we recommended fixing it. Frank and Lucy said it sounded like a good plan to them. Once I had their blessing, Jerry added his. The final report was published under his signature on February 9, 1978. The California Urban Strategy became the official land-use policy of the state of California. And still is to this day. Thank you, Frank and Lucy!

Note: It's too bad that land-use planning, such a hot topic in the '70s and '80s, has fallen out of favor. Because, like population control, it's one of the most basic environmental issues underlying all others. Just like so much noise and pollution wouldn't exist if we didn't have so damned many people crammed into so little space, we would not experience many environmental problems if we only had some commonsense laws or regulations— at the local, state, and maybe even federal level—about what development goes where. We should not be planting condominiums on good cropland.

We should not be siting refineries, chemical plants, or airports in wetlands. We should not be building power plants on earthquake faults. We should not be plowing freeways through and destroying vibrant, low- or mixed-income urban neighborhoods. We should not allow people to build homes in flood zones, fire zones, or barrier islands—and then bail them out when homes already built there are lost to natural disasters. All those problems could be solved by good, commonsense land-use planning. Which, I learned, would also be welcomed by developers and the business community. Why? Because then, at least, they'd have the certainty of knowing ahead of time what kind of development would be permitted and where— which would streamline the approval process and save them both time and money.

BROWN FOR PRESIDENT

Life around the governor's office, always so unpredictable, became even more so in the spring of 1976 when Governor Brown suddenly revealed he was going to run for president. He did so in classic Jerry fashion: no hoopla, no big rally of supporters, just casually letting the word slip out while talking to a reporter in his office. But of course, that announcement took the political world by storm.

Thus Jerry Brown, the most exciting politician in the country, joined an already crowded Democratic primary of fourteen candidates, including senators Frank Church, Lloyd Bentsen, Birch Bayh, Fred Harris, and Henry "Scoop" Jackson, as well as governors Terry Sanford, Milton Shapp, George Wallace, and Jimmy Carter—in what looked like a good year for Democrats to recapture the White House.

For Jerry, there was only one problem. A big one. The other candidates had been running for over a year and already had a campaign operation in place. But not Jerry Brown. He had no campaign operation and no plan, and, by jumping in so late, he'd missed the deadline to get his name on the ballot in all fifty states. Mathematically, it was almost impossible for him to win the nomination. Which is why so many of us dismissed his presidential bid as a foolish, ego-driven exercise that would soon be over. It wasn't the first—or last—time we underestimated Jerry Brown.

Jerry's first stop was the Maryland primary, where most political pundits gave him no chance. The morning of the primary, standing on the sidewalk outside OPR, Tony Kline and I laughed about Jerry's presidential campaign and assured each other, "At least, he'll be home tomorrow and we can get back to work."

But what we Sacramento insiders and national commentators ignored was the political reality in Maryland. One, Maryland Democrats didn't like any of the establishment candidates. They'd been looking for an outsider to run as "none of the above." Two, Democratic political power in Maryland was still controlled by former congressman and former mayor Tommy D'Alesandro, the father of Nancy Pelosi, then a Democratic National Committee member from San Francisco. All Jerry Brown had to do was get Nancy's father's blessing, and the primary was over. And that's exactly what happened.

The next morning, Kline and I met at the same spot in disbelief. Yes, Jerry was heading back to Sacramento that day, but not as a failed candidate. Instead, he was returning as the winner of the Maryland primary and a serious contender for the Democratic nomination.

For my part, I was happy to see the governor back in town for a totally unrelated reason. Four years had passed since Proposition 20 created the temporary State Coastal Commission. It was now time to make it permanent. I'd been working with Assemblyman Alan Sieroty and Peter Douglas on draft legislation, and I had an 8:00 a.m. appointment the next morning to get the governor's final approval.

I should have known better. When I walked into the governor's office the next morning with my notes on the coastal legislation, the ever-present Tony Kline was surprised to see me and asked, "What are you doing here? Didn't Jerry call you last night?" I told him I hadn't talked to the governor since before he'd left for Maryland.

Tony took me across the hall to Gray Davis's office, where we were soon joined by finance director Dick Silberman. There'd been a change of plans, they explained. I was no longer in charge of coastal legislation. In fact, temporarily, I was no longer director of OPR. In one hour, I would be leaving with the governor to join his campaign staff in the Oregon presidential primary. Whereupon they crammed me with all the details they could about the "emerging" campaign.

Sure enough, exactly one hour later, with nothing but the clothes on my back, I jumped in the blue Plymouth with candidate Jerry Brown. We were met at Sacramento Executive Airport by campaign aide LeRoy Chatfield and took off in a small private plane for Oregon: three former seminarians, like three missionaries, flying off to convert the heathens.

Our first stop was the University of Oregon in Eugene and my first introduction to Jerry's campaign magic. With little advance notice, thousands of students had turned out, many of them waving hand-made BROWN FOR PRESIDENT signs. They were wildly enthusiastic, and Jerry, fresh from his upset Maryland victory, was in top form. For the first time, I realized that his presidential campaign was not a fluke. This was a serious effort. And Governor Jerry Brown was a serious candidate.

In Portland, I was assigned as Brown's liaison to the powerful environmental community and offered a guest room in "the Rain House," headquarters of the local save-the-rain forest organization. Wally McGuire was in charge of the campaign, assisted by Judy Weisman, Byron Georgiou, and Mo Jourdain, veterans of Jerry's 1974 gubernatorial campaign. Marshall Ganz and Artie Rodriguez, César Chávez's son-in-law, led an army of volunteers, including dozens of United Farm Workers members from California.

Once in Portland, I finally had a chance to call Carol and bring her up to date. I went out and bought toiletries and underwear for a couple of days. Carol put a suitcase of clean clothes on a Greyhound bus to Portland. I returned home a month later.

Even for a popular candidate like Jerry Brown, the Oregon primary presented an almost insurmountable challenge. As in Maryland, Jerry's name was not on the ballot. But unlike Maryland, there was no "none of the above" option in Oregon. The only way people could vote for Jerry Brown was by writing in his name on the ballot. So our campaign handed out tens of thousands of pencils with the message: "Write in Jerry Brown."

And, once again, amazingly, it worked. Jerry didn't win. He came in second to Senator Frank Church, from the neighboring state of Idaho. But we achieved our goal, which was to beat establishment favorite Jimmy Carter and demonstrate how little enthusiasm there was for the peanut farmer from Georgia.

I stayed in Portland for another week while our lawyers camped out at the secretary of state's office, convincing officials to respect the intent of the voter and accept anything close to *Jerry Brown*, including Edmund G. Brown Jr.; G. Brown; J. Brown; or Gerry Brown. Once the secretary of state certified the election, I flew back to Sacramento to rejoin my family and OPR.

Or so I thought.

Less than two hours after I returned to OPR the next morning, I was again summoned to the governor's office and informed of the latest twist in Jerry Brown's ever-evolving campaign plans. The governor had decided to enter the Pennsylvania primary—and Byron Georgiou, Marshall Ganz, and I had already been booked on a red-eye flight that night from San Francisco to Philadelphia. I dutifully went back to OPR, told deputy director Mike Fisher he was still in charge, raced home to pack and say goodbye to Carol, and the boys headed to SFO.

Waiting in the bar for our flight, and laughing about Jerry's sudden change of plans, Byron, Marshall, and I had no idea they were about to change again—before we even boarded our plane. I suddenly heard my name being paged to a white courtesy telephone, where Gray Davis informed me Jerry was not going to compete in the Pennsylvania primary, after all. Our tickets had been changed. We were flying to Boston instead. Beyond that, destination unknown.

When we called early the next morning from Boston, we learned that, while we were in the air, on the Thursday night before Memorial Day weekend, Jerry had decided to compete in the Rhode Island Democratic primary the following Tuesday, just five days away. Our orders: Rent a car, drive to Providence, report to the local Brown office on Weybosset Street, and launch a blitzkrieg campaign.

As if that weren't daunting enough, we arrived in Providence to discover that the entire Rhode Island Brown campaign consisted of two people. Actually, two teenagers: Joey Paolino and Mark Weiner. But we also soon discovered, we couldn't have been in better hands.

Without Paolino and Weiner, we wouldn't be there. They had tracked down Jerry during the Maryland primary and encouraged him to come to

Rhode Island. Both knew the lay of the land in Rhode Island. Both were well connected. And both were nascent political pros. Joey Paolino went on to become mayor of Providence and ambassador to Malta under Bill Clinton. Mark Weiner worked in the Carter White House, handled merchandise sales at Democratic national conventions, and was a major Democratic donor until his untimely death in July 2016.

Together we embarked on one of the shortest and most successful primary campaigns in American politics. By Friday night, hundreds of farmworker volunteers from up and down the East Coast had arrived in Providence, led again by Marshall Ganz and Artie Rodriguez. They worked every crowd into a frenzy with their chant: "*Sí, se puede! Sí, se puede!*"—which Barack Obama stole in 2008 in its English version: "Yes, we can!" My favorite farmworker chant poked fun at a town just north of Providence: "Pawtucket. Ah, fuck it!"

Saturday night in Providence, we held a big rally in a downtown church. The next day, former governor Pat Brown and Kathleen Brown, Jerry's father and sister, campaigned from one end of the state to the other (not a lot of territory to cover). Meanwhile, we flooded the state with flyers for Jerry Brown, the "un-candidate"—since, for the third primary in a row, his name was not on the ballot.

Jerry himself barnstormed the state on Memorial Day, drawing big crowds on several public beaches. He also spoke to a gathering at Moses Brown School, hastily put together by Carol's parents, Tom and Mackie. The next day, after a five-day campaign and only one day of actual campaigning in the state, Jerry Brown came out on top. Without having his name on the ballot in any state so far, he had won three states.

Once again, nobody knew what was next. Byron, Marshall, and I headed to New York City and checked into the Gotham Hotel, awaiting instructions.

At least, when our next campaign assignment came, we didn't have to go too far, just across the Hudson River to New Jersey where, yet again, Jerry Brown had decided to run as the "uncommitted" candidate.

We had a little more time in New Jersey, maybe ten days, but we followed the same playbook. We joined forces with the existing loyal, but slim, Brown campaign, operating out of a former carpet showroom. Hundreds of farmworkers again flooded into the state. We printed up thousands of flyers for the unofficial "un-candidate." And we started lining up events for Pat and Kathleen Brown's one-day campaign swing through the state.

The big difference in New Jersey was the Democratic machine. State party leaders weren't hostile to Jerry. In fact, they liked him a lot more than Jimmy Carter. They just didn't want a bunch of amateurs getting in their way. So the word came down from on high. I got a call from one party leader telling me to keep our campaign workers out of Hudson County. When I protested there was no way we could ignore the biggest block of votes in the state, he was adamant: "I'm telling you, stay out of Hudson County and don't worry about it. We'll deliver Hudson County for Jerry Brown as long as you keep your volunteers the fuck out of there."

In the end, we did. And they did. We won Hudson County without making one phone call or handing out one single flyer.

Turns out we didn't have to worry about southern New Jersey, either. For Jerry's first stop in the state, I'd asked Angelo Errichetti, the mayor of Camden, to pull together a handful of civic leaders for an 8:00 a.m. meeting in his office. I met Jerry when he arrived from California at Philadelphia International Airport, and we proceeded to Camden to discover not some small meeting in the mayor's office but a rally of at least one thousand city workers in front of city hall, complete with signs, banners, and sharpshooters on the roof.

As we left, Errichetti pulled me aside and told me not to worry about hunting for votes in Camden or anywhere south of Camden. He promised he'd deliver those counties for Jerry Brown, and, based on what I'd just seen, I had no doubt he could and would. And he did.

Unfortunately for him, Errichetti played one too many political tricks in his career. In 1981, he and three others were convicted of accepting a $50,000 bribe from an FBI agent disguised as an Arab sheik, part of the classic Abscam sting operation. He served thirty-two months in federal prison. Jeremy Renner's character in the film *American Hustle* is based on him.

In New Jersey, Jerry Brown pulled off yet another political miracle, winning the state with just one day on the ground. A couple of days later, with the help of a real political scoundrel, Louisiana governor Edwin Edwards, Jerry also won the majority of delegates at the Louisiana state convention. But after that, he ran out of steam. With not enough states left whose rules would allow him to run as the "un-candidate," there was no way mathematically Jerry could win enough delegates to cinch the nomination.

But even outgunned and outnumbered, Jerry decided to carry his campaign all the way to the convention. Which, for me, was a dream come true. Ever since watching national conventions as a kid in Delaware City, I'd always hoped to attend one myself someday, and 1976 was my first. I've been to every Democratic convention, and most Republican conventions, since. But none as exciting as New York 1976.

In typical fashion, the Brown campaign established headquarters in the historic Hotel McAlpin, once the largest hotel in the world but now a run-down dump, at the corner of Thirty-fourth and Broadway. Its original grandeur was long gone. Mice overran the rooms. Toilets only sometimes flushed. The elevators often failed to operate. It was the perfect image and location for Jerry Brown. It closed forever the day we left.

With Carter all but officially the Democratic nominee, Jerry was the only story in town, so the media flocked to our wreck of a hotel. During one elevator shutdown, Walter Cronkite and his CBS crew huffed up the stairs to the eighth floor for an interview.

While the media may have enjoyed the Brown sideshow, national party leaders, led by DNC chair Bob Strauss, decidedly did not. The closer we got to the actual presidential balloting, the more pressure was applied to Brown delegates to switch to Carter. But Jerry still hung on. His name was officially placed in nomination by Louisiana governor Edwin Edwards, to the dismay of us liberal Brown staffers. California attorney general Yvonne Burke seconded the nomination. At that point, Jerry knew it was time to fold, so even before balloting began, he addressed the convention and, without endorsing Carter, freed his delegates to vote their conscience. Carter won with 2,239 delegates. Jerry came in third, with 301, just behind Congressman Mo Udall of Arizona, with 330.

Jerry Brown never hid the fact that he disliked Jimmy Carter. He once sniffed to reporters that Carter had "the mind of an engineer." He ended up endorsing him for president, then was mildly amused watching Carter's series of blunders as president. Carter clearly was not ready for prime time.

But I wonder: Were we? Brown was the smartest, most exciting political figure and best campaigner of his time. I have no doubt that, had he started a year earlier, in time to get his name on the ballot in every state,

Jerry Brown would have been the Democratic nominee in 1976 and elected the next president of the United States. He would have been only thirty-eight years old. I would have been thirty-six. Nobody around him was over fifty. None of us had any experience at the national level. Were we ready to run the country?

Which begs the question: Who is really ready to run the country? Nobody, perhaps, but an older, experienced, classic Washington insider. Somebody like Hillary Clinton. And they're the ones who can't get elected. It's one of the oldest and unresolved issues of American politics. Every candidate for president, even longtime members of the House or Senate, pretends to be an outsider and run against Washington. Why? Because we get so frustrated with the lack of progress in Washington, we want an outsider to come in and shake things up, or maybe even "drain the swamp." Think about it: Jimmy Carter, Ronald Reagan, Bill Clinton, George W. Bush, Barack Obama, Donald Trump. George H. W. Bush is the last member of the Washington establishment elected president, and he only lasted four years. The problem is, these outsiders take over and, for the most part, they don't know what the hell they're doing. They're bound to fail, like Jimmy Carter, unless they surround themselves with some savvy, experienced Washington insiders, which Clinton, George W. Bush, and Obama did—but which Donald Trump never has, which is why his presidency has been a disaster from day one.

CALIFORNIA TEA PARTY

Soon after returning to Sacramento, Jerry Brown was back on the campaign trail, and so was I. This time, for reelection as governor. Jerry had no opposition in the primary but what looked like a tough challenge in the general election from Republican attorney general Evelle Younger.

Late in spring 1978, I took another leave from OPR and moved to Los Angeles as deputy campaign manager under Gray Davis. Our campaign headquarters was in the Union Oil Company building in downtown Los Angeles, near what is now the Staples Center. Byron Georgiou and I shared an apartment in the Sunset Towers in West Hollywood, where one of our neighbors was Ray Charles.

South of the Tehachapis, of course, is where most of the votes are in California, so Jerry spent a lot of time in the Los Angeles area, and I traveled with him in the famous blue Plymouth to many campaign events. This was also the time he was dating Linda Ronstadt. After a full day of campaigning, our routine was for me to drop him off at Linda's house in Malibu, or Hancock Park, and pick him up there the next morning.

In many ways, Jerry and Linda were the odd couple. He was all into politics; she was all into music. But they were very much in love and very affectionate with each other. In her delightful memoir, *Simple Dreams*, Linda wrote, "He was smart and funny, not interested in drinking or drugs, and lived his life carefully, with a great deal of discipline. This was different from a lot of the men I knew in rock and roll. I found it a relief."

But I think Linda sells herself short. Their relationship, I believe, was a lot deeper than that. Yes, Jerry, with his brilliant, inquisitive mind, was way ahead of his time on key issues like opposition to the death penalty, need for sensible immigration reform, and protection of the environment. But Linda herself was a rare bird in the world of rock and roll: a phenomenal musical talent and superstar performer but also a serious intellectual and committed reader who felt passionately about important issues of the day, many of which Jerry was actively involved in.

In the end, Younger turned out to be a lackluster candidate, and Jerry easily won reelection. But that wasn't the biggest political story of 1978. That turned out to be passage of Proposition 13.

Prop 13 was a classic case of the entire political establishment getting it wrong—much like the political establishment in 2016 missed the widespread economic anxiety that fueled the candidacies of Bernie Sanders and Donald Trump.

In California, frustration over property taxes had been building for years. The state was sitting on a surplus. Democrats in the legislature talked about giving taxpayers a refund but never did. Governor Brown promised tax relief but didn't deliver. Meanwhile, homeowners saw their taxes soar every year. The bonfire was laid. Howard Jarvis lit the match.

Jarvis, a rumpled anti-tax crusader whom historian Richard Reeves called "the last, angry man," teamed up with Sacramento populist Paul Gann to gather enough signatures to place Proposition 13 on the June 1978 ballot. Powerful in its simplicity, Prop 13 did four things: immediately lowered all property taxes to their 1975 level; limited future tax increases to 2 percent a year; ruled that homes could be reassessed only at the time of sale, and then assessed at only 1 percent of the home's new cash value; and required a two-thirds vote by any government, state or local, to raise taxes in the future.

We didn't recognize it at the time, but this was the first manifestation of what decades later would become the Tea Party. Proposition 13 was opposed by the governor, most members of the legislature of both parties, every leading civic organization, and the overwhelming number of newspaper editorials statewide. Yet it passed with 63 percent of the vote.

Proposition 13 started a nationwide movement that led directly to the Tea Party and its opposition to any tax increase for any purpose, and to the GOP craze to cut taxes for the wealthiest of Americans, over and over again. It also contains a stark warning for us progressives: No matter how noble your cause, nor how important the issue, you have to be careful, if not conservative, stewards of the people's money. The American people only reluctantly part with their tax dollars and expect you to spend them frugally and wisely—or even, as in the case with Proposition 13, return any funds you don't need.

A chastened Jerry Brown got the message. He responded by cutting state spending with such fervor that reporters dubbed him *Jerry Jarvis*. But Proposition 13 had already done a lot of damage. Revenue to local governments was cut 57 percent, with devastating effects on schools, police and fire protection, health services, and public transportation—and California still hasn't recovered. That's what happens when politicians lose touch with the people.

Back at OPR, with Jerry's support, I took on a new project: lining up votes in the legislature for a bill to raise funds for public transit in California through a tax on "excess" profits of oil companies, which at the time were reporting the biggest profits ever. It was an uphill battle. Even though the measure had a lot of popular support, oil industry lobbyists were able to block it.

At the same time, my personal clock was ticking. As a young staffer, I'd seen senior legislative aides sitting alone at the bar every evening at watering holes near the capitol. I didn't want to end up like them. I knew there was a limit to how long you could spend in Sacramento before it was too late to move on. I wasn't sure how long it was—maybe four years, maybe ten. But after two years as Peter Behr's chief of staff, two years at PCL, and four years working for Jerry Brown, I knew I was getting close. I was also antsy to get out and do something on my own.

The oil profits bill provided that opportunity. After hitting a brick wall in the legislature, I proposed to Jerry that I leave the administration and head up a grassroots campaign to qualify an excess profits initiative for the next statewide ballot. We'd had a good run together. We'd accomplished some important things. We'd become good friends. And Jerry graciously agreed.

In December 1979, I resigned as director of OPR, and Carol and I moved with Mark and David to a beautiful passive solar home we had built in the magical little village of Inverness, on the shores of Tomales Bay in Marin County.

I hesitate to speak of Inverness, because it is such a special place that those of us who live there want to keep it a secret. As of 2010, Inverness had a resident population of about 1,300, which swells to maybe 1,800 on the weekend. Nestled in the boundaries of the magnificent Point Reyes National Seashore, it's not only spectacularly beautiful, it's one of the most liberal enclaves in California, the only precinct outside Santa Monica to cast a majority of its votes for Tom Hayden in the democratic primary for governor in 1994.

It was the ideal place to escape from Los Angeles on weekends and raise two outdoor-oriented sons, but Inverness became hell on earth in October 1995 with the outbreak of the Mt. Vision fire. Our house, on the eastern slope of Mt. Vision, was right in the line of fire. A fire truck was parked in our driveway and a fire crew camped out on our lawn. We were allowed to stay in our home, but our car, packed with everything we wanted to save, was parked heading downhill—and we were told we had to leave the moment they gave the orders to do so. Looking south, we could see the wall of flames advancing to within a half-mile of our home. In the end, the winds shifted and our house was spared. But the Mt. Vision fire consumed 12,354 acres of the Point Reyes Seashores and destroyed 45 nearby homes, including that of my former boss Peter Behr.

TAX BIG OIL

Today, the initiative process means big business and big money. But that's not how it started out.

The initiative was introduced to California in 1911 by the great reform governor Hiram Johnson. To counter the stranglehold that Southern Pacific and other big corporations had on the legislature, Johnson gave citizens equal power to enact new laws by initiative. Any petition signed by 5 percent of those who had voted in the last gubernatorial election (8 percent for constitutional amendments) could automatically place a measure on the next statewide ballot. If approved by voters, it would automatically become law, with no opportunity of the legislature to amend or veto it.

For our public transit initiative, the first step was assembling a campaign team. David Calef left OPR to serve as campaign manager. Paul Milne, a trained United Farm Workers organizer, led the signature-gathering campaign. And Marshall Ganz, the Farm Workers' top organizer with whom I'd worked in Jerry Brown's presidential campaign, agreed to train our volunteers.

Once we submitted the text of our proposed initiative to the California secretary of state, we had three months to collect the necessary signatures. With very little money, we had no choice but to rely on volunteers to gather signatures. But where and how?

In our first organizational meeting, Ganz came up with a great idea: We would focus on people coming in and out of supermarkets—where our volunteers would be standing behind ironing boards bearing a TAX BIG OIL sign. It was a great idea. We were the first initiative campaign to use ironing boards and the first to target supermarkets. Everybody loved it—except the managers of Lucky Stores, who called the police and ordered us off their property.

That posed a serious problem for our signature-gathering operation, so we decided to fight back. After researching the law on public access, John Phillips, head of the Center for Law in the Public Interest (and later U.S. ambassador to Italy), concluded we had a strong case against Lucky Stores and recommended filing a lawsuit for the right to collect signatures in front of their stores. We did. And we won. In a landmark decision, *Press v.*

Lucky Stores, the California Supreme Court ruled that grassroots organizations could petition the support of other citizens in shopping malls and in front of supermarkets.

That was our first victory. Our second was collecting enough signatures to get on the ballot. More than enough, in fact. We needed 325,000 valid signatures. We turned in over 500,000. The secretary of state ruled that Proposition 11, enacting a special tax on the "excess profits" of oil companies to pay for public transit, would appear on the June 1980 statewide ballot.

Our Prop 11 campaign made history in one way: We were the last initiative campaign to qualify for the ballot using all volunteer signature gatherers. Unfortunately, we didn't make history in another way: We didn't win.

We expected the big oil companies to spend millions of dollars against us, and they did not disappoint. They flooded the airwaves with misleading ads about how making oil companies pay their fair share of taxes would be bad for consumers. And we had no money—none!—to respond with our own TV ads.

There was only one bright spot. Thanks to a onetime contribution from Jake West, then president of the California Ironworkers union, we produced one classic TV spot, the brainchild of Sidney Galanty and his partner Bill Zimmerman.

Even though it appeared only one time, on only one cable channel, it was so controversial, and so laugh-out-loud funny, it was played over and over again on every TV news station in the state. Picture this: Open with a shot of pigs grunting noisily as they gobbled up slop from a feeding trough. Cut to an old-fashioned typewriter clicking out the words *Tax Pig Oil*. Then the typewriter backs up, erasing its "mistake," replacing the *P* with a *B* and typing *Tax Big Oil* instead. We lost the election, but that campaign spot won Sid and Bill a Pollie award from the American Association of Political Consultants.

We fought the good fight, but we lost. And here I was, again, without a job. But by this point in my life, only twelve years after leaving my teaching job at Sacred Heart High School, I already had a lot of exciting experiences under my belt. I'd run a San Francisco citywide campaign, managed a California State Senate campaign, served in the state legislature as chief of staff to a California state senator, worked the legislature as an environmental lobbyist, led a state government agency of over one hundred people, helped run a governor's reelection campaign, traveled around the country in a presidential campaign, served as press secretary in one statewide initiative campaign, and headed up another one.

Not bad for a former "canal rat" from Delaware. It was time to relocate this hard-charging progressive to a bigger stage.

5

BILL PRESS, TRUE AMERICAN

With the defeat of Proposition 11 in June 1980, I found myself at the dawn of a new decade with a new home in Marin County, a wonderful, supportive wife, two lively, healthy sons, a wealth of experience in statewide politics, and an extensive network of friends and allies—but no job.

At first, I took time out to volunteer for Jerry Brown's second presidential campaign in New Hampshire and Maine, then returned to Inverness to focus on my next career move.

I set three goals: I wanted to find a job that would keep me involved in public policy issues, keep me in the public eye—"If you're not appearing, you're disappearing"—and, needless to say, also provide a paycheck. After dismissing going back to teaching, running political campaigns, or leading another environmental organization, I decided to try to get a job in the media.

True, I'd never been to journalism school or worked in journalism, but I wasn't a complete stranger to the world of the press. In every job since teaching at Sacred Heart, I'd been involved with the media at some level. I'd written several op-ed pieces and given many interviews on radio and television. And it was clear to me that television was the most powerful medium for communicating any message. So television was where I set my sights, and I decided to start at the top: KABC-TV in Los Angeles, the number-one-ranked TV station in the state. If I didn't succeed there, I'd work my way down the list till I got a job in some smaller market. Maybe Fresno.

I started out by writing a letter to Dennis Swanson, news director of KABC-TV, warning him that his station might be number one in the ratings today, but would soon sink if they didn't hire me. After all, energy and the environment were the two biggest issues in California in the '80s, and I knew more about those issues than anybody else on the planet. It was, I admit, a rather brassy letter. But what did I have to lose? And what do you know? Score one for cojones. It worked.

A couple of days later, I got a call from Swanson, inviting me to meet with him in Los Angeles. At the old ABC studios on Prospect Avenue in Silver Lake, Swanson explained that his station was about to expand its evening newscast from two hours to three. They already had two political commentators, Bruce Herschensohn and Al Julius, and were looking for a third when my letter arrived. Swanson remembered me from the Prop 11 campaign and offered me a job as a political commentator on the evening news, starting two nights a week. A couple of months later, he made it full-time, five nights a week, delivering a two-and-a-half-minute commentary at 5:00 p.m. on KABC-TV's *Eyewitness News*. I stayed at KABC-TV nine years.

I'm often invited to speak to journalism classes, and every time, as corny as it sounds, I tell the story of that letter. Because there's an important lesson there—for me and, I hope, for other aspiring young people in every field of endeavor: Be sure of yourself and always go for the very top. The higher you aim, the higher you'll end up. Never start at the bottom. Never settle for halfway. Never sell yourself short. It worked for me at KABC-TV, it worked for me later at CNN, it's worked my entire life. As Robert Browning wrote, "Ah, a man's reach should exceed his grasp, or what's a heaven for?"

As exciting as it was, one big problem with landing a job at the number-one television station in the state was that KABC-TV was in Los Angeles, while my family had just settled into our new home in Marin County. But with Carol's understanding, we made it work. On Monday, I'd leave Inverness around noon and drive to Oakland International Airport for a 2:00 p.m. flight to Burbank, where I'd head directly to KABC for the 5:00 p.m. broadcast. I delivered my commentary live on set Monday, Tuesday, Wednesday, and Thursday evenings. Meanwhile, I'd pretape a commentary for Friday. Immediately after Thursday's newscast, I'd rush to Burbank for a 7:00 p.m. return flight to Oakland, arriving home in Inverness in time for a late dinner with Carol. That became my weekly schedule for the next nine years, until Carol moved to Los Angeles.

If finding a job was the first challenge, finding a place to live in LA was the second. Problem solved when friends Michael Nicola and Steve Smith introduced me to Clyde Cairns, an openly gay businessman, who offered me a basement apartment in one of his two fabulous mansions in the Hollywood Hills. Little did I realize what a colorful scene I was moving into.

At home, Clyde always walked around with Delilah, a green parrot, perched on his shoulder. He gave wild dinner parties, and he often rented the house out for photo shoots—usually porno flicks, gay or straight. I often came home to find the strangest collection of people walking around the house, some fully clothed, some not. Life at Clyde's was never dull. I'd come a long way from the Oblates!

Sadly, Clyde was an early victim of AIDS. If only we knew as much about AIDS then as we do today, with today's miracle drugs, Clyde might still be with us.

After Clyde's death, I rented a guesthouse in the Hollywood Hills, just outside of one of the hidden entrances to Griffith Park. Even though it was in the middle of Los Angeles, living in the Hollywood Hills was like living out in the country. Most mornings, I'd jog for three miles around nearby Lake Hollywood. Once a week, I'd join friends for an early-morning hike in the Santa Monica Mountains, occasionally running into then-just-an-actor Arnold Schwarzenegger, hiking with his bodyguard.

In addition to a fun job and a big paycheck, there was one other happy benefit of living in Los Angeles: the opportunity to reconnect with the Siciliano family and Seth and Margery Warner.

The Sicilianos had moved from Washington to Rodeo Drive in Beverly

Hills, where Rocco was now head of TICOR, the giant title insurance company. Once again, he took me under his wing, introduced me to several movers and shakers in the LA business community, entertained me often at the downtown California Club, LA's most exclusive business gathering place, and included me in many Siciliano family dinners.

Marion Siciliano, meanwhile, was involved in many local environmental issues. She recruited me to join the board of the Los Angeles TreePeople, which she chaired. I, in turn, enlisted her help in raising funds for the Wildlife WayStation, an animal rescue sanctuary located in Little Tujunga Canyon, north of Los Angeles.

Seth and Margery Warner lived on Point Dume in Malibu, about an hour away, just close enough that, once a month or so, I could bolt out right after the 5:00 p.m. news, dash to Malibu for one of Margery's great dinners, and rush back for the 11:00 p.m. broadcast. Those evenings were not only great fun, they were like graduate school with two great professors. I learned so much about the history of ideas from Seth and so much about the good things of life from Margery.

Seriously, I could not have had a better break than landing a job at KABC-TV. First, the job itself was the perfect fit. A lot of people have strong opinions about the issues of the day. But unlike everybody else, I not only got to express my opinions in front of a million people every evening, I got paid for it.

And in a way, it brought together both sides of my life so far. I started out studying to be a preacher, then switched to practicing politics. Now I had a job that gave this proud progressive the opportunity to preach about politics from one of the biggest pulpits of all.

I was also lucky to work with a great team of broadcasters. General manager John Severino and news director Dennis Swanson had assembled some of the best talent in the country: anchors Jerry Dunphy, Christine Lund, Paul Moyer, Ann Martin, Tawny Little, and Harold Greene; meteorologists "Dr. George" Fischbeck and Dallas Raines; sports anchor Ted Dawson; investigative reporter Wayne Satz; plus a whole arm of talented producers, writers, and editors.

Movie reviews were an important part of the news at KABC-TV, of course. After all, this was Hollywood. And our movie critic was none other than Regis Philbin—he started out as a page on *The Tonight Show* in the

1950s and went on to make television history as host of *Live! with Regis and Kelly* and *Who Wants to Be a Millionaire*. Regis still holds the Guinness Book of World Records title for the most time spent in front of a television camera.

My own introduction to broadcast journalism was rocky, at best. Arriving at KABC-TV, I showed the draft of my first commentary to Swanson, who leafed through it quickly, then handed it back with the warning "Looks okay. Don't fuck it up." And that was it! All the advice I received before appearing on the air for the first time, and all the journalism training I've ever had.

Next, I sought out political reporter Leo McElroy for his advice. "Just stare into the camera," he said, "and when the red light comes on, start talking." Which is exactly what I did. And the result was as stiff and awkward as it sounds.

At any rate, for what it's worth, here's my very first commentary on KABC-TV—September 16, 1980—in which I staked out my territory:

California. The last stop in the Far West. The first step to the Far East.

California is, in Carey McWilliam's memorable phrase, "The Great Exception." People do, in fact, accept and expect almost anything from California, whether it be the newest, the most expensive, the wackiest, or the most outrageous. They are seldom disappointed.

California today is America tomorrow. The events, the trends, the changes that began in California are the direction America is heading toward. If it exists, it started here: the semiconductor, the disco, the freeway, the smog, the martini, the United Nations, and the John Birch Society.

California is the land of plenty. We have more swimming pools, 450,000; more millionaires, 38,691; more dogs and cats, 50 million (that's 2.3 per resident); and more mobile homes, telephones, microwaves.

California is also the land of contradiction. Our water and politicians are in the north; our people and votes are here in the south. Agriculture is our number-one industry. Yet most of us have never seen a plow or touched a cow.

Yes, California is the great exception. Yet sometimes we become so blinded by the tinsel glare of what makes California so special that we never slow down to take a closer look.

We may have given birth to the electronics industry, but it's now abandoning California. There is no new housing that the average worker can afford. Agriculture may be our number-one industry, but we're paving over 20,000 acres of our best farmland each year. We may boast a concentration of wealth, but we can't deny large pockets of the poor and unemployed. We may live in the future, but we are ignoring the lessons of the past by building in flood zones, fire zones, and on top of earthquake faults.

And now California, faults and all, heads into the eighties. Is California still leading the way, or have we lost our way?

Those will be the questions before us in this and other commentaries that will follow. I'll be here twice a week. We'll take a close look at California's energy policy. We'll look at California's environment. We'll look at California's economy, health policy, housing, schools, and cities. And of course, the glue that holds them all together, California politics. I'm Bill Press.

Okay, let me admit: Looking back now, I'm almost embarrassed by that commentary. It was too soft, too philosophical, too mushy. Clearly, I was just feeling my way. But it didn't take long before I took the gloves off and my commentaries became a lot more pointed. Ronald Reagan had just been elected. I soon became his chief critic in Southern California, and I also spoke out on animal rights, gay rights, gun control, civil rights, nuclear weapons, the environment, and other hot-button issues. Why the change from philosophical to colorful? Because I recognized the importance of a rule I still live by: If you're given a platform, if you have the microphone, either at the local, state, or national level, don't waste the moment. Don't pussyfoot around. Don't hold back. Take no prisoners. Take full advantage of that opportunity to be as proud and strong and hard-hitting as you can.

One thing I did not expect: the outpouring of telephone calls and letters in response to each commentary. Even though they were, in my case, mainly negative, management always had my back. The first time I met general manager John Severino, he asked, "Press, do you realize how many complaints I get about you?" He told me there were two boxes of hate mail in response to my commentaries on his desk. "You know what I tell 'em?" he added. "I tell 'em to go shit in their hat!"

Actually, there were two operators in the middle of the newsroom who did nothing else but take calls from viewers and make notes of their comments. Most of the day, they just sat there, reading or manicuring their nails. Until I came on the air, when the phones would go bonkers. Most of them with callers screaming, "Why do you have Bill Press on the air? I'll never watch Channel 7 again until you get rid of that Commie!"

Right then and there, I discovered a few things about TV viewers and radio listeners that remain true to this day. First, if I did not piss a lot of people off, I was not doing my job. Second, in the media, you have to have the hide of an armadillo. If you can't take being regularly called an asshole, or worse, get out of the business. Third, sometimes people are weird in what they choose to listen to. There are some who will only tune in to programs they will agree with 100 percent and never hear a dissenting point of view: Fox viewers, Rush Limbaugh listeners, Rachel Maddow fans. But there are a lot of others who will turn on the opposition just to get their daily hate fix. They get off on getting pissed off and then lash out with angry letters or phone calls. In the movie *Private Parts*, Howard Stern is told that listeners who love him listen for thirty minutes. Those who hate him listen for two hours. Same for my viewers at KABC-TV: no matter how much they threatened to boycott the station, as long as I was on the air, they couldn't wait to tune in the next day. Go figure.

Not everybody hated my commentaries, I hasten to add. I actually got lots of positive responses, too. One day, I scorched LA coroner Thomas Noguchi for his tasteless handling of the tragic drowning of actress Natalie Wood off Santa Catalina Island—blasting him for speculating about drinking, drugs, or foul play. Why not just say, "*Requiescat in Pace*—Let her rest in peace!" Within minutes, Nancy Sinatra called to tell me her father asked her to call and thank me.

In August 1988, I defended Lew Wasserman, chairman of MCA, the parent company of Universal Studios, which had just released Martin Scorsese's movie *The Last Temptation of Christ*—and blasted right-wing Christians who were picketing outside Wasserman's home. The next day, Lynne Wasserman called to say her father wanted to take me to lunch.

That was the beginning of a great friendship with the legendary Wasserman who, in his days as a talent agent, had represented everyone from Bette Davis to Ronald Reagan. We often had lunch in the studio commissary. Because of his power and seniority, he may have been a feared figure in Hollywood, but he became a very warm, generous, and valuable mentor to me. Years later, when I ran for chair of the state Democratic Party, Lew gave me his private phone number and asked me to call him as soon as I learned the outcome of the vote.

A great raconteur, Wasserman especially loved telling one story about Governor Pat Brown and President John F. Kennedy. As Wasserman related, JFK once called and asked him to help organize a big fund-raiser at the Beverly Hilton. Wasserman delivered, even though it meant kicking a group of high school students out of the grand ballroom and moving them to a smaller ballroom.

That evening, before the event, Kennedy said he'd like to surprise the students by popping in on them, and sent Governor Brown to prepare the way. Brown soon returned, assured them the coast was clear, and proceeded to lead the president and Wasserman down to the ballroom level, where he ushered them into not the high school prom as expected but a wedding reception. Brown had scoped out the wrong ballroom. Kennedy seized the moment, first congratulating the stunned newlyweds and having his photo taken with them before moving on to greet the high school students.

It wasn't long before I encountered one other reality about appearing on television every night: being recognized almost everywhere I went in Southern California. And, usually, when I least expected it. That led to some funny experiences.

One evening, while checking out at the supermarket, the clerk was busy scanning my items when she glanced up, took one look at me, and blurted out, "Oh, my God. Do you know who you are?"

Another morning, I was enjoying breakfast in a neighborhood restaurant when a stranger walked up to my table. "I've been watching you ever since you walked in here," he volunteered. "You look so much like that guy who's on Channel 7 every night. Could that be your father?"

Being recognized increased exponentially once I landed on CNN's *Crossfire*—which led to the funniest experience of all. While waiting with friends to play golf in Winnapaug Country Club in Rhode Island, a member of the foursome ahead of us walked over and remarked that I looked just like that guy on television. I waved him off, as I often did, with a laugh. "Yeah, people tell me that all the time." A few minutes later, he returned to say he couldn't believe how much I resembled that guy on TV. Same comment from me. Then he came back a third time to insist, "I can't believe it. You look so much like that guy on CNN. I can't remember his name, but he's a real asshole!" By that time, I couldn't resist. I stuck out my hand and said, "Hi, I'm Bill Press." He slinked away, and I never saw him again.

Before Carol moved to Los Angeles in 1989, my home away from home was Jerry Brown's favorite hangout, Lucy's El Adobe restaurant on Melrose Avenue, across from Paramount Studios. Lucy's is where, as I recounted earlier, Jerry and I had sealed the deal on the California Urban Strategy with the blessing of owners Frank and Lucy Casado. I ate there at least a couple of times a week, often joining Jerry and Linda Ronstadt for dinner. Other regulars included Jackson Browne, Don Henley, Rosemary Clooney, Jimmy Webb, Jack Nicholson, and Lily Tomlin. John Belushi had dinner there a couple of weeks before his death.

We all felt a great loss when Frank Casado died suddenly in 1990. I was one of the pallbearers at his funeral. Linda sang a hauntingly beautiful "Ave Maria." Lucy passed away in 2017. Today, daughter Patty and son James Casado continue the Lucy's tradition of a friendly meeting place over great Mexican food and margaritas.

If politics makes strange bedfellows, so do radio and television. While at KABC, I made friends with people I never thought I could stand to be in the same room with. First on the list: Bay Buchanan, Pat's baby sister and an equally conservative firebrand. She and I squared off in a lively debate, and we both enjoyed it so much we scheduled several more.

I also ended up befriending the entire Reagan family, except for Ronnie and Nancy. Michael was a fellow talk show host and lively debate partner. For a while, his younger brother, Ron, was an intern at KABC-TV, and we both ended up at MSNBC together. Daughter Maureen and her husband, Dennis Revell, were fun to hang out with.

The Reagan sibling I got to know best was Patti Davis, the real renegade of the family. She eventually reconciled with her parents, but when I met her she was not on the best of terms. In her 1992 autobiography, *The*

Way I See It, she brutally recounts what a dysfunctional family she grew up in. Appearing on my radio show at KFI-AM, she admitted to smoking pot in the White House with her brother Ron. I asked her if she'd ever had sex on the rug in the Oval Office. She fessed up that she'd always wanted to but was never able to pull it off because there were too many Secret Service agents around.

Shortly after that interview, I was invited to Patti's fortieth birthday at her home in Santa Monica. On the way, I stopped in West Hollywood and picked up her birthday present, a T-shirt with the printed message: IF YOU THINK I'M A BITCH, YOU SHOULD MEET MY MOTHER. She loved it.

EYEWITNESS IN NICARAGUA

At the time, one story that interested me greatly was Nicaragua, where the Sandinistas under Daniel Ortega had overthrown American-backed dictator Anastasio Somoza. Now the right-wing Contras, allegedly with American assistance, were in turn trying to oust the Sandinistas.

After commenting on the war in Nicaragua and attending several meetings with Southern California peace activists—including businessmen Harold Willens and Aris Anagnos, Rabbi Leonard Beerman, producer Lila Garrett, and former priest Blase Bonpane, head of the Office of the Americas—I asked news director Dennis Swanson for permission to travel to Nicaragua with a video camera and report on the conflict.

Swanson agreed, but first I had to figure out how to get there. Problem solved when I spotted an ad in *The Nation* magazine for educational trips to Nicaragua led by one Alice McGrath of Ventura County. I called Alice and signed up for her next trip. But first, she said, it was important the two of us meet privately.

A week later, in the coffee shop of the Burbank airport, Alice told me that, early in her career, she'd been a member of the Communist Party. As a TV journalist, she wanted me to know that and would understand if I backed out of the trip. Even though she was the first "Communist" I'd ever met, I assured her I'd have no trouble traveling with her. After all, I'd often been accused of being a "fellow traveler" myself. And Alice proceeded to tell me her amazing story.

She was the very Alice McGrath of *Zoot Suit* fame. In 1942, Alice had been hired by attorney George Shibley to assist in the defense of twenty-two Mexican American youths charged with murdering a farmworker near Sleepy Lagoon in Los Angeles County. After all twenty-two were convicted and sent to San Quentin State Prison, Alice worked with the renowned journalist Carey McWilliams, executive secretary of the Sleepy Lagoon Defense Committee, making speeches, writing articles, and raising funds in support of the group—all of whom were eventually released after an appeals court ruled they'd been wrongly convicted on insufficient evidence. Alice's role in the Sleepy Lagoon case was the focus of *Zoot Suit*, the highly successful play (1978) and movie (1981) by Luis Valdez.

Alice later moved to Ventura County, where she founded a pro bono legal defense committee, earned herself a brown belt in judo, and became a peace activist—or, as she called herself, a "Sandinista in exilo." In spring 1986, our group, the eighty-sixth mission she'd led to Nicaragua, included Irish American actress Fionnula Flanagan and Lydia Brazon, a Nicaraguan American from Los Angeles with important high-level contacts in the Sandinista government.

In Managua, we met several top Sandinista officials, including interior minister Tomás Borge. We also met with business leaders, teachers, and mothers who'd lost their sons in the Contra war. We traveled to Estelí, where you could still see bullet holes from the revolutionary war in the walls of downtown buildings. In the beautiful mountain town of Matagalpa, we ran across Los Angeles contractor Steve Kerpen, who was working with a group of American volunteers, building housing for farmworker families.

We met and talked with Nicaraguans of whatever political persuasion. And our overwhelming impression was that, after suffering under Somoza for many years, and even though still mired in poverty, the people of Nicaragua were excited about the new opportunities they enjoyed under the Sandinista government. There was no reason—except the stale, meaningless fear of communism left over from the Cold War—for the United States not to recognize the Sandinistas, much less support the Contras.

Back at KABC-TV, I produced a five-part report on what I'd discovered in Nicaragua. I also arranged a screening of the documentary at the Dance Palace in Point Reyes Station, near our hometown of Inverness, after which our friends Jim Campe, Rufus Blunk, and Michael Mery organized a group of carpenters from West Marin to spend a month in Nicaragua helping Steve Kerpen build houses for farming families.

But ironically, it was only after leaving Nicaragua that I learned the most about what was really happening in that country. At the suggestion of a friend in Los Angeles, I moved on from Nicaragua to Costa Rica to meet with American freelance journalists Martha Honey and Tony Avirgan, Central American stringers for ABC Radio and NPR.

Tony was not only a veteran but a victim of the Nicaraguan conflict. He'd been severely wounded when a bomb planted by a Contra double agent exploded at a confidential press briefing with former Sandinista and renegade Contra leader Edén Pastora, deep in the rain forest. Four people were killed.

Martha was out of town, but over dinner in San Jose, Tony unveiled in great detail an incredible story of weapons being supplied secretly to the Contras by the United States, via airfields in northern Costa Rica, through a network of connections that led all the way to the Reagan White House. Nobody had yet reported this story.

I must admit that even as a severe Reagan critic, I had a hard time be-lieving Tony's wild, conspiracy-laden tale: the Reagan White House, defying the law by secretly arming the Contras? Indeed, returning to the States, I did not write or speak about it at all. Until, about a month later, I received a call from Tony telling me that he and Martha were coming to Los Ange-les. Would I organize a news conference where they could share their find-ings on illegal arms trafficking in Central America?

At my invitation, a respectable crowd of radio, print, and TV reporters showed up at the Los Angeles Press Club, where Martha and Tony out-lined for them the same elaborate chain of events Tony had laid out for me earlier: a covert plot run out of the White House to bypass Congress and secretly provide arms to the Contras for their campaign to overthrow the Sandinista government. It had all the elements of a great spy novel: Orders from the White House. Jungle hide-outs. Secret memos. Mysterious night-time flights into Costa Rica and Honduras. Yet, even for skeptical journal-ists, it seemed far-fetched.

As I had done a month earlier in Costa Rica, my friends and colleagues listened politely, asked a few questions, and then went back to the daily grind. Not one of them reported on Martha and Tony's press conference.

Little did we realize that we were sitting on what would soon become the biggest story in the country.

Less than two weeks later, news broke that a cargo plane carrying supplies to the Contras had been shot down over Nicaragua. Two pilots and a radio operator were killed in the crash. But American Eugene Hasenfus had parachuted to safety and was immediately arrested on suspicion of aiding the Contras. Sandinista officials then revealed that in the plane's wreckage they had discovered a phone book belonging to Hasenfus, which contained links to a Contra base in El Salvador and to Ollie North's office in the Reagan White House—exactly as Tony Avirgan and Martha Honey had reported.

The very next day, then White House counsel Ed Meese walked into the White House Briefing Room and admitted the entire operation to reporters. From his office in the White House, and with direct knowledge and approval of President Reagan, Colonel Oliver North had been leading an elaborate scheme to sell arms to Iran and then use that money to buy and ship arms to the Contras—in direction violation of the Boland Amendment, which banned American aid to the Contras.

Thus was born the Iran-Contra scandal that marred Ronald Reagan's second term. Suddenly, I started getting calls from reporter friends in Los Angeles: "Isn't this what Tony and Martha told us about at the Press Club?" The lucky ones had saved their notes and tape from their news conference.

BACK IN THE USSR

I guess travel to Nicaragua whetted my appetite for travel to Communist countries. But for whatever reason, in the summer of 1987, when I read that a group of American and Russian citizens had walked from Saint Petersburg to Moscow in the first annual Peace Walk, I decided to sign our family up for the next one, one year later: across Ukraine from Odessa to Kiev.

It was an incredible experience for all four of us. Our group numbered about two hundred Americans and two hundred Soviets (half of whom we assumed were working for the KGB), plus a support team of another hundred or so. Every morning, we'd walk ten or twelve miles, stop for lunch, then walk another few miles before setting up tents for the night in a field or city park. A small fleet of trucks carried our luggage and supplies from one site to the next.

For us Americans, especially, it was a heady experience. As the first Americans seen in Ukraine since American soldiers liberated the republic in World War II, everywhere we went we were received like rock stars. Crowds lined the sides of the road two or three deep in every town we passed through and piled our arms full of flowers, books, medals, photos, and other souvenirs.

The Ukrainians' ultimate expression of hospitality was to invite us to their homes for dinner and an overnight stay, which was, in fact, more of an ordeal than it sounds. Rather than a night off the beat, it turned out to be a night onstage. Our proud hosts would also invite all their neighbors to meet "real Americans" and enjoy a long and lavish dinner. And the entire evening, from start to finish, would be filled with toast after toast after toast—of vodka. After one of those "nights off," it was hard to keep up with the pace of the walk the next day.

As exciting as the Peace Walk was, Carol and I had another mission in what was then still the Soviet Union. Before leaving Los Angeles, I'd asked Rabbi Marvin Hier and Rabbi Abraham Cooper of the Simon Wiesenthal Center to put us in touch with some "Refuseniks"—Soviet Jews who'd been denied permission to emigrate—whom we might meet with. The people whose names they provided all lived in Leningrad, so once our group reached Kiev, without informing anyone, Carol and I went directly to the airport for a flight to Leningrad.

That's when we learned that in the Soviet Union "not a sparrow falls" without Big Brother knowing where it's going to land. Again, we had told no one where we were going or why. What a surprise, then, to be met at our gate in Leningrad by a government official with a car and driver, who whisked us directly to our hotel.

I immediately placed a call to the first name on the list, Lev Shieba, who turned out to be fluent in English and immediately invited us over to his apartment—assuring us there was no doubt we would be tailed. Nonetheless, we headed to the subway, and Lev met us at the assigned stop and took us to his home, where he and his wife, Vera, proceeded to tell us their sad story, similar to that of so many Jews in Leningrad.

Lev had been a senior acoustical engineer for the Soviet Navy until he applied for an exit visa to immigrate to the United States—at which point he was summarily fired and forbidden to travel anywhere outside of Leningrad. They were now living hand to mouth, without any income, depending on the charity of friends.

The next day, Lev and Vera showed us the sights of their magical city, including the Hermitage Museum, the Winter Palace, and the Peterhof Palace. That evening, they also organized a reception for other Refusenik families, after which Carol and I took the overnight train to Moscow. True to form, we'd no sooner pulled into the station when there was a knock on our compartment door. "Mr. and Mrs. Press, welcome to Moscow!" Another USSR official was waiting with a car and driver to take us to our hotel, where we were reunited with Mark, David, and the rest of the Peace Walk. It was amazing how the Soviet government could be so incomparably efficient about some things and so grossly incompetent about others.

We ran into even more Big Brother in Moscow. To celebrate the completion of our Soviet/American Peace Walk, we had applied for permission to hold a rally in Red Square. The Kremlin said no. We appealed, citing all the positive international publicity our joint appearance would generate. Still no dice. So we simply informed authorities that, with or without permission, we were going to show up.

As planned, we arrived early the next morning, expecting to be arrested. Instead, Kremlin authorities adopted a different strategy: They simply closed Red Square to everybody but us. With Soviet troops stationed on nearby streets, we held our little rally in the middle of a huge, eerily empty Red Square. We held hands, sang peace songs, and proudly waved the American and Soviet flags. Sadly, nobody was there to see it but us.

That wasn't the end of our adventure, however. Shortly after we returned to the United States, Vera Shieba obtained a temporary visa to visit her daughter, then living in the United States. We took Vera to see our friend Senator Barbara Boxer, who immediately went to work on behalf of Lev and Vera with the State Department. One year later, thanks to Senator Boxer, Lev and Vera were able to immigrate to the United States, where Lev soon put his acoustical engineering skills back to work—this time for the U.S. Navy. Now U.S. citizens, Lev and Vera are still here, enjoying their children and grandchildren.

TALK RADIO

For over thirty years now, I've enjoyed a career as a television commentator and radio host at the same time. So it seems strange that when I landed my first job in television, I never thought about appearing on radio as well. To me, they were two different worlds. How wrong I was.

I'd been at KABC-TV less than a year when Wally Sherman, program director of KABC Radio, asked if I might be interested in appearing as a guest or filling in as a guest host. I appeared on a few shows, enjoyed it, and before long I was a regular at KABC Radio, sitting in for Michael Jackson (the talk show host, not the moonwalker) and providing a two-minute liberal commentary via ISDN from my home in the Hollywood Hills on the morning show with Ken and Bob. For a couple of years, I also cohosted an afternoon, left-right debate show, appropriately called *The Dueling Bills*, with Bill Pearl. And, yes, our theme song was the dueling banjos from *Deliverance*.

I soon learned to love talk radio, loved working with the gang at KABC, and thought general manager George Green loved me—until the buildup to the first Persian Gulf War, when Green revealed himself to be a real asshole. When I argued against starting another war in the Middle East, George would walk into the studio, glare at me, and, as soon as I took a commercial break, start screaming at me.

Then one day, he walked me to my car, insisting that I stop opposing the war in order to provide "balance." I pointed out that, out of some dozen hosts on KABC, I was the only one who openly opposed the war. In other words, I *was* the station's balance. But Green would have none of it. He made it clear that if I didn't change my position, I'd be out of job. I didn't. And I was.

But actually, getting fired from KABC was a blessing. KABC had started to slip in the ratings, while KFI AM, offering a much livelier mix of talk radio over a much bigger signal, was climbing under the banner "More Stimulating Talk Radio."

It didn't take me long to knock on KFI's door. And, thanks to program director David Hall, I soon had my own show on KFI, Saturday and Sunday afternoons, following the weekend *Best of Rush Limbaugh* show. Hall was probably the youngest program director in the country, and still to this day, he's the smartest and most creative radio executive I've worked with anywhere.

It was Hall's idea to both enrage and engage Limbaugh's conservative listeners by branding me "Bill Press, True American." We peppered the Rush Limbaugh show preceding mine with corny promos created by assistant producer Tim Kelly. "He helps little old ladies across the street. Of course, he's Bill Press, True American." Or "He bakes a cherry pie. Of course, he's Bill Press, True American." As Hall predicted, Limbaugh's followers were pissed, but they couldn't resist tuning in.

KFI had a great team in those days, many of whom went on to bigger and better things: Dr. Laura Schlessinger; Stephanie Miller; Tammy Bruce; Hugh Hewitt; Tom Leykis; Bill Handel; John Kobylt and Ken Chiampou; and Marc Germain. They were fun to work with. They all helped me find my voice as a talk show host.

JOINING THE UNION

There was one other huge benefit to working at KABC-TV: I was required to join a union—in my case, the American Federation of Television and Radio Artists, or AFTRA. News director Dennis Swanson apologized when he informed me of this rule and was surprised when I told him it's something I'd always wanted to do.

It was one of the best decisions of my life. Seriously. With its health plan and pension plan, the union's been great for me and my family. It's even stronger now that AFTRA and the Screen Actors Guild (SAG) have finally merged, forming SAG-AFTRA.

My proudest moment as a union man came years later, after I'd moved to KCOP-TV, when the engineering staff and members of IATSE, the International Alliance of Theatrical Stage Employees, went on strike and set up a picket line outside the studio. As on-air talent and a member of AFTRA, I was technically not on strike, but I refused to cross the picket line anyway, out of solidarity. I even walked the line myself in support of my union brothers and sisters.

After the strike had dragged on for a week, KCOP's general manager called to suggest a compromise. I didn't have to cross the picket line, he proposed. He would send a camera crew to my home to record a commentary for the evening news. No way. As I pointed out, I would still be crossing the picket line, via videotape. I would still be a scab. I refused.

Over thirty years later, I'm still a proud union member. My commentaries reflect that because that's who I am. No matter the issue—living wage, collective bargaining, health care, workplace safety—if it's management versus working men and women, I'm on the side of the workers and their union. Because I realize, as all working men and women should, that many of the great benefits working families share today exist only because of the battles fought by our union brothers and sisters who came before us. Do you like weekends, health care, and the forty-hour workweek? Thank a union! And join one.

By this time, I'd been working on TV and radio for eight years and, if I may say so myself, I'd gotten pretty good at it. I had definitely found and established my progressive voice. And I'd learned a few basics about how to be a successful broadcaster. One, do your homework. Two, know your stuff. Three, be comfortable and relax. Four, tell the truth. Five, whatever you do, be yourself. Don't pretend to be anything else, because television can spot a phony a mile away.

I'd learned TV and radio so well, in fact, that I was ready for a bigger stage. But first, politics got in the way. Ever since high school, I'd had that proverbial political itch—and I finally had to scratch it.

6

BILL PRESS FOR SENATE

Why anybody puts himself or herself through the wringer of running for public office remains a mystery—especially with the demands of raising so much money, the total lack of privacy for you and your family, and the need to put up with all the insufferable party hacks you meet on the campaign trail. "You must be accessible to every fool who wants to see you," writes Gore Vidal in his classic novel *Washington, D.C.*, "since the only person who can never escape a bore is the man who needs his vote."

I guess I ran for office for the same reasons every other candidate does. It's mostly a desire to do some good and improve people's lives. It's also the burning need to be recognized, admired, approved, and fawned over. As my old boss Peter Behr used to joke, "Politics is the only fatal disease that those who have it want to die from."

So that's why I did it: the desire both to make a difference and to be the center of attention. In other words, I ran for office for the same reasons I joined the seminary.

In 1988, U.S. senator Pete Wilson was up for reelection. Wilson, former state assemblyman and former mayor of San Diego, was a good man, a moderate Republican, yet one of America's most boring politicians, with nothing to show after six years in Washington. To me, this looked like the chance to do something I'd been wanting to do for a long time.

My first move was to convince ten friends to contribute $500 each for a statewide public opinion poll that showed that while I had little name recognition statewide, I had far more name recognition than Pete Wilson in Southern California—and that's where all the votes were! National campaign strategist Bob Squier and his partner, Carter Eskew, flew out from Washington, reviewed the poll results, and encouraged me to take the plunge.

A few nights later, at the end of my commentary, I announced that I was leaving KABC-TV to run for U.S. senator from California—and headed directly to my very first fund-raiser, at the home of Ira and Adele Yellin. A few weeks later, Tom Hayden and then-wife Jane Fonda hosted a reception for me at their home in Venice.

My first break was a call from a dynamic young Beverly Hills developer named Albert Gersten, who volunteered to be chairman of my campaign. We sealed the deal the next day at his beach house in Malibu. Gersten was wealthy and politically well connected. He and I flew to Sacramento in his private jet to seek Assembly Speaker Willie Brown's endorsement but came home empty-handed. We then flew to Washington, where Gersten hired noted campaign strategist Ray Strother to produce our campaign commercials.

While in Washington, I made three obligatory stops for any senate candidate. First, a meeting with Senator John Kerry, then head of the Democratic Senatorial Campaign Committee, who promised me the DSCC's full support—*if* I won the primary. Next, Tom Dine, head of the powerful American Israel Public Affairs Committee (AIPAC), who told me that, even though Wilson might not be good on other issues, he was a solid vote for Israel and they were sticking with him. I also met with Jim Zogby, founder of the Arab American Institute, who promised to spread the word that I was open-minded on the Middle East and believed the Palestinian people, like the Israelis, deserved their own homeland.

Gersten and I eventually parted company over direction of the campaign, but he was a valuable, colorful, and wholly unpredictable ally. Out of the blue, he called me one day to say, "We have to do something about those bags under your eyes." He'd already made an appointment for me the next morning with a plastic surgeon. I declined.

My most embarrassing moment with Gersten came when he summoned me to his office in late 1987. I had no idea why. We chatted for a few minutes when, suddenly, the door opened and in walked Senator Al Gore, gearing up to run for president in 1988. I just sat there as Gore made his pitch on why he, a liberal Democrat from the South, was the party's best choice. Then, to my total surprise, Gersten told Gore he couldn't help him because he'd decided to support only one candidate in 1988—namely, me! Gore just glared at me.

RESCUE FROM NICARAGUA

My campaign team and I were convinced we had a good shot at Pete Wilson, but we had to win the Democratic primary first against Lieutenant Governor Leo McCarthy, another good man, but just as boring as Wilson. Our problem was that, as the establishment candidate, McCarthy had locked up all the endorsements of big-name Democrats and labor unions. The only way to win was to generate some buzz.

One evening, while we were brainstorming, good friend (and now state senator) Steve Glazer came up with a wild idea: I should go to Lebanon and rescue Anglican Church official Terry Waite, who'd been held hostage by Hezbollah since 1987. Great idea, I responded, but I had zero connections in Lebanon.

Then I remembered that, based on my previous visit, I *did* have several important contacts in Nicaragua, where American James Denby had recently been arrested by the Sandinistas. Bingo! Steve said, "Let's go to Nicaragua instead." And the race to free Denby was underway.

On one level, it was a noble cause to free an American citizen held captive by a hostile country. On the other level, politics. To be honest, we didn't know that much about Denby, and didn't care. He'd been shot down flying his small plane over Nicaragua on God knows what mission. Drugs? Aid to the Contras? Mere adventure? For all we knew he might have been a

CIA spy. All we really cared about was the good publicity we'd get for my senate campaign by springing him.

For such a bold and brazen move, we needed a bold and brazen team leader, and I had the perfect person in mind: fellow Jerry Brown colleague Llewellyn Werner, twenty years my junior, a freewheeling campaign aide who was always given the toughest assignments—and who always delivered.

Werner jumped at the chance. He and I flew to Nicaragua with Lydia Brazon, a native Nicaraguan from Los Angeles who was part of the group with whom I'd first traveled there. Thanks to her connections, we met first with Interior Minister Tomás Borge, where we laid out our case for freeing Denby. He was worth nothing to the Sandinistas in prison, we argued, but freeing him might win some goodwill in Washington, where Congress was about to vote on the Reagan administration's request for aid to the Contras.

Borge listened carefully, and then, after grilling us about whom we knew in Washington, he proposed a deal: We go back to Washington, see what promises we could wrangle out of our friends in Congress, and then come back and report to him. We agreed.

The next morning, before we left for the airport, Borge arranged a brief visit with Denby at a safe house in Managua. Denby was as surprised to see us as we were to see him. He assured us he was in good health and being treated well by his captors. But he refused to talk about what he was doing in Nicaragua in the first place. We didn't care. We just wanted to get him out of there.

After a brief stop in LA, I flew to Washington, where I met with good friend Howard Berman, ranking Democrat on the House Foreign Affairs Committee. He immediately grasped the potential payoff of a Denby release and promised to talk with other Democratic leaders in the House and Senate. That evening in our second meeting, he advised that, while Democratic leaders could offer no guarantees, they did believe that the release of Denby would greatly increase their chances of blocking financial aid to the Contras.

With that assurance, Llew Werner, Lydia Brazon, and I returned to Nicaragua, this time with a couple of extra players. I recruited a longtime friend, Dr. Mike Witte, founder of the West Marin Clinic and fluent Spanish speaker, to accompany us in order to examine Denby and assess his medical condition. Also at Llew's suggestion, we invited *Los Angeles Times*

Drafted near the end of World War II, Dad served with the occupation forces in Japan.

Mom was smart, funny, vivacious, and kept both family and Dad's business together.

Future media star? I was never camera shy, no matter what I was wearing. My views on guns have changed since this photo.

After Mom's death, Dad married Dorothy Miller. They enjoyed thirty-seven great years together.

Eugene McCarthy's the first candidate I volunteered for, in his 1968 presidential campaign. In April 2003, we celebrated the Senator's eighty-seventh birthday at our home in Washington. Linda Daschle is to Senator's right; Marie Arana, on his left.

President Clinton honored Carol and me with an invitation to a State Dinner on January 11, 1999, for Argentine President Carlos Saul Menem.

The Bernie Sanders campaign is born! November 19, 2014, a second meeting was held at our Capitol Hill Townhouse to explore the possibility of a Sanders presidential campaign. From left: Carol; Jane Sanders; Senator Sanders; Susan McGee; Alyssa Mastromonaco.

Holiday parties at the White House are always festive, and with a special treat: a quick photo op with the President and First Lady.

April 9, 1969. Carol and I celebrated our wedding with family and friends in San Francisco.

July 2017. The entire Press family gathers at the family vacation home in Weekapaug, Rhode Island: Carol and I welcome Mark and Cari, and Milo and Silas; David and Hez, and Prairie, Willow, and Django.

senior political reporter George Skelton, on one condition: that the entire adventure was "off the record" until and unless we told him otherwise. Finally, just in case, I asked Los Angeles businessman and leading peace activist Aris Anagnos to charter a private plane and stand by for a rescue mission if we proved successful.

Once in Managua, we informed the Interior Ministry we were back. And waited. And waited. Two nights later, we were having dinner in a downtown restaurant when the manager called me to the phone. Commandant Borge wanted to see us right away.

Lydia, Llew, and I informed Borge of my meetings with congressional Democrats and their belief that Denby's release could help block funding for the Contras. But, we emphasized, it was important to move quickly. He listened carefully, then, sphinxlike, said that while he could make no promise, things were looking good. We should make all necessary preparations, he advised, while keeping everything top secret. On the spot, like something right out of a Le Carré novel, we dubbed the entire operation "Bogey"—the name of Llew Werner's dog.

Acting on Borge's cautious assurances, I asked Aris Anagnos to fire up his chartered jet and get to Managua as soon as possible. As the final member of our team, he brought along Llew's girlfriend (now wife), Yale- and Stanford-educated attorney Martha Sanchez.

The next evening, our entire team met again with Borge, who told us Denby would be released to us the next morning, provided the government's decision was approved by the Nicaraguan Supreme Court. Borge then invited us all to join him (and his well-armed security guards) at a Managua dance hall, where he shamelessly hit on and danced with the attractive Martha Sanchez all evening, while Llew steamed nearby. When I teased Llew about it later, he groused, "What was I supposed to do? They were all slinging AK-47s."

We danced and drank until well after midnight. The next morning, with little opportunity to prepare, Martha went off to court by herself to argue for Denby's freedom before the Nicaraguan Supreme Court. Meanwhile, I called campaign manager David Calef and told him to inform reporters of our arrival that evening at LAX with a surprise guest.

A couple of hours later, Martha returned from court with good news: We'd won! Then things really went crazy. A government car picked us up and took us to the house where we'd met Denby a week earlier. We told Denby he was coming home with us to the United States. Mike Witte gave him a quick examination and declared him in good health. Sandinista officials then escorted us to the front door—and, to our surprise, a mob of reporters and TV cameras.

I made a brief statement, thanking the Sandinistas on behalf of all Americans for releasing American prisoner James Denby. Then Denby and I climbed into a jeep, escorted by Nicaraguan motorcycle police, sirens blaring, for a wild ride to the airport. Reporters on motorcycles buzzed all around us, edging up to the jeep to shout questions.

In the middle of that media madness, Denby turned to me with a big smile on his face and said, "I thought for sure Jesse Jackson was going to beat you to it!" I had no idea Jackson had already been to Managua and made his own pitch for Denby. What a riot. We had beaten Jesse at his own game.

Aris Anagnos was waiting for us at the Managua airport with his chartered jet, and we were immediately off to LAX, where we rolled up to the executive terminal and a huge gaggle of LA media, earning a front-page photo in the *Los Angeles Times* the next morning. Denby spent the night near the airport. I flew up to San Francisco to see Carol. Denby and I met again in Washington the following afternoon.

That evening, I briefed Howard Berman and several other members of Congress on the success of our mission. The next day, after Denby and I did a joint appearance on *CBS Morning News* from Washington, we held a news conference at the Capitol. Denby wobbled a little, saying he didn't really have anything against the Contras, but insisted he still opposed the war. But at that point, it didn't really matter what he said. His release had done the trick. The motion for Contra funding failed. Our Denby mission had achieved its most important goal.

Unfortunately, the second-most important goal didn't work out so well. Even though I enjoyed a brief burst of positive publicity, Leo McCarthy still led in the polls and fund-raising. I truly believed I could have defeated Pete Wilson in the general election, but I realized there was no way I could best McCarthy in the primary. So I dropped out of the race, endorsed Leo, and went back to KABC-TV and KABC Radio.

COMMUNITY SERVICE

As a political activist, I had always argued that progressives could not be content with sitting on the sidelines. To bring about true progressive change, they had to get involved in some form of community services. So now, no longer a candidate, with more time on my hands, I decided it was time to practice what I preached—and I enlisted in the fight for gay rights and civil rights.

In 1989, I joined the board of the Municipal Elections Committee of Los Angeles, or MECLA, the first PAC in the country dedicated exclusively to backing candidates who supported gay rights. That was our unique focus: to endorse and raise money for gay-friendly candidates, both Democrat and Republican—although it was hard back then finding gay-friendly Republicans to endorse. And, unfortunately, still is today.

MECLA's one big event was an annual fund-raising dinner at the Century Plaza Hotel, with many prominent state and national politicians in attendance. My first year on the board, Teddy Kennedy was our keynote speaker. The next year, our headliner was Texas governor Ann Richards, who brought the house down with her story about the importance of all political contributions, large and small.

As Governor Richards told it, Mae West was at a party in New York, when Tallulah Bankhead walked in, wearing a drop-dead, floor-length, silver fox coat. "Where'd you get that coat?" Mae wanted to know. Tallulah bragged, "Baby, I met a man with ten thousand dollars."

Flash forward. A couple of months later, roles were reversed. This time, it was Mae West who walked into a party sporting an identical drop-dead, floor-length, silver fox coat. "Baby, did you also meet a man with ten thousand dollars?" Tallulah asked. "No, honey," Mae proudly explained, "I met ten thousand men with one dollar."

Even though we did a lot of good work, had a lot of fun, and supported a lot of good candidates, my memories of those days at MECLA are filled with sadness. Tragically, this was the height of the AIDS epidemic, which struck LA especially hard, long before doctors knew what was causing this dreadful disease or how to treat it. So when I think back to our board meetings and look around the table, I see the faces of so many beautiful young men—David Quarles, Peter Scott, Clyde Cairns, Sheldon Andelson, Scott Hitt, and others—lost at an early age to AIDS. I went to too many funerals and sang "Amazing Grace" too many times.

At about the same time, I was invited to join the board of the Los Angeles chapter of the Southern Christian Leadership Conference, the historic civil rights organization founded by Dr. Martin Luther King Jr. The LA chapter was headed by its chair, Reverend James Lawson, who had organized the historic 1968 strike of sanitation workers in Memphis, and executive director Mark Ridley Thomas, who went on to hold just about every elective office available in Los Angeles: city council, state assembly, state senate, and county supervisor.

My experience at SCLC taught me a lot about the many challenges still facing African Americans in this country, especially regarding jobs, housing, schools, incarceration, and insurance. We also dealt with the serious divide between the Los Angeles Police Department and black residents of South Central LA.

I lived through the results of that divide during the O.J. trial and the riots following the verdict in the Rodney King trial. I also saw that divide, and the resulting tension, up close the first time I was called for jury duty in Los Angeles County: a drive-by robbery case in South Central LA. The defendant was a young black man.

The only witness for the prosecution was a white police officer who had made the arrest, but could not place the suspect at the scene. The only "evidence" provided of his guilt was the fact that he was black, had been seen in the general vicinity of the crime, and had the tattoo of a popular LA gang on his neck. He was young, he was black, he was a gang member, therefore, he must be guilty.

As a jury, we knew what we were expected to do: take the cop at his word and convict him. But we took our job seriously. We looked for evidence of guilt. There was none. We voted not guilty.

Hearing from a friend who was losing her eyesight how much she depended on audio books, I took on one more form of community service: volunteering once at a week at the Braille Institute in Los Angeles, recording books for the blind. Little did I realize that experience would have such a huge impact on my life.

Purely by chance, the first book I was assigned to read was *Hank: The*

Life of Charles Bukowski by Neeli Cherkovski. I had never heard of Bukowski, but I became a big fan, began searching for signed copies of his poetry in local bookstores, and started building a big Bukowski collection I still spend too much money on. Bukowski was still alive, living in San Pedro at the time. I regret not meeting him before his death in March 1994.

PRESS FOR INSURANCE COMMISSIONER

Two years after my aborted Senate campaign, running for political office wasn't yet out of my system. It wasn't long before I jumped back in.

In 1988, one of the big issues on the ballot was Proposition 103, which made the position of California insurance commissioner an elected office, rather than one appointed by the governor.

I often spoke about insurance issues on television. I also served as chair of the Los Angeles County Insurance Commission, appointed by supervisor Kenny Hahn. So when Prop 103 passed, I decided to run in June 1990 for the job of California's first elected insurance commissioner.

Again, I said goodbye on KABC, this time for good, and set about reassembling my campaign team. David Calef stepped back in as campaign manager. Joanne Ruden and Debbie Taylor headed up fund-raising.

Everybody agreed it'd be tough for a Republican to get elected insurance commissioner, so the real contest was in the Democratic primary, where there were four candidates: state senator John Garamendi; California Common Cause leader Walter Zelman; attorney/lobbyist Conway Collis; and me.

We each brought certain strengths to the campaign. But I was lucky to win the endorsement of most of California's leading trial lawyers, many of whom had helped me in researching material for my TV commentary, including Browne Greene, Bruce Broillet, Gary Paul, and Paul Kiesel in Los Angeles; Dave Casey in San Diego; Wylie Aitken in Orange County; and Joe Cotchett, Arnold Laub, and Mary Alexander in San Francisco. I also campaigned hard for and won the official endorsement of the California Democratic Party.

I took a lot of grief from some liberals for my close association with trial lawyers. But I make no apologies, because I was proud to stand up for trial lawyers and have them stand up with me. I still consider them to be one of the greatest forces for good in America today.

Let's face it. Most of the criticism of trial lawyers comes from big businesses who are out to screw their customers and resent lawyers getting in the way. A manufacturer marketing an unsafe baby crib. A carmaker selling a pickup truck that rolls too easily. An incompetent doctor who botches an operation and maims a person for life. The list of real, tragic cases goes on and on. Nobody would have a chance against those mighty powers without trial lawyers willing to take on the tough cases.

For average Americans, having access to a trial lawyer is more important than ever today, after the Supreme Court's 2013 ruling allowing corporations to force arbitration on consumers. It's more difficult than ever, without the assistance of a good trial lawyer, for customers to file a class-action lawsuit.

True, there are some trial lawyers who take advantage of the system, just as there are some dishonest doctors, bankers, and insurance executives. But they don't, or shouldn't, tarnish the reputation of trial lawyers in general. Every one of the arguments made against trial lawyers boils down to an argument made by the haves against the have-nots. Do they take cases with no money up front, on a contingency, roll-of-the-dice basis? Yes, but if they didn't, most people could not afford to hire an attorney in the first place. Do they and their clients get rich from punitive damages? Not as rich as you might think. But the truth is, there wouldn't be any need for trial lawyers if companies made safe products or if insurance companies only paid a fair settlement in the first place. Do they scare the shit out of doctors? Sometimes. But doctors who do their jobs diligently and carefully have nothing to worry about.

I also received a lot of support from leaders of the entertainment industry, including MCA's Lew Wasserman and Sidney Sheinberg; veteran Hollywood stars Ed Asner, Richard Dreyfuss, Ed Begley, Morgan Fairchild, Robert Foxworth, George Takei, and Leonard Nimoy; comedian Milton Berle; music legends Jackson Browne, Graham Nash, Don Henley, and Casey Kasem; and a passel of young actors led by Rob Lowe, his brother, Chad Lowe, and Sarah Jessica Parker.

By far my most colorful supporter was *Playboy* publisher Hugh Hefner. Two of my most successful fund-raisers, in fact, were held at the magnificent Playboy mansion in Holmby Hills. At both, Hef dutifully showed up in his trademark silk pajamas.

We four candidates battled down to the wire, but in the end, I came in second to Garamendi, who now represents California's Third District in the U.S. Congress.

Once more, I was out of a job—and also broke, since, in a dumb move I still regret, I convinced Carol to take out a second mortgage of $100,000 on our home in Inverness in order to pump extra cash into my campaign, thereby violating one of the cardinal rules of politics: OPM. Always and only spend Other People's Money!

But if I didn't know how to practice politics, I still knew how to talk politics. Thanks to program director Jeff Wald, I landed another TV job as political commentator on independent channel KCOP-TV, reporting to fabled news director Bob Long. *Fabled* because nobody seemed to know where Long came from. Sure, he was a brilliant news director. But before that? CIA? French Foreign Legion? All we really knew and appreciated was that he had a big set of balls running the newsroom. He once complimented an anchor for having a "three-testicle voice." A couple of times a week after the show, a clutch of us would gather with Long at the nearby Formosa Café, where he regaled us with wild stories. Bob lost a long battle to cancer in August 2016, leaving behind an army of television anchors, reporters, and producers he had mentored, now serving in TV stations across the land.

For me, a new job at KCOP, plus a weekend radio show on KFI, meant that I was, once again, back to full-time television and radio, a winning combination for me.

A SPIRITUAL HOME

As much as I enjoyed living in West Hollywood, where Carol and I now owned a townhouse, I realized there was still one thing missing: any comfort on the spiritual side. I decided to return to a church I'd first visited with Jerry Brown when he was running for reelection: the legendary First AME Church in South Central Los Angeles, led by Pastor Chip Murray.

After all my years as a Catholic, including all that time in the seminary, I never experienced a more meaningful official worship service than that first time at First AME. It brought me back to the sense of welcome and joy I knew at Glide Methodist Church in San Francisco. The congregation, literally, rocked with music and prayer. The choir was awesome. And Pastor Murray's sermon was both inspiring and down to earth. *This is what church ought to be*, I remember thinking that day with Jerry Brown. So I went back, hungry for more.

I didn't make a big deal of it. I didn't try to play the big shot TV star. I didn't call and announce my arrival. I just showed up one Sunday morning. The entire service and Pastor Murray's sermon were every bit as powerful as I remembered.

So I came back the following Sunday when, to my total surprise, Pastor Murray singled me out in the congregation, introduced me, and asked me to stand and be recognized. He did that several Sundays in a row until, finally, after services, I remarked to one woman how embarrassed I was but also how impressed I was that, without any advance notice, Pastor Murray knew I was there in the congregation. She laughed out loud. "Bill," she said, "think about it. When he looks down from that pulpit, it's not hard to spot the one white face in the house!" I begged Pastor Murray to stop singling me out, which he did.

First AME became my new spiritual home—and that's where I sought refuge during the Rodney King riots. Those six days were the scariest time of my life. It all started on the night of March 3, 1991, when Rodney King was pulled over by cops on the Foothill Freeway. King initially resisted arrest, whereupon he was Tasered, tackled, kicked in the head, and beaten with batons by four officers—all of it videotaped by a neighbor from his nearby balcony. That video sparked national outrage, leading to all four officers being charged with assault and use of excessive force.

The trial was moved from Los Angeles to Simi Valley, where on Wednesday, April 29, 1992, a mostly white jury acquitted all four officers—and all hell broke loose. Protestors poured into the streets, without incident at first. Then truck driver Reginald Denny stopped for a traffic light at the corner of Florence and Normandie. He was attacked by a mob, hit in the head with a rock, and dragged from the cab of his truck. Again, all of it caught on video. This time, broadcast over live television by KCOP-TV reporter Bob Tur, flying overhead in his news chopper.

Video of that violence sparked more violence, more outrage, more fear, and six days of lawlessness. After watching the video at KCOP, I proposed to news director Bob Long that I broadcast my commentary live that night from First AME, where Mayor Tom Bradley was expected to make a statement. Long agreed, and I drove to the church with the promise of a TV crew to join me later.

First AME was packed with local residents seeking refuge. There were reports of more looting and violence in the neighborhood. We could hear gunfire and smell acrid smoke from burning buildings nearby. It was soon clear that Mayor Bradley wasn't going to show, and I wasn't going to do my commentary, either. The area was too dangerous for the TV crew to enter.

Trapped like everyone else, I joined church members on the balcony behind the church. It was a frightening scene. From every side, we could hear gunfire and see buildings burning. Cars in the parking lot were covered with ash. None of us knew where to turn or what to do. One man asked me how I, the only white man in the crowd, was planning to get home.

"No problem," I said. "My car's right here in the lot. I'll just drive home."

"Oh, no, you won't," he shot back. "With that face, you'll never get out of here alive."

Whereupon that Good Samaritan proposed a different plan of escape. We very carefully made our way to his car, parked half a block away, where he told me to lie down on the floor of the back seat, covered me with a blanket, and warned me not to move, no matter what happened. Amid much noise and shouting, with many stops and starts, twists and turns, he drove me out of South Central all the way to our home in West Hollywood. I'm embarrassed to say I don't even know that man's name. But his courage and clear thinking may well have saved my life.

The next few days were pure hell. Life in the second-largest city in the United States was like living in a lawless zone. Any police presence, in effect, was either ineffective or nonexistent. One evening, Bob Long and I stood on the roof of the KCOP building and watched carloads of looters working their way north on La Brea Avenue, going from one side of the street to the other, breaking store windows, walking away with whatever they could carry, and then torching the businesses. No cops came. No fire trucks came. Nobody called 911, because nobody would respond.

Downstairs in his office, I told Long I was worried they might break into our studios, but Bob assured me he wasn't worried. "I've got my riot kit," he said with a big grin. He picked up his black briefcase, laid it on his desk, and opened it. Inside were three items: a bottle of scotch, a carton of cigarettes—and a handgun! "Let 'em come," he declared. "I'm ready for 'em." Classic Bob Long.

Outside of South Central Los Angeles, one of the hardest-hit areas was Koreatown, where our KFI radio studios were located. Koreatown became so dangerous that, for a couple of days, KFI's entire operation secretly relocated to the home of our chief engineer in the mountains above Pasadena, where we broadcast from his living room.

Eventually, things quieted down. But the riots left 53 dead and over 2,000 injured. Officials estimated that 3,600 fires were set, destroying 1,100 buildings. Total property damage neared $1 billion.

Years later, when protests against abuse of force by police officers broke out in Ferguson, Missouri, and Baltimore, Maryland, for me it was déjà vu. I flashed back to Los Angeles and the Rodney King riots. There were so many similarities.

Once again, peaceful protests soon turned to violence. Once again, the trigger was excessive use of force by white police officers against young black men. And, once again, all police officers involved escaped punishment. For a while, after Ferguson, Baltimore, and other examples of officer abuse, there was a lot of positive talk about police reform, but little action. And now Attorney General Jeff Sessions is going in the opposite direction: rolling back reforms already in place and letting all other police departments off the hook.

That is a serious mistake that will have disastrous consequences. Until we recognize the inherent racial bias of some white police officers and some white members of juries, until we accept the reality of white officers deliberately targeting young black men, even going so far as to kill unarmed black men with impunity, until we deal with that problem by getting rid of those bad apples, better vetting and training new recruits, and hiring new officers who reflect the face of the community they serve . . . the racial tension in many American cities will just continue to percolate until it breaks out again in violence. When will we learn?

Strangely enough, as traumatic as the Rodney King riots were, that turned out to be not the only war zone I found myself in that year.

WAR IN CROATIA

In fact, I was soon in the middle of an actual war, between Yugoslavia and Croatia, thanks to a long friendship with Orange County businessman Milan Panić.

I could write a whole book about Milan Panić, and several have. He's led an incredible life and played a big part in mine.

Panić is a true American success story. Born in Belgrade, and champion of his country's national cycling team, Panić defected from Yugoslavia to Austria and then Germany. A year later, he arrived in New York with his wife, two children, two suitcases, and $20 in his pocket. From the East Coast, he made his way to Los Angeles and Caltech. In 1960, with $200 cash, he founded ICN Pharmaceuticals, which he built up into a multibillion-dollar business, best known for developing the miracle drug ribavirin, or Virazole. Panić resigned as chairman in 2002 and founded MP Biomedicals, which he led until selling the company in 2016.

I met Milan in 1978, during Jerry Brown's reelection campaign. He counts among the most generous Democratic donors in California. He's also a brilliant, hard-driving, phenomenally successful businessman. Ever looking for new business opportunities, Milan saw a ready-made one with the collapse of communism in Eastern Europe. He began in Serbia, his former homeland, by convincing Yugoslavia's dictator Slobodan Milošević to sell him Galenika, the state-owned pharmaceutical company.

For the first time anywhere in Eastern Europe, Milan offered employees stock ownership in the company, and he even published a pamphlet on how capitalism worked. He next expanded operations into Russia, with pharmaceutical labs in Moscow and Saint Petersburg. At the time, in an interview with the *Los Angeles Times*, I called him "the Ross Perot of the Balkans."

Milan invited me to Belgrade in August 1991 to interview Milošević and report on the war in Croatia for KCOP-TV. News director Bob Long gave his approval, so off I went, after dutifully promising Carol I'd go nowhere near the combat zone.

The night I arrived in Belgrade, Dušan Mitević, the head of Radio Television Belgrade, Yugoslavia's state-owned media, met me in the lobby of my hotel to inform me that Panić would be an hour late for dinner. Over drinks, and later over dinner, he proceeded to bore me with the history of Serbian-Croatian relations, starting in the twelfth century.

The next morning, I discovered it was all part of the plan. When I showed up at the presidential palace for my interview with Milošević, we were all ready to go when a press aide opened the door to the president's private office—only to reveal Milošević talking with Mitević, the man who'd briefed me the night before. He was prepping Milošević on prepping me.

In flawless English (he had, after all, worked in New York as a banker for several years), Milošević defended Serbia's war against Croatia as only one step in a righteous campaign to keep Yugoslavia intact. It was just like America's own Civil War, he insisted, which we fought to prevent the South from seceding from the Union. He attacked the Croatian people as antidemocratic forces who supported the Nazis in World War II and even operated a concentration camp on Croatian soil.

At the end of the interview, Milošević beamed. "Good, now we drink." He clapped his hands, and in walked an aide bearing a silver tray filled with shot glasses of whiskey and orange juice. It was only 9:00 a.m., I'd been in Belgrade less than twenty-four hours, and here I was, knocking back shots with Slobodan Milošević.

Early the next morning, with a TV crew and translator, I secretly left Belgrade for the Vojvodina area of Serbia. Our plan was to sneak into Croatia and interview residents of Vukovar to get their side of the Serbia-Croatia conflict. Because of the war, there was no direct access to Croatia, so we hooked up with a local partisan who took us to a remote spot on the Danube where, for a price, a local fisherman agreed to ferry us across the river.

Walking to a little village on the outskirts of Vukovar, we were surprised to find stores closed, streets deserted, and, aside from a couple of other journalists, nobody in sight. We soon found out why. A couple of Serbian military officers rounded us up and took us to a nearby elementary school, where they informed us that the Serbian Army was about to launch a siege of Vukovar.

Sure enough, we soon heard fighter planes overhead and the sound of bombs dropping nearby. The school had been requisitioned as a triage station, and as we were leaving, the first victims of the bombing were being brought in, including one soldier who'd lost a leg. We decided to get the hell of there.

First, ignoring my promise to Carol, we walked a few blocks closer to Vukovar, where I quickly did a stand-up with fighter planes dropping bombs behind me. Then we hurried to the river and our fisherman friend, who advised us to lie in the bottom of his boat to avoid getting shot on our way back to Serbia. It was my one and only time anywhere near the front lines of a war. I had no desire to become another Peter Arnett.

That first trip to Serbia was not the last. But on my next visit, I was engaged in a different kind of war: a political war between Slobodan Milošević and Milan Panić for president of Serbia, which actually had its roots in the first Bush White House.

POLITICS SERBIAN-STYLE

About a year later, Milan Panić called again with an intriguing new twist: Slobodan Milošević had offered to appoint him prime minister of Yugoslavia—on the promise that Milošević would step down in six months so Milan could step up as president, which I didn't believe for a minute. "Stop! Don't agree to anything," I pleaded with Milan, "until we can talk."

When I caught up with Milan the next morning, it was clear he'd already decided to accept Milošević's offer. The only question was how. Because there were U.S. sanctions against Yugoslavia, Panić would need a waiver from the George H. W. Bush White House—all the more difficult since, out of all the hundreds of thousands of dollars in campaign contributions he'd made over the years, Panić had never given one dollar to a Republican.

Never having learned to say no to Milan, I agreed to help. My first call was to campaign strategist Bob Squier, who said he didn't have any more access to the Bush White House than I did. But Bob suggested that I call his then weekly debate partner on *CBS Morning News*: Roger Ailes, former political adviser to both Richard Nixon and Ronald Reagan, who then, long before Fox News, had his own consulting firm.

Using Squier's name, I managed to get Roger on the phone and made my pitch. For the White House, there was no downside to this proposition,

I argued. If Panić were successful in replacing Milošević and ending Serbian aggression, Bush could take credit for it. If Panić failed, Bush could say he'd done everything possible to bring an end to the war in Croatia. Roger promised to make a couple of phone calls and called me back ten minutes later. "I can't tell you who," he reported, "but I talked to somebody high in the White House. I think we may be able to do something. But I have to meet your guy first."

After a red-eye flight from California, Panić and I showed up in Roger's midtown Manhattan office the next morning. We were still making small talk when Roger excused himself to take a call from the White House. He came back five minutes later to tell us President Bush would grant Panić a waiver from U.S. sanctions. In early July 1992, he was sworn in as the Serbian-born, American-bred, millionaire prime minister of Yugoslavia. That's when the fun began.

Once in office, Panić called for ending Milošević's latest war, against Bosnia, within one hundred days, thereby setting up an inevitable clash with Milošević—who, of course, reneged on his promise to resign. Panić then decided to run against Milošević for president of Serbia and summoned his political allies from the United States to Belgrade. Political strategist Doug Schoen led the campaign team, assisted by former senator Birch Bayh and my former campaign director David Calef. I parachuted in for a couple of weeks.

Panić turned out to be a born candidate. His campaign slogan was "Change Now!" His message of nonviolence and economic optimism was exactly what the Serbian people were yearning for after years of war and recession under Milošević. His speeches, delivered in a mix of American-accented Serbian and Serbian-accented English, were amusing and endearing. And crowds loved him. Twenty thousand showed up for his first campaign rally in the city of Niš, a Milošević stronghold. His final campaign rally in Belgrade drew a crowd of 150,000—bigger than Donald Trump or Bernie Sanders!

Obviously worried about Panić, Milošević tried to suppress the vote in every way possible. As documented by campaign manager Doug Schoen in *The New York Times*, Milošević's apparatchiks began by cleansing the voter rolls of anyone who had not voted in the spring elections, which the opposition had largely boycotted. As a result, on Election Day, December 20,

5–10 percent of voters were turned away because their names were no longer on the voter rolls. And college students, who were overwhelmingly Panić supporters, were curiously required to report to campus on Election Day to qualify for subsidized student housing, preventing many of them from getting to their local polling places.

Exit polls nationwide showed Panić and Milošević in a dead heat at 47 percent. In Belgrade, 80–90 percent of voters said they'd voted for Panić. Yet, in the end, official returns showed that Milošević crushed Panić, 56 percent to 34. Bullshit! There's no doubt what happened: Panić won that election, but Milošević counted the votes. Even the Helsinki Commission concluded that the presidential election was "neither free nor fair."

The day after the election, a top general warned Panić that he should leave the country immediately or end up a dead man. Panić went back to California and ICN Pharmaceuticals. A decade later, Milošević was arrested, charged with war crimes, and tried at The Hague, where he died in his prison cell of a heart attack in March 2006.

DEMOCRATIC STATE CHAIR

Once you're bitten by politics, you're bitten forever. At least I was. Even after running unsuccessfully for the U.S. Senate and California insurance commissioner, I still couldn't get politics out of my system. All I needed was an office I could run for and win. Early in 1993, one dropped into my lap.

Phil Angelides, a good friend from Sacramento, was chair of the California Democratic Party. With his term about to expire, Phil called and asked if I'd be interested in running to succeed him.

For me it was, I must admit, a stretch. Despite all my political experience, I'd never been involved with the party as such. I'd never been to a state convention. Never walked into a party headquarters. On the other hand, Bill Clinton had just been elected president. Dianne Feinstein and Barbara Boxer were the newly elected senators from California. It looked like a fun time to be California Democratic chair. So I decided to go for it.

But it wasn't automatic. First, you had to run and win. I teamed up with labor leader Arlene Holt of AFSCME, running for vice chair. Michael Ganley, a labor organizer from San Francisco, ran the campaign. Our opponent was Steve Barr, a young graduate student from LA. We traveled up and down the state, appearing before county Democratic committees, meeting with members of the party's executive committee, and debating the issues. When the votes were counted at the state convention in Sacramento, Arlene and I prevailed.

The next three years were an exciting blur of politics by day and TV by night.

During the day, I worked at party headquarters in West Hollywood; in the evening, I offered my political commentary on KCOP-TV's 10:00 p.m. newscast.

At least once a month, I'd spend the day in Sacramento at northern party headquarters.

Phil had left the state party in good shape, under executive director Susan Kennedy. When she left to work for Senator Feinstein, Kathy Bowler took over the reins. Brian Wolff was my capable executive assistant. Political director Bob Mulholland rounded out the team. I still can't believe some of the crazy stunts he talked me into as state chair, most of them aimed at Republican governor Pete Wilson. I once appeared at a Republican convention in Orange County, carrying a large box marked *Preparation H*, claiming Wilson was going to need it if he continued to straddle the fence on every issue. And in 1996, when Wilson announced his run for president in New York's Battery Park, I was on the scene, dressed in a lizard costume, accusing him of being a political chameleon.

We also had a great team of officers at the CDP: Arlene Holt, first vice chair; Angela Alioto, second vice chair; controller Tal Finney; and state treasurer Gary Paul. Former chair Nancy Pelosi pitched in whenever we needed help in California or Washington. Christine Pelosi, born with her mother's zest for politics, served as chair of the rules committee.

At the time, Reverend Jesse Jackson was the best orator in the Democratic Party. Richard Nixon even praised him as "the only real poet in American politics today." We enlisted Jackson's help in voter registration drives, where he'd fly in, give a great speech, inspire the crowd, and then take off. To those who complained he never stayed around for the hard work, Jackson merely shrugged. "I'm a tree shaker, not a jelly-maker," he once told columnist Clarence Page.

Hands down, the most fun of being state chair was hanging out with President Bill Clinton. He came to the West Coast often, and every time he showed up, north or south, I was there. Over time, we became friends. He turned one state convention into a party for my fifty-fifth birthday. Even though his visits were usually on official government or national party business, he always took time out to help the state party. And he filled his administration with California transplants, including chief of staff Leon Panetta, White House aides John Emerson and Tom Epstein, and DNC secretary Alice Travis Germond.

There were many memorable moments with Clinton, one of which turned into a near disaster. When the president started to gear up for his reelection campaign, Harold Ickes asked me to help with his fund-raising effort in California, long the ATM for Democratic candidates. Not wanting to organize yet another fund-raising dinner, I suggested a different approach: ten donors who would contribute $100,000 each to spend an hour "discussing the issues" with the president. The White House agreed.

A couple of weeks later, Clinton was in San Francisco for some official event, after which, right on time, he walked into my suite at the Fairmont Hotel, shook hands with the ten donors I'd recruited, sat down, and asked each of them to introduce themselves and tell him what was on their minds. Everything went smoothly until Doug McCarron, then president of the Southern California Conference of Carpenters, got his chance. Known for being an effective but outspoken labor leader, McCarron told Clinton how disappointed his members were, after having worked so hard to get him elected. "When I go to my union halls today," he said, "All I hear is: 'Bill Clinton, asshole!'"

Did he just call the president of the United States an asshole? I wanted to crawl out of the room. I looked over at Clinton. His face was red. You could see the veins in his neck throbbing. I half expected him either to jump up and punch McCarron or storm out of the room. But he did neither. For what seemed like forever, he just nodded. Then he calmly said he was sorry to hear that, he understood their frustration, and he'd look into the issues McCarron's members were concerned about. Nuclear warfare narrowly avoided.

Later, the president told me that, with that one exception, he actually enjoyed the format. With little hassle, and nothing but an hour of his time, we'd raised a cool $1 million. We followed up with a similar event in Los Angeles and one in Washington, where ten donors contributed $100,000 each for lunch with the president at the Hay-Adams hotel.

The truth is, President Clinton loves getting out and meeting people.

Period. One evening, I joined him and the First Lady for a big fund-raiser at the fabulous Hotel del Coronado in San Diego, preceded by a private reception for major donors at the beach club. I was walking with Hillary from the earlier event up to the hotel when I noticed the president was missing. *Where's the president?* I wondered. I asked her.

"Oh, he's probably still back there, shaking hands," Hillary said.

Sure enough, when I walked back to the beach, there was nobody left—no donors, no White House aides, no hangers-on—nobody but the president of the United States and the waitstaff. Clinton was going from serving table to serving table, shaking hands with every one of them.

The day before one of Clinton's visits to Los Angeles, the deputy chief of staff, Harold Ickes, called to tell me the president was going to play a round of golf the next afternoon and asked me to find another player to round out his foursome. I immediately called supermarket king Ron Burkle, head of the Yucaipa Companies and one of our major donors. At first, Ron tried to beg off, insisting he hadn't played golf in years. But I persisted. "Ron, this may be your only chance ever to play golf with the president of the United States. Get your ass out to the nearest driving range and practice your swing." Which he did.

The next evening, I asked the president how Burkle made out on the course. The ever-political Clinton smiled and said, "Let me put it this way. Ron's a fast learner."

Which reminds me of my favorite Clinton golf tale. A couple of years later, when I was already cohost of *Crossfire*, Susie and Mark Buell, our good friends from Bolinas, came over for breakfast in Washington, after which Susie and I drove Mark to the White House for a golf date with the president. They played on the blue course at the Congressional Country Club, a course I knew well. Just before the green on the ninth hole is a huge swale, into which Clinton sank his second shot. His three partners made it across and walked to the green to wait for the president.

Mark relates how the three of them watched as the most powerful man on the planet walked up the fairway and disappeared from view down into the swale. A couple of minutes later, a ball comes soaring out of nowhere and lands on the green. Then they see Clinton—first the top of his hat, then his head, then his shoulders, and finally his whole body emerge from the swale. Clinton walked over, spotted his ball lying on the green, broke into a big grin, and remarked, "Look at that. I get myself into some deep shit sometimes, but I'm pretty good at getting out of it!" He didn't have to mention Monica Lewinsky.

President Clinton was also up to speed on pop culture, far more than I was. On one visit, I flew with him on Air Force One from Los Angeles to Oakland, where I introduced him at a big rally. At the end of his remarks, he was still waving to the crowd while I was staring at the program, wondering what the hell I could say about the next speaker, somebody named Queen Latifah, whom I'd never even heard of.

Suddenly, over the noise of the crowd, I heard a husky voice whispering in my left ear. "Let me do this." I looked up and, sure enough, there was the president, asking me to let him introduce Queen Latifah. Which, of course, I happily did. They were already best buds.

On one of his first visits to California, Carol had given the president one of her beautiful, hand-woven scarves, which he proceeded to wear on every outdoor winter occasion, including meetings with foreign leaders. Years later, on December 31, 2003, we were dismayed to see a photo of him arriving with Hillary the night before at a Broadway theater, wearing a different, rather god-awful scarf. So, for the first time, I used a private number I'd been given and called him at home in Chappaqua.

Clinton himself answered the phone. I wished him Happy New Year, we chatted, and then I told him there was another reason I'd called: "Obviously, we've let you down." A puzzled Clinton asked: "How'd you let me down?"

When I explained we'd let him down by not sending him a new Carol Press scarf, so he was forced to wear that ugly one, Clinton said: "Well, you know something about that scarf? It was Hillary's Christmas present."

Needless to say, my face was red and my foot firmly planted in mouth. I laughed and said: "I take it back. It's the most beautiful scarf I ever saw— and be sure to tell Hillary."

Next to Bill, the most fun was spending time with First Lady Hillary Clinton. She didn't come to California quite as often, but every time she did, like Bill, she was most generous with her time for the state party. She did a couple of fund-raisers for us. She also appeared as a guest on my radio show.

Two things I quickly learned about Hillary Clinton. One, in private, she has a wicked sense of humor and an infectious laugh. I once rode on Air

Force Three with her and then Assembly Speaker Willie Brown for the short flight from Sacramento to San Francisco. She kept us both in stitches.

Two, she's brilliant, a real policy wonk, and knows the issues better than anybody. No, she's not as good a campaigner as her husband, Bill. But who is?

The first time I noticed this about Hillary was at a Los Angeles fund-raiser for Kathleen Brown, Jerry's sister, who was running for governor of California. I was sitting alongside Hillary at the head table. Brown spoke first and in her remarks briefly touched on the notion that the more women succeed, the better the nation succeeds. There's a direct cause and effect between the two. Hillary turned to me and said, "That's a very important point, but I never thought of it that way before."

Hillary spoke next and, without any prepared remarks, picked up on Kathleen's theme and expanded it, speaking for at least twenty minutes on how important it was that women do well, in politics as in any other field, because when women do well, America does well—and citing several examples to make her point. I was blown away, because I knew she was doing it off the cuff. And I knew at that moment that her career in public service was not going to end with the end of her term as First Lady.

I once introduced Hillary as one of the people I admire most in the world, and I still mean it. She was an outstanding First Lady of Arkansas, First Lady of the United States, U.S. senator from New York, and secretary of state. I supported her over Barack Obama in the 2008 Democratic primary. I supported Bernie Sanders over her in the 2016 Democratic primary, but I enthusiastically threw my support to Hillary Clinton once she secured the Democratic nomination. She would have made an outstanding president—but why and how she lost the election to Donald Trump is the subject of a thousand other books, not this one.

During my three years as state chair, I also spent a lot of time with Vice President Al Gore, went to the World Cup match between Brazil and Italy with him, flew on Air Force Two, and introduced him at several events. I encouraged him to run for president in 2000 and promised to sign up full-time for his campaign—but by that time, I was already at CNN and unavailable.

Juggling my volunteer position as state Democratic chair with my paid position as TV commentator and radio talk show host was a challenge, but

I managed to pull it off for the most part—with one notable exception. One Saturday, I left our executive committee meeting in San Diego and flew to LA to host my regular radio show. One of our topics that afternoon was a recent statement by some conservative Christian preacher that parents should never be seen naked in front of their children, which I thought was ridiculous. Carol and I often stepped out of the shower in front of our sons when they were young, and they thought nothing of it.

When one woman called and accused me of setting a bad example for our sons, I went ballistic. "What are you ashamed of?" I asked. "Are you ashamed of your body? I'm not ashamed of my body. I love my body. I love every part of my body." Then, in an affirmation heard not only across Southern California but all the way across the country, I added, "I love my genitals!"

What was I thinking? Obviously, I wasn't thinking at all. On Monday morning, the Reliable Sources column of *The Washington Post* featured the headline I LOVE MY GENITALS, with a photo of Michelangelo's David and a full transcript of my colorful remarks on KFI. And I soon got a call from the White House suggesting that—in light of the fact that I was California Democratic Party chair and, therefore, President Clinton's unofficial representative in the Golden State—I might try to be more circumspect in my public remarks.

That's one lesson I didn't learn. I would continue to get in hot water for things I said on the air. With one big difference. Soon, I not only got in trouble in California. I got in trouble everywhere. Because now I was playing on a national stage.

7

"PAT, YOU IGNORANT SLUT!"

On Monday, February 26, 1996, I got the luckiest break in my life: making my debut as the new liberal host on CNN's *Crossfire*.

After sixteen years on Los Angeles radio and television, it was exciting to be at last on the national stage, but it wasn't easy to get there. Making the leap from local to national television involves a lot more than a change in geography. I tried several times to get myself booked on any of the national political shows but, most of the time, didn't even get the dignity of a reply.

I learned the hard way that, for many people who live in Washington, D.C., especially those in the media, their narrow universe is almost exclusively limited to people who live inside the BosWash corridor. They book their guests not on knowledge or experience but on geography alone. Those who live outside Manhattan, Cambridge, or the Beltway need not apply.

My lucky break came early in 1996, when *Los Angeles Times* TV critic Howard Rosenberg reported that Michael Kinsley was stepping down as cohost of *Crossfire*—and CNN was holding auditions for his replacement.

Among those being considered, according to Rosenberg, were campaign guru Bob Shrum, pundit Juan Williams, New York City public advocate Mark Green, and environmental lawyer (and famous son) Bobby Kennedy Jr.—all members of the East Coast media establishment.

So I decided to strike another blow for the West Coast. I picked up the phone and placed a cold call to Rick Davis, executive producer of *Crossfire*. To my surprise, he actually took my call. I told him I thought I could bring a fresh, new perspective to *Crossfire* and asked him to give me a shot. Fortunately, Davis remembered having seen me debate Pat Buchanan at a talk radio conference in Los Angeles and agreed to add me to the mix.

A couple of weeks later, I flew to Washington for my first audition as *Crossfire* cohost on the left. Bob Novak, whom I had met a couple of times in Los Angeles through a mutual friend Democratic strategist Joe Cerrell, was hosting on the right. The topic was taxes, and our guest was conservative senator Don Nickles of Oklahoma. Tax policy was not exactly my strong suit, but I'd boned up well enough to ask some pertinent questions and poke a few holes in the senator's argument.

Novak, on the other hand, relished debates over tax policy and, far in advance of the Tea Party, was also against any new taxes whatsoever. Period. Full stop. During the back-and-forth comments that ended every show—which our producers irreverently called the *yip-yap*—Novak threw me his favorite conservative taunt: "Do you think Americans pay too much in taxes, or not enough?" Somehow I managed to blurt out what remains the only answer to that question: "Some Americans pay too much, but some don't pay their fair share."

After the show, Rick Davis's only comment was: "At least you didn't back down." But I must have done well enough for Davis to invite me back the next night to debate global warming—in the middle of a blizzard that shut down Washington! Our guest was a University of Virginia "scientist" who, I was only too happy to point out, was also on the coal industry payroll and therefore not credible in any discussion of climate change.

After one more audition, I was back in California when Rick Davis called again, this time offering me the position as one of two new cohosts on the left. I would share the job, he explained, with former vice presidential candidate Geraldine Ferraro, one of my all-time heroes. And the job was mine on two conditions. One, that I move to Washington, D.C., at

CNN's expense. Two, that I resign as Democratic Party chair of California. Not only that, this was Tuesday morning. I had to begin my new job on *Crossfire* in CNN's Washington bureau the following Monday!

Talk about a no-brainer. The choice between dialing rich California donors for dollars and debating the issues on national television was not difficult. And besides, after serving for three years as a volunteer state chair, the idea of a paycheck was extremely appealing. I checked in with Carol, then called Davis back to accept.

All I had to do now was find a new state party chair, which turned out to be more complicated than I'd thought. According to party bylaws, a vacancy for the chair would be filled by the first or the second vice chair. But our first vice chair, Arlene Holt, had already moved to Washington, and the second vice chair, Angela Alioto, was running for state senate in a Democratic primary.

Under party rules, I had no authority to name my replacement, but given the time constraints and the unavailability of either first or second vice chair, I decided to appoint a new chair, anyway—and dare anybody to sue me. My choice was Art Torres, former state senator and recent candidate for state treasurer. Both Senator Dianne Feinstein and Senator Barbara Boxer agreed, so I met with Art and offered him the post.

We scheduled a news conference at party headquarters the very next morning, where I announced my resignation and introduced the new chairman of the California Democratic Party. Art Torres went on to serve as state chair for the next fourteen years! And Carol and I moved to Washington, bought a house on Capitol Hill, and started a whole new life.

WELCOME TO *CROSSFIRE*

With every bit of bias I'm capable of, let me repeat: *Crossfire* was the first—and is still the best—of all political debate shows. And no other political show today is as good or compelling.

Several factors combined to make the original *Crossfire* so successful. First, its laser-like focus. The show was a half hour long and dealt with one issue only, examined from both sides. When it was over, viewers may not have been convinced either way, but they sure knew a whole lot more after a lively give-and-take on the topic and had all the information they needed to make their own decision.

That singular focus of *Crossfire* was underscored by the simple but dramatic set. No fancy graphics. No moving wall of video. No fake Washington background. Just one desk, four chairs, and a black curtain behind the desk. The emphasis was on content, not flash. What a novel concept.

The second big factor was the guests. As the most popular political show on TV and the second-highest rated show on CNN, after *Larry King Live*, we consistently lined up the biggest newsmakers every day. If it was politics, you could count on John McCain, Mitch McConnell, Tom Daschle, Dick Durbin, Arlen Specter, John Boehner, Newt Gingrich, Dick Armey, Orrin Hatch, John Chafee, Tom Delay, John Kasich, Dick Gephardt—or whichever Republican or Democrat was leading the most hotly contested issue du jour.

If it was religion, Jerry Falwell, Pat Robertson, Ralph Reed, or Gary Bauer took the conservative seat. On women's issues, Eleanor Smeal versus Phyllis Schlafly. On sex, Dr. Ruth. On diets, Dr. Atkins. Two Florida congressmen, Joe Scarborough and Robert Wexler, were our favorite tag team during the Monica Lewinsky scandal. The guests made the show, and we were able to round up the best.

During my *Crossfire* days, I was often asked if there was a politician I admired. And my answer was always the same: Among Republicans and Democrats, the one I admired most was John McCain. Not because I agreed with him on every issue but because he was thoughtful, had a great self-deprecating sense of humor, and, at least in his earlier years, was known as a maverick—not afraid to take on and vote against leaders of his own party if he thought they were wrong. As he did, for example, in opposing George W. Bush's plan to give millionaires a special tax cut.

Coming from Arizona to Washington, McCain often quipped, he quickly learned the difference between a cactus and a caucus. "With a cactus," McCain pointed out, "the pricks are on the outside." By 2008, McCain's star had fallen. For a while, he became more of a predictable Republican, and we can never forgive him for foisting Sarah Palin on the nation. But McCain later redeemed himself by reclaiming his role as a maverick and casting that dramatic and deciding thumbs-down vote against Donald Trump's plan to repeal Obamacare.

Pennsylvania's Arlen Specter, another maverick, was also a frequent guest, albeit an oft-frustrating one. Specter had a way of making headlines early in the day, which won him the nickname of "Snarlin' Arlen," but later backing down. One morning, I remember, he demanded that President Clinton immediately fire Attorney General Janet Reno. We rushed to book him for *Crossfire* that evening, but once under fire (from me), he said he didn't really want Clinton to "fire" her, he just wanted him to give her "a good talking-to." Around *Crossfire*, we started referring to "Snarlin' Arlen" as "Spineless Specter." (Either way, may he rest in peace.)

Because *Crossfire* was only broadcast in the United States, we rarely entertained foreign guests, but my job as cohost did result in encounters with two of the more controversial international players around. Carol and I were having dinner at the Palm restaurant one evening when Vladimir Putin walked in with an entourage of about twelve people. His press secretary spotted me and invited me to come over and shake hands with Putin. Later, we were still enjoying our meal, the Putin party having left the restaurant, when his press secretary reappeared at our table and asked me to come outside with him so President Putin could say goodbye. Sure enough, there was Putin, standing alongside his limousine, his entire motorcade waiting, until he could shake hands again and tell me how much he liked CNN.

Same thing with Palestinian president Yasser Arafat. On one of his official visits to Washington, I attended a big dinner for Arafat at the Washington Peace Center, where Jim Zogby, founder of the Arab American Institute, offered to introduce me to the guest of honor. I was nervous about what I might say to the man once accused of being the world's number-one terrorist—or what he might say to me. No worries. I almost laughed out loud when Arafat shook my hand and said in his raspy—almost feminine—voice, "Say hello to all my good friends at CNN!"

It was not only foreign leaders we had a chance to rub shoulders with. Even as a Democrat, I was a big admirer of former president George H. W. Bush. While I disagreed with many of his policies, I knew he was a good, decent man who conducted himself with great dignity and purpose. So I was excited when my good friend and mentor Rocco Siciliano offered to introduce us at the annual Eisenhower Award dinner.

Bush actually got up from the head table and walked over to greet me with a big grin. "Bill Press, you're a famous man."

I blushed. "Oh, I don't know about that, Mr. President."

And he immediately shot back, "Well, you're sure a famous man in the Bush household."

Then he asked me where his former chief of staff John Sununu was. I told him I'd just left John at CNN, where we'd cohosted *Crossfire*, but wasn't sure where he'd gone after the show.

In his best commander-in-chief tones, Bush growled, "Well, call him up and tell him to get his ass over here!"

I first met the second President Bush shortly after he arrived in Washington at the annual luncheon of the American Society of News Editors. In the middle of his remarks, Bush spotted me sitting at a table directly in front of the podium and, without missing a beat, pointed at me and gave me a wink. After lunch, he was working the rope line when he again spotted me and waved me over. I shook his hand and playfully said, "You don't have to worry about me, Mr. President. Mary Matalin keeps me in line."

Bush reached up, grabbed my shoulder, pulled me close, and whispered, "Bullshit!"

Caught on videotape, it looked like Bush was planting a big kiss on my cheek. So, of course, ever eager to rub it in, Tucker Carlson played that tape of "Bush giving me a kiss" over and over again on *The Spin Room*.

My second encounter with George W. Bush was decidedly less friendly. When I showed up for his first White House Christmas party for the media, the first thing I noticed was that many of my more progressive friends in the media were missing. In fact, it seemed like I'd mistakenly walked into the holiday party for Fox News. The entire Fox lineup was there, starting with Roger Ailes himself.

Like everyone else, I lined up for a photo with the president and First Lady. But when the marine in charge announced my name, President Bush turned, glared at me, and said, "Press, how'd you get in here?"

"Mr. President, you invited me," I responded. "Merry Christmas."

Hand shaken. Photo taken. Orders apparently given. I was never invited back during the Bush presidency.

Of course, what really put *Crossfire* on the map were the hosts. *Crossfire* actually started in Washington, D.C., as a late-night radio debate show on WCR-AM between Pat Buchanan and Tom Braden. That's where Ted

Turner first heard about it and made it part of the original lineup on the revolutionary, twenty-four-hour, all-news cable channel he launched in 1982.

At first, *Crossfire* appeared late nights on CNN with only one guest per show. Bob Novak joined Pat Buchanan on the right, while Tom Braden continued to hold down the fort on the left. But producers soon added a second guest and moved the show to early evening. Why? Because, Novak once told me, given the late-night time slot, too many guests showed up drunk. Tucker Carlson and I later experienced the same problem on CNN with *The Spin Room*.

In its new time slot, *Crossfire* thrived and grew stronger every year. Tom Braden retired in 1989, replaced by Michael Kinsley, a brilliant debater, thinker, and writer who single-handedly held down the liberal slot for seven years, until Geraldine Ferraro and I arrived in 1996. One year later, CNN president Rick Kaplan named me sole cohost on the left when Ferraro left to run for the U.S. Senate against Al D'Amato of New York

Meanwhile, several cohosts rotated in and out of the conservative chair. John Sununu, former governor of New Hampshire and former chief of staff to President George H. W. Bush, filled in for Pat Buchanan while he was off running for president. Mary Matalin and Tucker Carlson also joined the team after Pat's return. Bob Beckel and Lynne Cheney cohosted the weekend edition of *Crossfire*.

Funny thing about *Crossfire*. I was often asked the same two questions about the show: How far ahead of time do you decide what topics you're going to debate that day? And how much of the show is scripted and read from the teleprompter? Both questions floored me.

Wasn't it obvious? Since our goal was to debate the hottest issue of the day, there was no way to plan ahead. Occasionally, we could settle on a topic the day before, but most of the time we couldn't decide until the morning of the show. So our standard procedure was to hold a conference call at 9:30 each morning, when cohosts and producers would weigh various options and decide on that night's topic. Some days, it was obvious. There was only one big story. Other days, things were so slow we'd have to wait until later to decide. Which resulted in one of my funniest memories of *Crossfire*.

On this particular morning, Pat Buchanan and I weren't excited by any of the suggested topics, so we decided to let the decision float for a couple of hours to see what might pop up. Meanwhile, I spotted a story out of Kansas City, where the city council had voted to broadcast on cable television the names and faces of men who'd been arrested the evening before for soliciting prostitution. Airing this damning information prior to any trial or determination of guilt, it seemed to me, raised certain privacy and due process issues. I told our producers. They liked it. They checked with Pat. He liked it. And the producers went to work booking guests.

An hour later, one of the producers called with our first guest: Reverend Jerry Falwell, appearing via satellite from Liberty University. Perfect! But whom should we book to argue the other side, she wanted to know. Smart-ass as always, I suggested, "How 'bout a prostitute?"—adding that I had no idea where to actually find one, until . . . I remembered an organization in San Francisco called COYOTE—acronym for Cast Off Your Old, Tired Ethics—which was, in effect, a union for sex workers. And, within an hour, the president of COYOTE was booked by satellite out of San Francisco as our second guest.

Months earlier, to help keep the show moving, we'd all agreed on rules of the road for questioning guests. One host would open the show and set the topic. The other host would begin the questioning by posing one main question, with two follow-ups. Then the other host would take over the questioning. That evening, it was Pat's turn to start.

He began by asking the head of COYOTE, who very much looked the part, "Are you really a prostitute?"

To which she cautiously replied, "Well, I'm not going to admit I break the law, but I'm also not going to lie on national television." Which I thought was a very candid and carefully calculated answer!

Pat's first follow-up: "Have you always been a prostitute?"

Her answer: a quick no.

Pat: "And what were you before you became a prostitute?"

She: "A Los Angeles police officer."

Note: Pat was now out of time. He'd exhausted his quota of opening question and two follow-ups. But I also knew Pat was on a roll. Clearly there was no way to stop him. Nor did I even try.

Next question. Pat: "And why did you change jobs?"

Ms. COYOTE: "Because I felt I needed a more honorable profession!"

At which point, for all practical purposes, the debate was over. Pat was speechless. The pained expression on Jerry Falwell's face was priceless. I don't even remember the rest of the show. Nor am I sure we ever got around to talking about Kansas City. Score one for sex workers!

The second most often asked question ("How much of the show is scripted and read from the teleprompter?") also surprised me. Seriously? I can't believe anyone who actually watched the show—with its lively back-and-forth between hosts and guests, bouncing off in directions nobody anticipated—could honestly think we'd scripted it all ahead of time. Besides, we cohosts were too independent and too hardheaded to follow any script. Once we'd fixed on a topic, we did our own research, talked to sources, plowed through a background file prepared by staff, prepared our toughest questions, anticipated arguments the opposition guest and cohost might make, made notes on good rebuttals—and then went out on live television and gave it our best shot.

Each of us believed deeply in the positions we took. We argued both from the head and from the heart. But we also respected each other and actually liked each other. And that, I believe, was the hidden secret of *Crossfire*'s success: the fact that, despite our differences and our deeply held and passionately expressed opinions, we *Crossfire* cohosts were all good friends, on the air and off. If only that same mutual respect existed in Congress today.

Yes, our debates were often heated, but only very, very rarely did they ever get personal. Unlike Dan Aykroyd's famous put-down of Jane Curtin on SNL's *Point-Counterpoint*, I never turned to Buchanan—or Novak, Carlson, Sununu, or Matalin—and fired back, "Pat, you ignorant slut!"

During my six years at *Crossfire*, in fact, I recall only two times when things got too personal—once with John Sununu, once with Bob Novak. I honestly don't remember what they said, but I thought they had crossed the line. I called them on it. They both admitted it. Both times, we gave each other a hug and vowed not to let it happen again. "The show's too short, and life's too short, to take it personally," advised Sununu. And he was right.

Mary Matalin and I enjoyed many good times together, even though she's a hopeless Republican and I'm a yellow-dog Democrat. We share the same irreverent approach to most issues and the same jaundiced attitude toward politics in general. As a result, we laughed our way through many interviews, including a strained Thanksgiving Day taping with Dr. Robert

Atkins of Atkins diet fame, whom neither one of us took seriously. After yukking it up on the set one night, Mary whispered to me off camera, "Our problem is, you and I could sit here all night and tell dick jokes!"

THE SPIN ROOM

Tucker Carlson and I became fast friends from the first time he appeared as a conservative guest on *Crossfire*, while still a young reporter with *The Weekly Standard*. I lobbied for him to take Mary Matalin's seat on the right when she left for the George W. Bush presidential campaign.

In 2000, Tucker and I were tapped to offer left-right spin—online, not on camera—during the vice presidential debate between Joe Lieberman and Dick Cheney. Our exchange generated such a good response that CNN decided to turn it into a daily prime-time show called, appropriately, *The Spin Room*.

Hands down, *The Spin Room* was the most fun I ever had in broadcasting, mainly because Tucker and I treated it as our own creation and defied management's attempt to control it. We refused to use a teleprompter. After too many interruptions, we banned our producer in Atlanta from speaking in our ears during the broadcast. Every night, we skewered politicians on the left and right for their ridiculous spin, and the show actually acquired an almost cultlike status.

On many college campuses, students religiously gathered to watch our antics. We shamelessly begged for gifts—and were promptly swamped with cookies, cakes, fudge, candles, beads, T-shirts, and hats. When we complained that CNN wouldn't provide us *Spin Room* mugs, viewers made their own and sent them in. We spontaneously launched a defense fund for one of our favorite guests, Congressman Jim Traficant, when he was indicted for bribery—soliciting contributions on the air until we were told it was illegal and ordered to stop. For some reason, we also attracted a large Canadian following, even though Tucker poked fun at them for curling and once suggested the United States should invade Canada in order to provide more satellite parking for American sports events.

We could tell viewers were really getting into the spirit of the show from their emails, and we read many of them on the show. One of my favorites: After Tucker and I had ranted about how ridiculous it was to introduce a piece of legislation only in order to change a comma in an existing law, the so-called Comma Bill, we received this warning from viewer Robert Reynolds:

Messrs. Press and Carlson:

I find it shameful for you to abuse the poor comma! Below, you will find an illustration of the worth of a comma:

Go on, shoot, Bill and Tucker.
Go on, shoot Bill and Tucker.

Which sentence do you prefer? You scoff at the poor comma? For shame!!

But our favorite came from an anonymous voter in West Palm Beach, on the heels of the long 2000 Florida recount:

Honk if you voted for Al Gore. It's the large button in the middle of the steering wheel.

In many ways, I believe, *The Spin Room* was the forerunner of *The Daily Show* and *The Colbert Report*—a freewheeling, irreverent look back at the political news of the day. I know we put on a damned good show. We also had a lot of fun, and we were getting good ratings. But after several months, CNN suddenly—with no announcement or reason given—pulled the plug. I think we were just too "un-CNN-like," too daring and different a show for the uptight CNN brass. But here again, the network made a big mistake. To this day, wherever Tucker or I travel, we meet former fans of *The Spin Room*. CNN could use that kind of unorthodox spirit today.

One of our most memorable *Spin Room* shows took place the night of the Supreme Court's 2000 *Bush v. Gore* decision. For over a month, since election night November 7, we'd talked about almost nothing else but the vote-count circus in Florida, where election officials were painstakingly re-checking every ballot in George W. Bush's slim 327 vote lead out of nearly six million votes cast.

It was great fodder for radio and television talk shows: Were Florida seniors too confused to follow instructions on the butterfly ballot? How could conservative Pat Buchanan rack up 3,407 votes in ultraliberal Palm Beach County? And should a hanging chad be counted as a legitimate vote or not?

On December 11, the case was argued before the Supreme Court of the United States. And, in a highly unusual move, the court said it would announce its decision the next day. That evening, Tucker and I broadcast *The Spin Room* from the grounds of the U.S. Capitol, directly across the street from the court. It was bitterly cold. Thousands of people had gathered in front of the court. Tensions were understandably high. Tucker almost got in a fistfight with one obnoxious bystander. It wasn't until around 11:00 p.m. that reporters raced out of the court with news that the court, 5–4, had declared George W. Bush winner of the Florida primary—and thus president-elect of the United States.

We immediately went live with two guests we just happened to find in the crowd in front of the Supreme Court, Colorado governor Bill Owens and Florida Republican congressman Mark Foley. We opened the show with Owens. Curious, I asked him what the governor of Colorado was doing hanging around the Capitol grounds so late at night. The official lighting of the congressional Christmas tree had taken place earlier that evening, he explained, and since that year's tree had come from Colorado, of course he was there, leading the state's delegation.

Next up, Florida congressman Mark Foley. As our producer was putting Foley's mike on, Foley, who was then still a closeted gay member of Congress (he came out in 2003), joked: "Bill, please don't ask me what I was doing trolling the Capitol grounds so late at night!" Foley later resigned from Congress when accused of sexting congressional pages.

The Supreme Court's ruling was a historic moment, and it was exciting to be part of it, even though, as I said that night, and still believe, it was the worst Supreme Court decision since 1896 and *Plessy v. Ferguson*, which upheld the constitutionality of racial segregation. The issue was finally resolved the next evening, December 13, when Al Gore, speaking to the nation from the vice president's residence, said he would accept the court's decision, even though he strongly disagreed with it. That was, without a doubt, Gore's finest moment.

Another *Spin Room* highlight was our Valentine's Day 2001 interview with Dr. Ruth—who else?—to discuss—what else?—whether there was too much sex in Washington or not enough. Before Tucker could ask the first question, Dr. Ruth immediately stole the show by announcing that she had a challenge for both of us. "When I watch the two of you," she told the world, "I can visualize what you do in your bedrooms. Did you ever think of that?" So, for Valentine's Day, she announced, she wanted us to go home and try something new sexually. Not with each other, she hastened to add, but with our respective spouses.

In his own book, *Politicians, Partisans, and Parasites*, Tucker recalls what happened next: "Unlike Dr. Ruth, I had never visualized Bill's bedroom activities, so I had no real idea what she was talking about. But Bill apparently did. He shifted in his chair. Even through his makeup I could see that his face had turned red."

But I remember it differently. It was Tucker who got so red he couldn't talk. So I jumped in and asked, "Dr. Ruth, we've both been married a long time. I think by now we know every possible trick in the book. What did you have in mind?" She recommended that Tucker try a new position he'd never done before. For me, her advice was: "Try not talking so much." How did she know?

Marriage proclivities aside, it was strangely a bout with the flu that first sealed my and Tucker's friendship. It hit me as we were preparing for the show. In his book, Tucker takes it from there: "Bill's schedule caught up with him from time to time, and he'd get sick. One night he showed up with a terrible case of the flu. Walking to the studio, he stopped off at the men's room. 'Hold on a second,' he said, and went inside and threw up. Ten minutes later we were on the air. Bill did the entire show with a trash can between his knees just in case it happened again. He must have felt horrible, but you couldn't tell. He never said a word about it." To this day, Tucker swears that's when he decided we'd be pals forever.

BUCHANAN AND NOVAK

Pat Buchanan and I also hit it off right away and still do. After all, he and I come from the same roots: raised strict Catholics, graduated from Catholic schools, and both seriously considered the priesthood before turning to journalism and politics. We often laughed about the fact that, after both starting out as altar boys, he veered so far to the right—and I, so far to the left.

Pat was the perfect *Crossfire* host: always prepared, a brilliant debater, with an infectious sense of humor. He has the one important gift lacking in so many conservatives and liberals alike: the ability to poke fun at himself. After being bounced from *Crossfire*, Pat and I went on to host our own two-hour program, *Buchanan & Press*, on MSNBC, and for years we still enjoyed sparring from time to time in paid speaking engagements and on various MSNBC political programs.

As the years went by, Pat actually mellowed on some issues. On gays, guns, or abortion, he remained a true take-no-prisoners right-winger. But he reversed his position on trading with Cuba, for example. He used to be against it; now he's for it. Same with medicinal marijuana. He's a strong proponent of keeping jobs in America and rebuilding our manufacturing base, which won him a surprising amount of support among union workers during his presidential campaigns. Like me, Pat's also a firm anti-interventionist. Which eventually got both of us in trouble at MSNBC.

At *Crossfire*, despite our political differences, Pat and I usually agreed on what topic we should tackle that day and which ones were getting stale. Which led to one big embarrassment. In the middle of the Clinton-Lewinsky scandal, when our producers suggested yet another program on the latest Monica gossip, Pat and I both groaned. Having sliced and diced the topic every night for two weeks straight, Pat and I knew we had nothing new to say about Lewinsky. We argued, instead, for something new and different (and unbelievably wonky): the expansion of NATO. Which we did—and, of course, the ratings bombed. The next night, we were back on Monicagate—and, like the rest of Washington media, never left it for weeks.

In the end, what brought Pat's colorful TV career to an ignominious end was his assertion that demographic change meant that we were experiencing the end of the American dream, if not the end of Western civilization as we know it. It's a theme he'd previously articulated in several books, but his views never received serious public attention until the 2011 publication of *Suicide of a Superpower: Will America Survive to 2025?*

Even though he said nothing in this book he hadn't said before—in books and articles, on radio and TV—Pat's latest book was widely criticized as homophobic, anti-Semitic, and racist. After suspending him for four months, MSNBC president Phil Griffin fired Buchanan in a public statement: "The ideas he put forth aren't really appropriate for national dialogue, much less the dialogue on MSNBC."

Without endorsing his views, many and most of which I strongly disagree with, it's worth noting that, less than ten years later, many of Pat's ideas, good and especially bad, were embraced by Donald Trump and propelled him all the way to the White House.

I disagreed with MSNBC's action at the time and still do. No matter how vile or incorrect, Pat's views deserved to be aired. The correct answer was not to silence Pat but to challenge him, debate him, and prove him wrong in the public arena, which I had enjoyed doing for years. Even though he's often been accused of it, I do not believe that Pat Buchanan is a racist. In my opinion, he's just wrong and paranoid about the inevitable forward march of humankind and the danger of changing demographics—which have been changing as long as America has existed.

Over the years, the debate partner I became especially close to was Bob Novak. As mentioned earlier, I'd met Novak a couple of times, so I called him for advice when I sought to join the *Crossfire* team. Bob confessed that he was supporting another friend, Democratic strategist Bob Shrum, but said he'd be happy to work with me if I got the job. And he made good on that promise. In fact, I soon turned to him again for advice.

In December 1996, just ten months after starting on *Crossfire*, Carol and I returned to Inverness for the holidays, where I found five messages from Karen Skelton, one of Al Gore's top aides, saying the vice president wanted to speak to me urgently. I first called Karen, who told me that David Wilhelm was stepping down as chairman of the Democratic National Committee, and Gore planned to recommend to President Clinton that I take Wilhelm's place—but wanted to check with me first.

Before calling Gore, I tracked Novak down in Hawaii, where he'd traveled with his favorite basketball team, the University of Maryland Terrapins. With the noise of the game in the background, I explained my dilemma: Yes, I'd enjoyed my stint as California State Democratic chair. And, yes, at one time I'd dreamed of becoming chair of the DNC. At the same time, I loved my new job at CNN. What to do?

Novak listened politely and then gave me his blunt advice. "It's about time you decided what you want to be when you grow up," he told me. "Do you want to be a journalist? Or do you want to be a politician?" I'd be good at either one, he said, but I couldn't do both. I had to choose one or the other. I hung up from Novak and called Al Gore to thank him for the honor—and tell him I was staying at CNN. Thank you, Bob. That was the right decision.

I never knew anybody who worked harder than Bob Novak. When I first came to CNN, Bob was cohost of *Crossfire*, host of *Capital Gang*, and host of his own show, *The Novak Report*. In addition, he and Rowland Evans published a popular weekly political newsletter, he wrote a weekly column for *The Washington Post*, and he provided two or three weekly columns for the *Chicago Sun-Times*. In his spare time, he made probably fifty paid speeches a year for the Washington Speakers Bureau.

Many times, in fact, Novak and I went on the road together in a mini-version of *Crossfire*, where he was always the crowd favorite because the only groups that could afford our lecture fees were big corporations or industry associations. We flew out together, usually had dinner together, put on a good act, and then flew home together—once, with a hilarious finale. Coming home from Phoenix, we stopped to change planes in Chicago. I went off to buy a paper while Bob immediately boarded the next flight. But when I returned to the gate, passengers were blocked from reboarding because of the arrival of a celebrity. And suddenly, surrounded by security guards and waving gaily to the crowd, arrives Little Richard!

When I was finally able to board, there was Little Richard seated in the very front row of first class, on the aisle. I said hello, told him I was a big fan, then took my seat in the third row alongside Novak, who promptly asked me who that big shot was. When I said I was surprised he didn't recognize Little Richard, Novak snarled, "Well, you may know who he is, but I'm sure he has no idea who you are."

Fast-forward to Washington's National Airport. No sooner had the plane pulled up to the gate then Little Richard stood up, turned around, and handed me a paperback copy of a book, saying, "Bill, so nice to see you. I signed this book just for you." I still have that book, a Christian prayer book Little Richard wrote called *Finding Peace Within*, with his handwritten inscription: "To Bill. God loves and cares for you."

But that wasn't the end of Bob's comeuppance. As we stood up to deplane, the man across the aisle spoke up and said, "Well, now that Little Richard has broken the ice, I want to say hello to one of my real heroes, Mr. Evans." I laughed out loud.

Bob snorted, "I'm not Evans, I'm Novak!"—and stormed off the plane.

Novak and I were very much the odd couple. I think we became such good friends because we both loved politics and felt passionately about and loved debating the issues. Yet we also respected each other and realized it was, in some sense, all a game on television. We never took ourselves that seriously. At the end of one *Crossfire* broadcast, while we were still sitting on the set after a particularly heated exchange, I turned to Novak and said, "Boy, that was really a good show!"

Novak just stared at me.

"What's wrong?" I asked.

"Do you realize," he said, "in seven years Michael Kinsley never once said that to me!"

Even before I arrived in Washington, stories about Bob Novak were legend. Al Hunt, panelist on Novak's *Capital Gang* and the husband of then-CNN anchor Judy Woodruff, loved to tell about the time he called Bob to tell him he and Judy had just adopted a little baby from Korea. Novak immediately barked, "North or South?"

Al was also invited to the special Mass where Bob, who grew up a Jew, converted to Catholicism and was received into the Catholic Church. Walking out of the church, Al remarked to John McLaughlin, host of *The McLaughlin Group*, how remarkable it was to see Novak, at his age, become a Catholic. "Yes," grumbled McLaughlin, "now if we could only make a Christian out of him!"

In his personal life, Bob was a real fighter. He had survived two bouts with cancer and a broken hip before being diagnosed with a brain tumor in August 2008. Again, he determined to fight it—and did, for a whole year. It was painful to visit him in those last few months and see him going downhill so rapidly. When he died a year later, August 2009, I surprised a lot of my readers with this column.

My Friend, the Prince of Darkness

It wasn't supposed to happen this way. In 1996, I came to Washington as the new liberal cohost of CNN's *Crossfire* to do battle with Bob Novak. And I did, hammer and tongs, almost every night, for six years. But along the way, I also became his friend.

His nickname was "the Prince of Darkness," but Bob never

complained about it. In fact, he relished it and he earned it, with every scowl and cutting remark. In those *Crossfire* days, Bob and I often went on the road together as a traveling dog-and-pony show. I used to begin every appearance by telling the audience, "I know the first question on everyone's mind: Is Bob Novak as obnoxious off the air as he is on the air?" Bob would laugh out loud when I said, "The answer is yes!"

For me, every *Crossfire* show with Bob was a challenge, because he was the sharpest, toughest, best-prepared, and sometimes meanest debater one could ever face. He might seem warm and fuzzy during show prep, but once the lights went on, he was a tiger.

At the same time, I learned a lot from him. I learned, first of all, that being a good journalist takes a lot more than just showing up, getting makeup on, and preening before the camera. Becoming a serious journalist is a lot of work. And, right to the end, Bob Novak was, without doubt, the hardest-working journalist in Washington.

Indeed, I didn't realize until I read his memoir, *The Prince of Darkness*, how long and how hard he'd been working the Washington beat. He came to Washington in 1957 as a string reporter for the AP, soon made his mark, and never slowed down. When I joined him at CNN, forty years later, he was still writing five columns a week, doing three TV shows a week on CNN (in addition to frequent guest appearances), writing a weekly newsletter with Rowland Evans, and giving two or three speeches a week.

In between, at breakfast, lunch, and dinner, he was working his sources. To the end, Novak had more and better sources than anybody in Washington, because he worked them, thanked them, and never double-crossed them. He was truly the last of Washington's tireless, fearless, hard-digging, shoe-leather reporters. He also produced perhaps the last column that actually included real reporting and real news, not just one writer's opinion.

From Novak, I also learned that liberals were too quick to endorse an American war, especially when launched by a Democratic president. No matter who was in the White House, Novak believed the use of force should be reserved for direct threats against this country and not for unnecessary displays of military strength around the world. And he was consistent. The first Gulf War under Bush 41, the bombing of Bosnia under Clinton, and the War in Iraq under Bush 43: Novak opposed them all.

He was a true conservative, even a paleoconservative. But Novak was never a party man. He was fiercely independent. Unlike many commentators today, he wouldn't consider leaving journalism to work in government. Indeed, he prided himself on never having been invited to! His advice to young people was: "Always love your country—but never trust your government." Good advice to live by.

Yes, I regret that he allowed himself to be used by George W. Bush and Dick Cheney in their nefarious plot to wreck the careers of Valerie Plame and Joe Wilson. In this case, I believe, his zeal to break a big story clouded his usually strong suspicion of government leaks. The irony is that Novak couldn't resist reporting what he saw as a hot news item, even though it had been leaked by Richard Armitage and confirmed by Karl Rove to help build the case for a war that he personally opposed. But that one mistake on his part does not negate or diminish a long career as one of America's best journalists.

Many of us who worked with Bob Novak learned a big secret about him: under his gruff exterior beat a big and generous heart. He was a man of deep faith who loved life, his family, and his friends. And I was lucky to be one of them.

Okay. Stop right there. Every time I appeared anywhere as the liberal cohost of *Crossfire*, somebody was bound to ask, "How can you stand sitting across the desk from Bob Novak?" (Or Pat Buchanan, or Tucker Carlson.)

My ready-made answer, which always got a big laugh, was "Because Ted Turner pays me a lot of money!"

Which, while true, wasn't the real answer. The truth was I loved sitting across the table from Novak, Buchanan, Matalin, Carlson, and others. I loved debating the issues with them and with all the conservative guests we had on the show, and many of them became friends.

This book, in fact, is chock-full of names of people you might think I would not even shake hands with, let alone enjoy lunch, a drink, or a conversation with: Buchanan, Carlson, John Boehner, Joe Scarborough, Orrin Hatch, Jerry Falwell, Ralph Reed, Sean Hannity, Ann Coulter, Chris Christie, and many others. But I actually got along with all of them.

It's a lesson I learned early on, when I spent two years as an environmental lobbyist for the Planning and Conservation League in the California legislature. There weren't enough liberal Democrats to pass our bills. I had to round up the votes of a lot of conservative Republicans, too. So I learned to get along with everybody. Unlike most lobbyists, I didn't have any big checks to hand out. But I could provide all the facts members needed on any environmental legislation and the promise that, liberal or conservative, we'd make sure they got full credit for voting with us—or absolute fury for voting against us.

I've taken that lesson with me wherever I've gone, and it's served me well. After all, there's some good in almost everybody if you look hard enough and, often, more that unites us than divides us. I always cringed when Jerry Falwell called me "[his] favorite Democrat," but I knew he meant well—he was just wrong about everything, especially what Jesus taught in the Gospels.

So my approach is to look for the good in everybody and try to get along with everybody at some level. Life is too short to make it any more difficult than it already is.

Having said that, don't think I roll over for everybody. There are still a few people I really despise. If I saw them coming, I'd cross the street to avoid having to say hello. Not to mention names, but they include Bill O'Reilly, Dick Morris, and Rudy Giuliani. And, of course, at the very top of the list, Donald Trump.

One final note on *Crossfire*: We could never have tackled the issues so effectively without our stellar team of producers and camera operators, led by executive producer Rick Davis and his deputy, Daniel Silva, who soon left to pursue his blockbuster career as a spy novelist. Producers Jennifer Zeidman, Sue Bennett, and Nancy Segerdahl hammered together each show. Susan Toffler helped with booking. When Rick Davis moved to Atlanta as vice president of CNN, Jennifer Zeidman, now Jennifer Zeidman Bloch, moved up as executive producer, assisted by Kristy Schantz and Kate Farrell.

CHRISTMAS IN CUBA

One of our favorite, go-to topics on *Crossfire* was America's relations with Cuba. Novak and Buchanan argued for continuing the embargo, in place since 1960. I agreed with the U.S. Chamber of Commerce that the embargo was ineffective and only hurt American farmers and businesses, and it was long past time to end it. Besides, if we could trade with "Communist North Vietnam" and "Communist China," why not trade with "Communist Cuba"?

My support for lifting the embargo led to a meeting with two staffers from the Cuban Mission to the United States, organized by Llewellyn Werner, my partner in freeing James Denby from prison in Nicaragua. That resulted in an invitation to dinner at the home of Fernando Ramírez de Estenoz, then Cuba's "ambassador" to the United States, whose official title, since we had no diplomatic relations with Cuba at the time, was head of the Cuban Interest Section of the Swiss Embassy.

Carol and I reciprocated by hosting a dinner party at our home for Ramírez and his wife. And, before we knew it, with Ramírez's help, we were planning a family vacation in Cuba over the 1998 Christmas holiday.

Under the boycott, American citizens were forbidden to travel on their own to Cuba, so we signed up with a group called Global Exchange for an educational tour led by the dynamic Medea Benjamin, later cofounder of Code Pink. The travel program was very well organized and very informative. We spent a lot of time in Havana, visiting local businesses and community organizations. We walked in Ernest Hemingway's shoes, enjoying a mojito at La Bodeguita del Medio and a daiquiri at El Floridita. We learned to dance the salsa on a Havana rooftop. We sought out and enjoyed several meals at *paladares*, unofficial, yet government-sanctioned restaurants in people's private homes. We traveled south of Havana to visit a farmers' cooperative. Everywhere we went, we were free to talk to anybody about any topic. We had no meetings with government officials, either Cuban or American. And we danced our asses off.

Cuba's a beautiful country with enormous potential. Everywhere we looked, we saw construction projects or new hotels operated by the Spanish, Dutch, British, Germans, French, and Canadians. Cuba's the next big economic center in the Western Hemisphere. Every other country recognizes that. Again, only American farmers and businessmen were missing out on the action—and profits. It made no sense. And everybody knew that the only reason both Republican and Democratic presidents had been afraid to change our policy and lift the embargo was the perceived political clout of Miami's large but diminishing anti-Castro Cuban American voting bloc. I returned to the United States more convinced than ever that the embargo had long ago outlived its usefulness.

It was one of President Obama's smartest moves to restore diplomatic relations with Cuba and lift restrictions on American businesses. It's one of President Trump's dumbest moves to reverse those new rules and go back to the failed economic boycotts of the 1960s. It means the Cuban people and American companies will continue to suffer.

At various White House events, I seized the opportunity to make that case personally to President Clinton and to Secretary of State Madeleine Albright. I'm disappointed they didn't do anything to restore relations with Cuba. I believe they would have liked to. But they both told me that any rapprochement with Cuba had been rendered impossible by the Cuban government's shooting down of two small planes and the ensuing deaths of four pilots from the anti-Castro group Brothers to the Rescue.

Debate over the embargo was one matter. Before I left *Crossfire*, however, Cuba was back in the news because of a much more explosive issue: the saga of little Elián González.

On November 21, 1999, five-year-old Elián was taken by his mother, her boyfriend, and eleven other friends on an unseaworthy aluminum motorboat, fleeing Cuba for Florida. A storm came up, and the boat took on water and soon sank. Elián and two others floated for hours on inner tubes before being rescued by fishermen and turned over to the Coast Guard. Elián's mother and ten others drowned.

At first, the Coast Guard placed Elián in the care of paternal relatives in Miami. But things soon became complicated when his father, Juan Miguel, sought the return of his son to Cuba and his Miami relatives refused to release the boy. A heated battle for legal custody began, while Republicans in Congress tried to rush through legislation granting Elián immediate U.S. citizenship.

On March 21, 2000, a federal court rejected the Miami family's request for asylum for Elián and ordered the boy returned to his father. Elián's relatives ignored the court's order, however, and the Miami Police Department, under direct orders from Mayor Alex Penelas, refused to enforce it. Enter U.S. attorney general Janet Reno, who issued a deadline for Elián's Miami relatives and local authorities to fulfill the judge's order by April 13.

On April 21, the press secretary of the Cuban Intersection invited me and Carol to dinner at his home to meet a special guest: Juan Miguel, Elián's father, who had come to Washington to plead his case. I readily accepted and, given my limited Spanish-language skills, invited journalist friends Tony Avirgan and Martha Honey, both fluent in Spanish, to join us.

Juan Miguel was no fiery political activist. He was very low-key, soft-spoken, and uncomfortable being in the media spotlight. But he was also eager to tell us all about his meetings at the Capitol—where, he explained, contrary to most media reports, he was not always surrounded by Cuban security guards. Except for a translator, he was alone in his meetings with senators, where he could have requested asylum at any time. In fact, he said, at every meeting he was asked if he wanted to stay in the United States. He told them all he wanted to do was return to Cuba with his son.

Over a round of mojitos, Martha and Tony suggested that one way we could help was to recruit a group of high-profile supporters to form a cocoon around the Miami house where Elián was being held captive by his distant relatives. Juan Miguel liked the idea. And Martha, Tony, and I vowed to get on the phone in the morning and start lining up volunteers. But that plan never got off the ground, because suddenly everything changed.

We were just about ready to sit down for dinner when Juan Miguel received an urgent call, summoning him to the Justice Department. He took off, alone again, except for a translator and Justice Department driver. He returned two hours later, tight-lipped except to confirm that he'd just met with Attorney General Reno.

The next morning, I was startled out of sleep by a call from our friend Lucie Gikovich with the greeting: "Good for Janet Reno!" I quickly turned on CNN to learn that early that morning, federal agents had swooped into the Miami home of Elián's relatives and rescued Elián, who was on his way to Andrews Air Force Base to be reunited with his father.

At first, I was furious, believing we'd been set up into providing cover for Juan Miguel while the undercover operation took place. I called our host of the night before, who assured me that nobody, not even Juan Miguel in his meeting with Reno, had been informed of her plans ahead of time. It was, he insisted, a surprise to everybody.

Soon, CNN called to confirm rumors that I'd met with Juan Miguel the evening before. An hour later, I was on the set at CNN, talking about our meeting, Reno's operation, Elián's reunion with his father, and what legal battles still lay ahead. For the next two months, Juan Miguel and Elián stayed at the Aspen Institute's Wye River Conference Center on the Eastern Shore, awaiting action by the courts. On June 7, the Eleventh U.S. Circuit Court of Appeals confirmed the lower court's decision, granting custody to Juan Miguel. On June 28, the Supreme Court declined to take the case. Later that day, Juan Miguel and Elián were flown back to Cuba.

MONICAGATE

For over twenty years, *Crossfire* was where Americans turned every evening to debate the most important issue of the day. During my tenure, two issues dominated public debate over all others: the impeachment of President Bill Clinton and the terrorist attacks of September 11, 2001.

One evening in late December 1997, executive producer Rick Davis called me into his office after the show and closed the door. CNN had received a tip from *The Washington Post*, he told me, that a major story was going to break later that night or early the next morning regarding President Clinton. He didn't know what it was all about; he just knew it was big news and was going to be bad news for the president. As cohost on the left, he wanted to warn me that I might find myself in a tough spot over the next few days.

The "next few days," of course, turned into the next year as the soap opera called Monicagate metastasized from rumors of an affair with an intern to Clinton's stormy denial, to recorded phone conversations between Monica Lewinsky and Linda Tripp, to the discovery of Monica's blue dress, to the investigation of independent counsel Ken Starr and publication of his steamy report, to hearings in the House of Representatives and Clinton's impeachment, and to the eventual finding of not guilty by the U.S. Senate.

Every new development in Monicagate consumed dozens of *Crossfire* programs. Indeed, for months, except for the misfire NATO expansion program mentioned earlier, we debated nothing else. It was all Monica, all the time.

I never found myself in a tough spot, however, because from the very beginning I took the position that, no matter what transpired between Bill Clinton and Monica Lewinsky, it was something agreed to by two consenting adults. It was not a "high crime" or "misdemeanor. It was therefore definitely not an impeachable offense.

Unlike many others on the left, knowing Clinton's past history, I believed Monica was telling the truth. Which is why I shuddered one evening, early in the drama, when *Newsweek*'s Eleanor Clift was a guest. "My president says he didn't do it, and I believe my president," she asserted. I thought to myself, *Eleanor, someday you're going to regret those words.*

Whether the truth was what "he said" or "she said," I stuck to what I said on the very first night of the Lewinsky scandal: If, indeed, the rumors of Clinton's sexual romp with a White House intern were true, I argued, what the president did was wrong and monumentally stupid—but it was not illegal and it was not an impeachable offense. And that's still my position. Even when it became clear that Clinton lied under oath about his relationship with Monica Lewinsky in his deposition in the Paula Jones trial, I stuck to my guns. There's no way that getting or lying about a blow job amounts to "treason, bribery, or other high crimes and misdemeanors"—and neither does any other sex act between two consenting adults.

One unexpected result of Monicagate: As cohost on the left, I suddenly found myself the focus of a lot of attention from the White House war room. Clinton made a very smart move in allowing press secretary Mike Mc-Curry, one of the best ever to hold that job, to divorce himself completely from questions on the Lewinsky scandal—in order to pretend that business at the White House continued as normal.

To handle press inquiries about Monicagate, Clinton instead brought in attorney Lanny Davis, who won a lot of respect from the media by promptly responding to all inquiries, releasing all documents, and rebutting all charges. Almost every afternoon, I'd receive a call from the White House telling me there was new information I should be aware of. Within an hour, a black town car would pull up in front of our house and an aide would jump out with a brown envelope marked WHITE HOUSE. The Clinton spin machine was in overdrive.

Apart from Lanny's operation, I also received frequent calls from Clinton aide Sidney Blumenthal, who was apparently running his own defensive operation. Sid often called me at CNN shortly before we went on the air to make sure I knew the latest developments in the Lewinsky case or to propose certain lines of questioning. Once, he called to suggest that Monica Lewinsky was no choir girl, that she had, in fact, acquired a reputation at Lewis & Clark College for being promiscuous—thereby implying that Clinton was the innocent victim of a notorious flirt. I refused to go there, but never said anything about it—unlike the late Christopher Hitchens, who testified before the House Judiciary Committee that, in conversations with him, Blumenthal had accused Lewinsky of being a stalker.

Whatever else, the Lewinsky scandal certainly made for a lot of colorful *Crossfire* shows—especially during the House impeachment hearings. I especially enjoyed pointing out the hypocrisy of certain Republicans, beginning with Chairman Henry Hyde and Congressman Dan Burton, who were trying to impeach the president of the United States for sexual transgressions they themselves were guilty of.

Later, we learned that former Speaker Newt Gingrich was among the most prominent offenders, carrying on his own affair with a House staffer—whom he later married—while leading the charge against Clinton for the same offense. "Now we know," liberal commentator Mark Shields observed, "that Newt was banging something more than the gavel."

The circus in the House ended on December 19, 1998, when the House voted to impeach the president of the United States on two counts: for perjury to a grand jury, 228–206; and for obstruction of justice, 221–212. Clinton thus became only the second president to be impeached, and the first since Andrew Johnson in 1868. (Richard Nixon resigned from the presidency before the House could impeach him over Watergate.)

But Clinton was far from down and out. Following the House vote, over a hundred Democratic members of Congress, led by leader Dick Gephardt, headed for the White House to stand in solidarity with the president and show support for Clinton's political and legislative agenda, whatever his personal weaknesses.

Ironically, a White House Christmas reception for Democratic Party activists, to which Carol and I had been invited, was scheduled for that very same evening. At first, we decided not to attend, fearing it would be too much like a wake. But then we changed our minds. This was no time to desert the president. This was a time to stand by our friend. So we showed up at the White House, and Clinton did not disappoint.

The mood that evening was far from somber. Just the opposite. It was almost celebratory. Everybody knew we'd lost a battle, yet we all felt we were on the verge of winning the war. After all, Clinton enjoyed over a 60 percent approval rating nationwide. It was highly unlikely the Senate would convict him. And Republicans in the House had clearly overplayed their hand. Maybe impeachment was politically survivable, a sentiment Clinton had already figured out.

When Carol and I saw our chance to say hello, I told Clinton how sorry we were for what had happened, but admired how he'd conducted himself throughout this ordeal—and were sure he and his presidency would carry on.

Clinton's face lit up. "Yeah, you know," he said, shaking his head, "all things considered, I think we had a pretty good day!"

We walked away, not believing what we'd just heard. Only a few hours earlier, Bill Clinton had suffered a disgrace that would forever be a black mark on his presidency. Yet he didn't sulk away and cry. He wasn't depressed. He threw a party for his friends, where he remained resolutely upbeat. It reminded me of the famous scene in Monty Python's *Life of Brian*, where prisoners hanging on crosses alongside Jesus cheerfully sing out, "Always look on the bright side of life."

As it turned out, Clinton was right. He beat the charges, voters turned on the Republicans in 1998, and today he's a much-beloved former president. All in all, he did indeed have a pretty good day.

SEPTEMBER 11

Those of us alive at the time always remember where we were when we learned President John F. Kennedy had been shot. Those alive on September 11, 2001, will always remember where we were when four planes hijacked by terrorists were flown into the Twin Towers, the Pentagon, and a field in rural Pennsylvania.

Washington woke to a magnificent early Indian summer day. Following my normal routine, I'd gone for a run, come home, had breakfast, and pored through the morning paper. But then, instead of turning on the TV, I started making notes for a noon speech scheduled before the National Automobile Dealers Association at the Capital Hilton. So I was stunned to learn from producer Kristy Schantz on our 9:30 conference call that we probably wouldn't have a show that evening because, now that a second plane had crashed into the World Trade Center, authorities were sure it was an act of terrorism. Like millions of Americans, I immediately turned on CNN to follow the horrific events of the day.

I sat there in a state of shock and disbelief over the unspeakable death and destruction. At the same time, I was also trying to think of what I could possibly say to that audience of auto dealers, and I decided I would just make a few brief comments about how horrible this attack on America was and then suggest they adjourn the meeting so we could all huddle around the nearest television sets.

But first I had to determine if the speech was still on. Which proved impossible. There was no phone service, either landline or cell phone, and no way to reach the Washington Speakers Bureau, the Capital Hilton, or representatives of the auto dealers. Meanwhile, news from New York got worse with the collapse of the first WTC tower. When the time came, I grabbed my speech notes and jumped in a waiting car for what turned out to be one of the scariest experiences of my life.

We hadn't gone two blocks before we heard over the radio that the second tower had collapsed. Every couple of minutes, it seemed, there were reports of another disaster, all frightening, some hard to believe. We were on Constitution Avenue, right alongside the U.S. Capitol, for example, when it was reported that a major explosion had just rocked the building. Which clearly was not true. I could see the Capitol from the car. There had been no explosion. There was no damage. Next came news of a car bomb exploding at the State Department, which was also false. Meanwhile, I could see heavy black smoke coming from across the Potomac. That turned out to be from American Airlines Flight 77, which had crashed into the Pentagon.

Washington and the nation were clearly under attack. And I was trying to make up my mind whether I was safer in a car on Pennsylvania Avenue or getting out and running for cover. That decision was soon made for me. By this time, the streets were so clogged we couldn't move at all. Cars were pouring out of parking garages and going in all directions at once. Drivers, ignoring traffic signals or one-way street signs, blocked intersections. Security officials with assault weapons suddenly appeared on sidewalks in front of federal buildings. It was total chaos. So, about a mile away, I got out and walked the rest of the way to the hotel, where an auto dealer official informed me that the entire program had been canceled.

So, like a good team player, I hopped on the Metro, which to my surprise was still working, and headed for CNN, where I walked up to the assignment editor and asked if there was anything I could do to help. Yes, he said. They'd just received a tip that conservative commentator Barbara Olson had been aboard the plane that crashed into the Pentagon. Could I try to confirm the news?

Suddenly the reality of September 11 hit home in a very personal way. A fiery conservative, Barbara was often a guest on *Crossfire*. I admired her lively debating style, and over the years we'd become friends. Just two days before, on Sunday, September 9, we'd appeared together on C-SPAN's *Washington Journal* in what turned out to be an awkward experience for both of us.

As always, Barbara and I disagreed on almost everything. But when several viewers called to attack Barbara personally, I leaped to her defense, accusing liberal callers of going over the line and reminding them we should be able to debate the issues and still remain friends—just like the two of us.

As we walked to our cars together after the show, we agreed to have lunch and talk about how the two of us might work together to improve the tone of political discourse in Washington. Barbara told me she was heading for Los Angeles on Tuesday, September 11, but would call as soon as she got back in town to set a date for lunch.

We hugged, said goodbye—and here I was, two days later, September 11, trying to find out if she was still alive. After striking out on several calls, I finally got confirmation from conservative commentator Kate O'Beirne, who had just left the Olson home. Barbara had, indeed, been on board American Airlines Flight 77 bound from Dulles to LAX. She'd called her husband, solicitor general Ted Olson, on her cell phone to report that the plane had been hijacked. Barbara was one of 2,977 good, innocent people killed on that terrible day, 59 of them on AA 77.

At CNN, I told the assignment editor what I'd learned and who my source was. He suggested that, as a friend of Barbara's, I should be the one to break the news on the air, but I declined. I was afraid I'd break down. I handed him my notes, left the building, and went home alone to cry. Carol was in California, unable to get a flight back to Washington.

September 11 and its aftermath—the cleanup, the search for survivors, the portraits and stories of the victims, the emerging news about Al Qaeda—continued to dominate the news for weeks. And, for the next month or more, *Crossfire* was off the air. Nobody was in the mood for the same old political bickering.

Still, it was such a big and important story, some of us weren't happy not to be part of the coverage. It certainly demanded analysis and commentary, in some appropriate format. So Tucker Carlson and I came up with the idea of substituting the traditional *Crossfire* format with a television "town hall" in front of a live audience. CNN executives approved, and our producers quickly lined up an auditorium at George Washington University.

For the next couple of weeks, we met every night at GWU not for a debate but for an honest discussion about all the issues stemming from the terrorist attacks of September 11. The auditorium was packed with students and local residents, many of them Muslims. We spent the first half of the show with a panel of experts and members of Congress. The second half was devoted to questions or statements from the audience.

Everybody wanted to talk about what had happened, what it meant, how it impacted them, what lessons we should learn, and how we could move on from those terrible events as a country united. I still remember leaving campus every night, shaken by the volatile mix of emotions—anguish, fear, anger, despair, confusion, yet hope and determination—expressed by our audience. To this day, it's the most powerful and meaningful television I've ever been part of.

LIGHTS OUT FOR *CROSSFIRE*

I had a great six years at *Crossfire*. Yet all good things must end. And, for me, the end wasn't pretty. It came when Rick Kaplan left and was replaced as president of CNN by *Time* magazine managing editor Walter Isaacson.

Isaacson's a brilliant journalist, but he had zero experience in television—and it soon showed. By that time, *Crossfire* had been on the air for twenty years. It was, by far, the most popular political debate show on television. It was, along with *Larry King Live*, one of two signature programs on CNN. It was producing both ratings and revenue for the network. But TV novice Isaacson thought he had a better idea.

When I first heard rumblings of change, late in 2002, I called Isaacson and asked him what was going on. He told me he loved *Crossfire* and thought I was the best cohost on the left in its history. But he believed he could make it an even better show by staging it in front of a live student audience with James Carville as cohost.

Talk about awkward! James was, and still is, a friend of mine. He was a frequent guest on *Crossfire* and married to my friend and former *Crossfire* cohost Mary Matalin. Nonetheless, I told Isaacson he was dead wrong. James was a great guest, I pointed out, but he would never cut it as a cohost because he lacked both the discipline to do his homework and the courtesy to listen to his guests' responses. But Isaacson was stubborn. As president, he had none of the leadership skills he later profiled in his masterful biography of Steve Jobs and all the shortcomings Jobs detested among other so-called leaders of technology companies: those whom Apple's fallen leader considered nothing but poseurs.

Isaacson went ahead with his plan, fired me, hired Carville and Paul Begala as new cohosts on the left, and moved the program from CNN studios to George Washington University, in front of a student audience. It remains one of the dumbest decisions ever made in television.

Yet in the end, I dodged a bullet: Isaacson's revamping of *Crossfire* was a disaster. On special occasions, like September 11, *Crossfire* could work in front of a live audience. But Isaacson turned a serious, highly respected debate program into a daily gong show. Literally. Boxing gloves became its new logo. A gong sounded between rounds of questions. And hosts and guests, rather than explore or probe the issues, now tossed out provocative one-liners instead, playing for the biggest hoots and hollers from the crowd. Many of our more prominent guests understandably refused to appear on the new format.

It was amateur hour. It was embarrassing. It was doomed. And its end was only hastened when *Daily Show* host Jon Stewart, appearing as a guest in October 2004, begged Tucker Carlson and Paul Begala to "stop, stop, stop, stop hurting America" by encouraging divisiveness, accused them of offering nothing but "partisan hackery," and topped it off by calling Tucker "as big a dick on your show as you are on any show."

Two months later, Tucker, embarrassed by the new format, quit the show. After another month of agony, in January 2005, Jonathan Klein, the new president of CNN after Isaacson, announced that he agreed with Stewart and pulled the plug. *Crossfire* was dead.

It was tough, leaving CNN. I'd been fired before, but this time it really hurt, because I loved the show and because I knew I'd done a good job at it. I didn't want to have to face friends the next day when the announcement was scheduled. So I was glad I'd agreed to speak to journalism students at Shepherd University in nearby Shepherdstown, West Virginia. I was driving to Shepherdstown when the shit hit the fan and my cell phone started going crazy.

My very first call? From Roger Ailes, then head of Fox News. "What the fuck are they thinking?" were the first words out of his mouth. Ailes, by the way, had always been friendly to me. I made a point of stopping by his office whenever I was in New York. But I was surprised as anybody when Gretchen Carlson filed her sexual harassment lawsuit against him in July 2016. There must have been truth behind her charges, and those of several other female Fox employees, because I never saw anyone topple from power as fast as Ailes did.

Roger's call was followed by a shout-out from none other than Sean Hannity, political adversary but fellow talk show host. And all day long the calls poured in from Buchanan, Novak, Matalin, and others, all conservative friends expressing their regrets and offering to help. Not a peep from my fellow liberals.

With one big exception. A few weeks later, checking our answering machine at home, I heard a familiar voice. "Hi, Bill. This is Bill Clinton. I was just in town, and I called to say hello and to say thanks for all the great work you did on *Crossfire*. I don't know what we'd have done without you. And I just wanted you to know I was thinking about you." Thank you, Mr. President.

So there I was, fired from the job that had brought me to Washington. But I knew by then that CNN was not the only game in town—and I set out to prove it.

8

MSNBC AND BEYOND

Pick your favorite cliché: You can't keep a good man down. When one door closes, another one opens. Whatever. Soon after being fired by CNN, I called Pat Buchanan, who had not returned to CNN after his most recent presidential campaign, and suggested we try to land a show together on a rival network.

Pat was eager to give it a shot, but there weren't a lot of options. Fox News was out of the question. His recent, friendly call aside, there was no way Roger Ailes was going to alter the network's conservative slant by hiring me. That left MSNBC. I called Erik Sorenson, then president of MSNBC, and told him Pat and I wanted to discuss a possible new show. Within a week, he came down to Washington and offered us a two-hour afternoon show: *Buchanan & Press*.

For the next year and a half, Pat and I owned cable television in the afternoon. We broadcast 2:00–4:00 p.m. from 400 North Capitol Street, directly across from the Capitol. We interviewed big-name guests. We debated the issues of the day. And we did so in a gentlemanly, civil, serious tone. Howard Stern called *Buchanan & Press* "the best show on cable television."

The life of *Buchanan & Press* overlapped with the buildup to the war in Iraq, and that one issue dominated the show. Which made for an interesting dynamic, because neither Pat, from the right, nor I, from the left, supported going to war. We didn't see any evidence to support President Bush's claim of weapons of mass destruction. We didn't buy Condi Rice's warning about a nuclear "smoking cloud." We laughed out loud at Bush's argument that Saddam Hussein's military posed a direct threat to the United States. They didn't have a navy or air force. And we were convinced that the administration, led by Dick Cheney, was cherry-picking intelligence to justify a decision to invade that had already been made. All of which turned out to be true.

Like millions of Americans, however, our confidence was shaken by Secretary of State Colin Powell's powerful presentation to the UN Security Council on February 5, 2003. While Pat and I still had our doubts, we knew the argument against the war was lost once Powell finished his presentation. And, sure enough, public opinion soon swung in support of the war in Iraq. Nobody else could have made the case so convincingly. It was little relief when, two years later, Powell admitted he'd relied on false information provided him by the CIA and called the speech a "blot" on his record that he would always regret.

Nevertheless, both Pat and I stuck to our anti-war guns, and I'm convinced that's what prompted MSNBC to cancel *Buchanan & Press*, even though we were beating every other cable show in the ratings. MSNBC also killed Phil Donahue's late-afternoon show because of his opposition to the Iraq War.

If my favorite moment on *Crossfire* was the joint appearance of Jerry Falwell and a San Francisco prostitute, my favorite *Buchanan & Press* moment was a confrontation with right-wing talk show host Michael Savage, still probably the most venal radio personality in the country.

When I heard that MSNBC was considering giving Savage his own afternoon show, I called Sorenson and warned him not to hire him, especially after, in his book *The Savage Nation*, Savage had trashed MSNBC's Ashleigh Banfield, calling her "the mind slut with a big pair of glasses that they sent to Afghanistan" and adding, "She looks like she went from porno into reporting."

Sorenson ignored my advice. So when Pat and I were obliged to include Savage in our lineup one day, to help "welcome" him to the network, I decided to go for the jugular. How could he agree to work on MSNBC, I asked Savage, when he'd slimed the network in general, and Ashleigh Banfield in particular, in his book? Would he now apologize for calling her a slut?

Savage went apeshit, refused to apologize, and even called Banfield a slut again. Which I had a hard time hearing because somebody from the control room in Secaucus was screaming in my ear, "No, no, no! You can't ask him about that! End this interview now!"

After the broadcast, I was ripped a new one for challenging Savage, but it wasn't long before management had to admit I'd been right about not hiring him in the first place. It was only four months later when he had the following exchange with a viewer.

Savage: "So you're one of those sodomites—are you a sodomite?"

Caller: "Yes, I am."

Savage: "Oh, you're one of the sodomites. You should only get AIDS and die, you pig. How's that? Why don't you see if you can sue me, you pig. You got nothing better than to put me down, you piece of garbage. You have got nothing to do today—go eat a sausage and choke on it. Get trichinosis."

Savage was gone from MSNBC within two days. Pat and I lasted a lot longer, but eventually the ax fell on us, too.

With the indefatigable Tammy Haddad as executive producer, backed up by Ann Klenk and Diane Robinson, *Buchanan & Press* dominated afternoon cable for about a year and a half, when for some crazy reason—was it our opposition to the war?—MSNBC decided to terminate the show. Another stupid decision made by TV management. *Buchanan & Press* was over. And so, for me, were the days of cohosting a daily TV show.

At the same time—when it rains, it pours?—WMAL-AM radio also decided to change its format. Which is a nice way of saying I was fired from my morning job, too, hosting morning drive on WMAL with Andy Parks and Jane Norris from 5:00 to 9:00 a.m.

How ignoble to be fired from two jobs in one month. But that double-barreled firing actually turned out to be a blessing. I was finally free to pursue a longtime dream of hosting my own nationally syndicated radio show.

THE BILL PRESS SHOW

One of the questions I'm most often asked is: "Which do you prefer, radio or television?"

Having made a career of both, it's not an easy question to answer. The truth is, I enjoy both. Yes, partly for the ego gratification. But more important, for the opportunity to debate the issues, express my views, explain and defend a strong liberal position on the issues of the day, and, hopefully, make a few converts along the way.

But if forced to choose—even though there's a lot more money in television, unless you're Rush Limbaugh or Glenn Beck—I would choose radio. Why? Because it's so much more intimate, so much less structured, and generates so much more of an immediate response than television.

Whether you're listening at home, at the office, or in the car, the essence of talk radio is: one person, at the other end of the dial, talking to *you*. And you alone. It's a conversation. You can listen. You can be amused or disgusted. You can agree or disagree. You can pick up the phone, talk to that person, and continue the conversation. You can tell him or her you think he or she is an idiot. Or you can simply change stations.

For the talk show host, it's an equally personal experience. There's no hiding behind the microphone or makeup. You say what you think. You tell that person across the dial how you feel. You bare your soul. And then— wham!—by email, Facebook, Twitter, or phone, listeners are in your face and you're forced to respond.

Not on television. There, you can say something outrageous and then simply take off your microphone, wipe off your makeup, walk out of the studio, and go have a couple of drinks and dinner without ever having to confront your viewers. The camera never talks back. The microphone always does.

Which is why talk radio became such a powerful force. At one time, more people listened to talk radio than read the daily newspaper, watched the network news, or tuned in to cable television. Until recently, it was even more powerful than the internet. But while popular news and political websites have more reach and influence today, talk radio hosts still have a lot of clout, especially those on the right.

By and large, conservative talk radio has always been a powerful political force, while progressive talk radio never really took off. As I document in my 2010 book, *Toxic Talk*, ownership's the main reason. Right-wingers own 95 percent of news talk stations, and right-wing owners won't put progressives on the air. It's as simple as that.

All a prospective conservative talk show host has to do is announce, "I'm here, I'm a certified right-winger, and I want to be on the radio," and presto, he or she starts off with over two hundred stations. For liberals, it's just the opposite. There is no progressive talk radio network. There are only dozens, not hundreds, of progressive talk stations. Miami doesn't have one. Neither does New York City, Philadelphia, Seattle, Los Angeles, San Francisco, Portland, Buffalo, Denver, or Atlanta. There's no Rupert Murdoch or Koch brothers on the left willing to buy radio stations and put liberal talk radio on the air.

There are a couple of other reasons, too. The basic format—a lone voice yelling into a microphone—appeals especially to angry white males, the vast majority of whom are conservative. They don't want to hear a mix of voices or opinions. They just want their daily hate fix. Many progressives, on the other hand, value a diversity of opinion—which is why they gravitate to NPR, rather than liberal talk, further shrinking the number of potential listeners to progressive talk.

So, from the beginning, it's always been an uphill battle for progressive talk radio. Several progressive talk show hosts—Ed Schultz, Thom Hartmann, Stephanie Miller, Randi Rhodes, Joe Madison, and others—have known great success, pulling in a lot of revenue, and even trumping Rush Limbaugh and Sean Hannity in certain markets. But their success often gets overshadowed by a cloud of failure still hanging over from Air America.

When first announced, Air America provided a spark of hope for progressive talk radio. At last! A strong, nationwide, progressive talk network! But soon that bright star crashed and burned.

Air America began as the brainchild of Anita and Sheldon Drobny of Chicago, who knew that if liberals were going to succeed in talk radio, they had to have their own network of stations. A great idea, but before launching the network, the Drobnys ran out of money and sold Air America to Evan Cohen. A shady character, Cohen lied about how much money was available, partially financed Air America through an illegal loan from a nonprofit boys' and girls' club, and ended up getting charged with money laundering. Air America, launched in 2004, declared bankruptcy in 2006 and eventually collapsed.

Air America did achieve two great things: It provided a launching pad for Al Franken to catapult himself all the way to the U.S. Senate, and it first introduced Rachel Maddow to a national audience, where she now presides as host of MSNBC's top-rated prime time program.

But Air America also did more damage than good. The failure of the first national progressive talk radio network—failure due to management incompetence, not to lack of broadcast talent—gave conservatives a lasting talking point. Still today, they insist: Nobody's interested in progressive talk radio. Just look at Air America. They tried it. They failed. Progressive radio doesn't work.

Before its collapse, I had been in discussions about joining the network. Now, with Air America out of the picture, I decided to launch a show on my own. I enlisted the help of veteran radio producer Paul Woodhull. Together we created a new morning show, convinced Jones Radio Networks to syndicate the program, and arranged to broadcast from the Center for American Progress. Thanks to a few good friends from California, I was able to raise enough money to get started and keep us going for at least a year. Within a week, we signed up our first local affiliate—Akron, Ohio— and we were off and running. Twelve years later, we're still at it.

For eleven years, we broadcast from 6:00 to 9:00 a.m. EST, which meant getting up at 4:00 and arriving at the studio by 5:00. Even though we now broadcast from 7:00 to 9:00 a.m., which allows for sleeping an hour later, it's still a pain in the ass. But it's worth it. The big advantage of morning drive radio is having the first crack at the day's news: telling people what's happened overnight and getting their first reactions. It's exciting, it's fun, it's fresh. Plus, sometimes we not only report on the news, we make news ourselves.

One morning in 2009, Michigan congressman John Conyers expressed his disappointment with President Obama on several issues. He was getting tired, he told me, of "having to save Obama's butt." The next morning, his complaint made the front page of *The Hill* newspaper. One day later, *The Hill* reported that Conyers had received a phone call from President Obama, telling him he was unhappy with comments made on *The Bill Press Show*.

That was one of the proudest moments of my career because it was great publicity for the show and because somebody had finally called Obama out on his lack of leadership on several key progressive issues.

While still strong, talk radio is a dying format. Many talk stations have gone out of business or been converted overnight to sports or religious programming. And more and more people get their news and music online or on their smartphones, not on something as old-fashioned as a radio.

So our show, like every other talk show, has had to adjust and add new platforms. We're no longer just on the radio; we're simulcast on Free Speech TV. We broadcast the entire show online on YouTube. We post every show as a daily podcast on our website so people can listen to it on their own schedule. We keep our Twitter followers up to date on guests, topics, and breaking news throughout the day. And we took a huge step forward in December 2016, when we joined the Young Turks Network founded by Cenk Uygur, the nation's most popular progressive broadcasting platform.

From the beginning, *The Bill Press Show* has been 100 percent sponsored by major labor unions: the Laborers, Machinists, United Steelworkers, International Association of Sheet Metal, Air, Rail and Transportation Workers (SMART), Firefighters, UFCW, AFSCME, AFT, NEA, AFGE, Ironworkers, Teamsters, Communications Workers of America, and Ullico. As a thirty-year-plus union member, I'm proud to stand with my brothers and sisters of organized labor every day in broadcasting a strong, pro-union, pro–working families message. Solidarity Forever!

CURRENT TV

As implied above, talk radio is even more effective when you can not only listen to the program on the radio but see it on TV. Which is why I've always looked for opportunities to simulcast my show, as we do today on Free Speech TV. But before Free Speech there was Current TV. And that's a story in and of itself.

Al Gore did not invent the internet. Nor, contrary to conservative critics, did he ever pretend to. But he and Joel Hyatt did invent Current TV. They launched their new network in August 2005 with the noble goal of creating the nation's first unapologetically progressive TV channel. After floundering for six years, they finally found their groove in 2011 by hiring David Bohrman, former Washington bureau chief for CNN, as president and Keith Olbermann, who had recently been fired by MSNBC, as their star anchor.

Suddenly, Current TV was on the map. And I pounced. I suggested to Bohrman that he needed a progressive morning show—and we were it. (Actually, it didn't take a lot of convincing. As president of MSNBC, Bohrman's the one who put Don Imus's morning radio show on television.) We quickly made a deal. On March 26, 2011, we started on Current TV.

Like both CNN and Fox News before it, the start-up network was a favorite target of industry humor. At the 2012 White House Correspondents' Dinner, Jimmy Kimmel noted that Current TV was founded by Al Gore and "took off like a North Korean rocket!" He'd be happy to watch Current, Kimmel confessed, except that "I don't get Channel One Million."

But for me, while it lasted, the move to Current TV was a big plus. It carried our show into areas of the country we never could reach before, vastly expanding our potential audience. The problem is, it didn't last long enough. As it turned out, Gore and Hyatt were more interested in making a quick profit than building a progressive television network. On January 2, 2013, I learned from a friend that Current TV had been sold to Doha-based, country of Qatar–owned Al Jazeera TV for $500 million. And the rug was summarily pulled out from under us.

Now, there's nothing wrong about a successful business venture. What bugged me about the sale of Current TV was the spin Gore and Hyatt tried to put on it. In a self-serving statement, Hyatt insisted Al Jazeera was just like us: "When considering the several suitors who were interested in acquiring Current, it became clear to us that Al Jazeera was founded with the same goals we had for Current."

Bullshit! That's not what it was about at all. Why not be honest? This was a big business deal, pure and simple. Al Jazeera was smart to buy Current TV because it gave them a presence in American media without having to build an entirely new network from scratch. It was a good business decision for Joel Hyatt, and especially for Al Gore, who reportedly walked away with $100 million in his own pocket. God bless America! Every small business owner dreams of being gobbled up by a bigger player for a lot of money. Just don't try to sell it as a victory for progressives.

I must admit, I couldn't resist saying, "I told you so!" when Al Jazeera America shut down in April 2016, just two and half years later, although the rest of Al Jazeera remains on the air. The sad part about the whole Current/Al Jazeera deal was that Americans were once again deprived of a strong, viable progressive media network. It was another Air America disaster.

ON TO THE WHITE HOUSE

Life's too short to slack off. There's never been a time when I declined to take on another job or responsibility because my plate was too full. So in 2009, when C-SPAN's Steve Scully, then president of the White House Correspondents' Association, suggested I attend daily White House briefings to expand the reach of my radio show, I jumped at the chance.

The first thing you notice about the White House Briefing Room: it's a lot smaller than it looks on television. It only has forty-nine seats, seven rows of seven, with standing room along both sides and in the back. Behind the briefing room are the cramped working quarters of the press corps, on two floors, with most reporters working out of space smaller than a broom closet. In other words, it's not a glamorous place to work. The basement floods during heavy rains. And sometimes there are as many mice running around as reporters.

But it's still an exciting place to work, because that's where the action is. When President Obama was awarded the Nobel Peace Prize, we were in the Rose Garden to record his first response. When David Souter told the president he was leaving the Supreme Court, Obama popped up unannounced in the briefing room to give us the news. When a frustrated Obama finally released his long-form birth certificate to placate the Trumps of the world, when he commented on the capture and killing of Libyan dictator Muammar Gaddafi, when he announced the withdrawal of all American troops from Iraq by the end of 2011, when he responded to the terrorist attack on our embassy in Benghazi, when he reported on the return of POW Bowe Bergdahl, when he declared our mission to "demean and destroy" ISIS—we were his audience, reporting from the front lines to our readers, listeners, and viewers around the world.

Most days, of course, it's not that newsworthy. At the average briefing, we're not learning and reporting big news. We're just trying to get a straight answer out of the White House press secretary—which isn't always easy, no matter who's at the podium. When somebody asks me, "How's Sarah Huckabee Sanders or Sean Spicer doing?" or, previously, "How's Josh Earnest, Jay Carney, or Robert Gibbs doing?" my answer's the same: If you understand that their role is to say nothing and make no news, they're doing a great job.

No matter how hard we push or prod, it's rare that any news emerges from the daily White House briefing, for one simple reason: because the press secretary steps up to the podium determined *not* to make news on any topic, *unless*, of course, it's a topic on which the White House wants to make news.

I discovered that in one of the first briefings I attended, on July 27, 2009, when I asked Robert Gibbs about the flap over the president's birth certificate.

"Robert," I began, "I hate to ask this, but I guess somebody has to. Is there anything you could say that would make the birthers go away?"

"No." Gibbs sighed, shaking his head in frustration. "I mean, the God's honest truth is no." He insisted that "nothing will assuage" those who continue to pursue what he called "made-up, fictional nonsense." And then he launched into a tirade about what lengths they had gone to during the campaign to shoot down rumors that Obama was not an American citizen, including posting a copy of Obama's birth certificate on the campaign website and publishing two contemporary Honolulu newspaper announcements of Obama's birth.

A week later, Gibbs himself raised the issue, denouncing as "totally crazy" the suggestion that even those two newspaper notices were part of a wider conspiracy. As he clumsily summed it up: "A pregnant woman leaves her home to go overseas to have a child—who there's not a passport for—so is in cahoots with someone—to smuggle that child, that previously doesn't exist on a government roll somewhere back into the country and has the amazing foresight to place birth announcements in the Hawaii newspapers? All while this is transpiring in cahoots with those in the border, all so some kid named Barack Obama could run for president forty-six and a half years later."

And, remember, this was even before Donald Trump appointed himself czar of the birther movement for the next five years.

The point is: On the birther issue, Gibbs wanted to make news, and he did. He was just waiting for someone—me!—to ask the question. But more often than not, all we get from the podium is evasion, obfuscation, or pure talking points.

Which is not to say we should just give up. No way. I disagree with former press secretary Dee Dee Myers that we should cancel daily press briefings. And I strongly disagree with the Trump administration's early decision to ban cameras from most briefings. No matter how routine, no matter how frustrating, no matter who sits in the Oval Office, the job of the press corps is to push for answers, to challenge assumptions, to question every assertion, and, ultimately, to discover the truth. Any good press secretary understands that. His or her job is to protect. Our job is to push and probe.

Of all those I've observed at the briefing room podium, Mike McCurry stands out. He was close to President Clinton. He knew what was going on in the White House, even though he wouldn't always spill the beans. He respected reporters and tried hard to keep them informed. He was very comfortable in the spotlight and never lost his sense of humor.

Of White House reporters I've seen up close, I believe ABC's Sam Donaldson was the best. Fearless, Sam didn't hesitate to challenge President Reagan, whom most reporters treated with kid gloves. Plus, he had a megaphonic set of lungs that allowed him to be heard even over the roar of the blades of Marine One. On LA's Channel 7, many are the times I defended Leather Lungs during those Reagan years.

But to be honest, we don't always see the White House press corps at its best. Under George W. Bush, they were nothing but a bunch of pussycats. Day after day, Dick Cheney, Condi Rice, Donald Rumsfeld, Colin Powell, and President Bush himself lied to the American people about things like Iraq's weapons of mass destruction, nuclear weapons, mobile long-range missile systems, and existential threat to the American mainland.

It was all a pack of lies. But with the exception of NBC's David Gregory, almost nobody in the briefing room challenged them at the time. Reporters simply took notes and then repeated and recycled those lies in their print or broadcasting stories. *The New York Times* even printed the administration's warning about mobile missile launchers on its front page, without first checking its accuracy.

Quite simply, the media was not doing its job and thereby shares responsibility for the disastrous war in Iraq that dragged on for years, cost over a trillion dollars and almost five thousand American lives, and paved the way for today's Islamic State, or ISIS. Had reporters done their job, I believe, neither Congress nor the American people would have been so quick to swallow Bush's lies about Iraq.

Perhaps White House reporters learned their lesson. It got a lot better during the Obama administration. Reporters questioned and challenged everything President Obama said. When he claimed that the stimulus, or Recovery Act, saved or created over two million jobs, we asked, "Where's the proof? How many new jobs are there? Aren't most of the ones you claim as new just keeping local government workers in preexisting jobs?"

White House reporters were also at their best in May 2013 when news broke of the Justice Department's seizure of phone records of Associated Press reporters and editors as part of a leak investigation. Their outrage only intensified two days later when it was reported that under yet another leak investigation, the private emails of Fox News reporter James Rosen had been captured by DOJ and Rosen himself had been labeled a criminal coconspirator. Reporters jumped all over press secretary Jay Carney, refusing to accept the administration's defense that national security trumped all other issues, even our First Amendment freedoms.

Every president, Republican or Democrat, has a rocky relationship with the media. But I was surprised it didn't go better with President Obama. After all, he started out ahead of the game because most reporters clearly liked him as a person—and because, when he does talk to the press, he's so damned good at it. But his administration, despite a promise to be the "most transparent" presidency in history, assumed a defensive posture, granted less access to the president than ever before, and hid behind the flimsiest of excuses for not answering straightforward questions.

For example, when Peter Baker of *The New York Times* asked Jay Carney a direct question about James Rosen—"Do you believe a reporter doing his job is a criminal coconspirator?"—all Carney would say is: "I can't comment on an ongoing criminal investigation." That's nonsense. It makes the president look shifty. And, by the way, that particular criminal investigation was soon over and Rosen was not charged with anything.

Then, things got far worse. Whatever problems existed with White House briefings under President Obama only increased a hundredfold once Donald Trump took over. For a while, we weren't even sure briefings would continue. During the transition, Trump officials openly proposed moving briefings out of the White House or canceling them altogether.

As of this writing, they still haven't canceled briefings, but they've done everything possible to render them meaningless. Briefings were not necessarily held every day. Under Sean Spicer, when they were scheduled, they were sometimes on camera, sometimes not. And, ironically, the Trump White House, which complains daily about "fake news," stuffed the briefing room with "fake reporters" from many obscure right-wing websites nobody had ever heard of and who would never qualify for a press credential under any other administration—and some of them get called on before the major networks or wire services.

Most damaging, of course, is that neither Spicer nor his then deputy, now press secretary, Sarah Huckabee Sanders made any effort to tell the truth. It started when Spicer, with no evidence, angrily defended Trump's claim that he had attracted the biggest Inauguration crowd ever. Once she took over, Sanders continued to evade the truth or just outright lie.

Take for example June 2017, when Sanders, asked to defend a mock video of President Trump pummeling a CNN reporter, insisted, "The president in no way, form, or fashion has ever promoted or encouraged violence." When, in fact, at his campaign rallies, candidate Trump encouraged supporters to punch protestors in the face and promised to pay their legal fees if they did so. Even today, as president, he continues to attack the media at almost every public appearance, encouraging his supporters to mock and boo them, if not worse.

The combination of Trump staffers' hostility toward the media and reporters' skepticism toward anything Trump's spokespersons say makes every briefing an open combat zone. Which is not surprising, given that President Trump seemingly devotes half his time and tweets to not just complaining about what he perceives to be unfair coverage but to openly attacking the media. Everybody in the media, that is, except Fox News.

Which raises a new and troubling issue for every member of the Fourth

Estate: how to be a fair and objective reporter while covering a president who does not tell the truth and who hates you and has declared war against you. Every journalist in Washington today has his or her take on that reality. Here's mine, as expressed in this column from July 6, 2017.

The Enemy of the American People

We always knew Donald Trump would start a war in the first six months of his presidency. We just thought it would be against North Korea or Syria. Silly us. We should have known it would be against the media. After all, his latest outbursts against MSNBC and CNN are nothing more than a continuation of the hostility he waged against the media as a candidate.

Attacking the media, in fact, was a standard feature of every Trump campaign rally. He banned many reporters from rallies because they wrote critical stories. Journalists who were allowed in were herded into pens like cattle, where Trump pointed at them and urged the crowd to taunt them. He even criticized several reporters by name—to the point where some media organizations hired security guards to accompany journalists to campaign events.

Those attacks didn't stop once he took office. They actually increased in frequency and vitriol, reaching a new low last week when Trump first lashed out at the cohosts of MSNBC's *Morning Joe*, calling Joe Scarborough "crazy" and Mika Brzezinski "dumb as a rock," and then tweeted a fake video of himself decking and punching out what looked like a CNN reporter.

Meanwhile, the First Lady and White House staffers defended Trump's bullying of the media as "you hit him, he'll hit you back." Trump himself characterized his childish, nonstop tweeting as "modern-day presidential." And over the Fourth of July weekend, at what was billed as a veterans' rally, he seized the opportunity to goad the media yet again: "The fake media tried to stop us from going to the White House. But I'm president, and they're not."

What to make of President Trump's war against the media? There are three takeaways. First, let's remember: Every president, indeed every politician, whines about the media. At some point, they all see themselves as victims of unfair coverage. They all complain. And, indeed, if they didn't complain, we in the media wouldn't be doing our jobs.

So Donald Trump isn't alone. He just makes his attacks against the media more personal than anybody else and even meaner than Spiro Agnew's. Trump's blasts on the media are ugly, obnoxious, and juvenile. They're also dangerous because they undermine the legitimacy of the press and could incite physical violence, as we saw in the case of Greg Gianforte, now a Republican congressman from Montana, body-slamming a *Guardian* reporter. In fact, the Committee to Protect Journalists, which has protested the arrest, torture, and assassination of journalists in countries like Russia and Venezuela, is now focusing on violence against reporters in the United States.

Second reality: Of course, Donald Trump could learn from other presidents. From George W. Bush, for example, no fan of the media, who admitted, "Power can be very addictive, and it can be corrosive. And it's important for the media to call to account people who abuse their power, whether it be here or elsewhere."

Yes, Donald Trump should grow up and grow a pair and recognize that criticism comes with the territory. But he won't. Because that's who he is. This man who was made by the media—who wouldn't be president without having his own TV show and being fawned over by the media—can't stop attacking the media because it's the only way to cover up his abysmal lack of accomplishments as president.

Third lesson: As disgusting as Trump's attacks against them are, it's a mistake for the media to take them too seriously. Otherwise, we play right into his hands. That's why he tweets. That's what he wants. For us to be talking about Joe, Mika, CNN, MSNBC, *The New York Times,* or *The Washington Post*—instead of about why Donald Trump can't round up fifty-one Republican votes in the Senate or why he still hasn't condemned Russia's attempts to sabotage the last election.

The best way to deal with Trump's attacks against the media is for reporters to ignore them and continue to do their job: Hold the powerful accountable. Dig out the facts. Report the news, good or bad. Let the chips fall where they may. Tell the American people the truth.

There's nothing more critical to the functioning of our democracy than a fearless, independent media. It's so essential that our founders enshrined it in the First Amendment to the Constitution.

So it's important that, despite all the criticism, we in the media continue to do our jobs. If only Donald Trump would do his.

After some twenty years in Washington, I'd managed to juggle a lot of media jobs: on television, at CNN, MSNBC, Current TV, and Free Speech TV; on radio, at WMAL and my own syndicated show; in print, writing a column for Tribune Content Agency and *The Hill*. But what I found even more challenging than navigating Washington's media world was navigating the city itself.

9

LIFE INSIDE THE BELTWAY

Working in Washington means living in Washington. Ask people what it's like living here and you'll get two responses: "It's great!" or "It sucks!" Both are true.

Moving to Washington, it doesn't take you long to discover that the phrase *inside the Beltway* is more than a geographical reference. It's the whole mind-set of many people who live in D.C. (or the tony suburbs of Potomac and McLean). There are more phony, self-important people per square inch here than anywhere else on the planet.

Remember, Washington's a one-industry town. And that industry is politics. People here practice, chew, eat, breathe, sweat, and talk politics twenty-four hours a day, seven days a week. And the sad fact is many people who thrive in Washington—politicians, lobbyists, government officials, bureaucrats, and journalists—are simply obnoxious human beings.

They suck up to you when you have a good job but don't even remember your name when you lose it. They go to restaurants to be seen, not to enjoy the food. They plan their dinner parties around who can create some buzz rather than who's actually a good friend. In fact, they don't have any real friends. All they have is the internet equivalent of a Rolodex, which is scrubbed regularly to get rid of any deadwood, a.k.a. former "friends" who are not considered hot anymore. It's so obvious, so sick, and so disgusting. As they say, "New York's a tough town; but Washington's a mean town."

New York Times reporter Mark Leibovich painted a damning picture of this Beltway crowd in his 2013 book *This Town*. These are the politicos and lobbyists who live to get their faces on television and their names in the gossip columns. They thrive on what Gore Vidal once told Dick Cavett was the rule he lived by: "Never turn down an opportunity to have sex or appear on television."

To that end, they flit from party to party, shaking hands—all the while looking over your shoulder to see whom they're going to glad-hand next. And they practically have a nervous breakdown if there's an A-list party they're not invited to.

Long before Leibovich, in his classic novel *Washington, D.C.*, Vidal captured what professional Washington's all about: "Peter meditated on the nature of the game all played, which was, simply, war. A conquers B who conquers C who conquers A. Each in his own way was struggling for precedence and to deny this essential predatoriness was sentimental; to accommodate it wrong; to change it impossible." Welcome to Washington!

The last thing these attention-grabbing bastards need is anybody new coming to town. They look down on outsiders or interlopers, whether it's a new president and First Lady coming from Arkansas or Chicago, a Seattle billionaire buying *The Washington Post*, or even just a new face on television from California. They resent anybody else trying to join the club.

Which I learned the hard way. One of the first things I did after arriving in Washington was call a few journalists I'd met and invite them to lunch, merely to seek their advice. "What's Washington all about? How do you fit in here?" A few—Juan Williams, Cal Thomas, Chris Matthews, Jack and Alice Germond, and Dan Balz—readily agreed to get together and were very helpful. But too many—I won't name names; you know who you are!—said they were simply too busy to have lunch with me. Not this week. Not next week. Never.

Instead, many of them were asking themselves, *How'd he get here, any-*

way, and with such a plum job? One snarky answer came in *The Washingtonian* magazine. In his Capital Comment column, Chuck Conconi noted that many insiders were surprised when a total unknown from California landed the job as cohost of *Crossfire*. But now, Conconi breathlessly reported, the secret could be told: Bill Press was a friend of Jane Fonda's from California. And Jane Fonda was married to CNN's founder, Ted Turner. So I had been hired thanks to pillow talk!

I called Conconi and set him straight. Yes, I'd known Jane when she was married to Tom Hayden, but I hadn't seen or spoken to her since their divorce, and I'd never even met Ted Turner. *Crossfire* executive producer Rick Davis is the one who made the decision, approved by CNN president Tom Johnson. Chuck apologized, we had lunch, and we've been good friends ever since.

What too many Washington insiders forget or ignore is a lesson I learned shortly after arriving in town from the legendary Tommy Boggs, then the Capitol's most powerful lobbyist. Tommy held court every day at the Palm. I joined him there for lunch one day with our mutual friend Chuck Manatt, former chair of the DNC.

Tommy gave me a bit of advice I didn't quite understand at the time but I've come to appreciate more and more. "Despite what people may tell you," he warned, "what counts in Washington is not *what* you are, but *who* you are." As I soon learned, that's a mistake many people make. They once had a powerful job and an impressive title, they were invited everywhere, yet they treated people like shit. Then they lost their job—and suddenly nobody would even return their phone calls. They never learned that basic lesson: It's not *what* you are, but *who* you are.

That's the "It sucks!" side of Washington. But remember, there's also the "It's great!" side of Washington.

As I discovered, there are two kinds of Washingtonians, the phony and the real: those who only want to use you, and those who genuinely want to be friends. But once you realize this is how the game is played here, and resign yourself to the inevitable social climbers and self-important snobs flitting around, there's still a lot of good fun and good friends to make in Washington. And Carol and I are lucky to have many great friends, some of whom you'll meet in the acknowledgments.

One thing about Washington reminds me of Los Angeles, and that's seeing celebrities in the most unlikely places. The only difference: In Hollywood, it's movie stars; in Washington, it's politicians or government officials. I remember running into Attorney General John Ashcroft shopping for a light bulb at Frager's Hardware; Speaker John Boehner out for a Sunday stroll on the Mall or at Trattoria Alberto; Barney Frank holding hands with his husband across the table at Banana Café; Justice Elena Kagan dining with a friend at Centrolina; and Justice David Souter replenishing his liquor supply at Schneider's on Capitol Hill.

As excited as I was to meet Milton Berle and Lawrence Welk, two early TV heroes of mine in Hollywood, I was equally excited in Washington to get to know my journalism heroes: Sam Donaldson of ABC, Tim Russert of NBC, Bob Schieffer of CBS, Bernard Shaw and Judy Woodruff of CNN, and especially the legendary Daniel Schorr of NPR, who loved regaling dinner audiences with the story of how he ended up with the first satellite dish in the nation's capital.

Schorr was one of the first people Ted Turner hired as anchor on CNN, but shortly after signing up, he told Turner his family would never be able to watch because the District of Columbia had no cable television. Turner vowed to fix that.

Within weeks, workers showed up at the Schorr residence to install a satellite dish. Remember, satellite dishes were then as big as a house, so installation was a major undertaking requiring several days of tearing up and replanting the landscaping. Also, because it was D.C.'s first satellite dish, the project received a great deal of media attention.

It didn't take long for Dan Schorr and Ted Turner to butt heads. Schorr, in fact, lasted only about a year at CNN and left with nothing but his satellite dish. Imagine his surprise, then, when several years later, he received a disturbing call from CNN's Washington bureau chief, Bill Headline (yes, that really was his name!), informing him that CNN executives in Atlanta had ordered that the dish be removed from Schorr's home.

Schorr promptly fired off a letter to Turner saying he'd be happy to return the dish, but only on three conditions. One, since the satellite dish was a personal gift from Ted Turner, he wanted a letter from Turner asking for its return. Two, he wanted to make sure that Turner realized that removing the dish would require tearing apart and restoring the Schorrs' garden—which CNN would have to pay for. Three, he also wanted to be sure Turner understood that, since installation of Washington's first satellite dish had received so much media coverage, its removal would also, no doubt, be of great interest to the media, especially TV cameras from competing networks.

A few days later, Headline called back with a terse message: "They say, 'Keep the fucking dish.'" So as far as I know, it's still there, outside Dan Schorr's old home in Cleveland Park.

THE PEOPLE'S HOUSE

Given how hard it is to meet people the usual way in D.C., Carol and I were lucky to land in Washington during the Clinton years, when we had many friends in the administration, starting at the very top. As recounted earlier, as Democratic state chair of California, I had seen President Clinton, First Lady Hillary Clinton, and Vice President Al Gore on almost every one of their many visits to California. Once we were in Washington, we saw them often at the White House.

Twice, we were invited to formal sit-down Christmas dinners at the White House. And we were invited to one state dinner, in honor of Carlos Menem, the president of Argentina.

It's a thrilling experience to have lunch or dinner in the White House anytime, but state dinners are as close to royalty as we get in this country. There are only 150 or so guests, because that's all the State Dining Room can hold. As Joe Biden might say, it's a "big fucking deal." Not to mention a great honor and a lot of fun.

With George Healy's powerful portrait of President Abraham Lincoln above the fireplace, the State Dining Room is as beautiful as it is historic. Carol was seated at one table, alongside navy secretary John Dalton. I sat at another table with my dinner partner, Secretary of State Madeleine Albright, whom I badgered the entire evening about restoring diplomatic relations with Cuba.

After dinner and the obligatory toasts by each president, everyone filed into the East Room for the evening's entertainment: for the President of Argentina—what else?—a tango demonstration. First, by a beautiful, wild, and sexy young couple from Argentina, flown in especially for the occasion.

Then a much more reserved, but no less beautiful, tango performed by actor Robert Duvall and his Argentine wife, Luciana Pedraza.

After the official entertainment, everyone else was invited to the dance floor. We partied until long after the presidents and their wives had retired for the evening, when White House ushers gently herded us down the stairs and out the door. But what the hell? You probably only attend one state dinner in your entire life. You might as well stay until they throw you out.

Next to state dinners, White House Christmas parties are the most fun— for everybody but the president and First Lady, who have to stand, shake hands, and have their photos taken with every guest at some two dozen parties every Christmas season.

The White House is ablaze with Christmas cheer. The main Christmas tree, with decorations from every state, is in the Blue Room. But every room is magnificently decorated—and the entire first floor open for guests. A couple of open bars and a long table adorned with piles of shrimp, lamb chops, and other delicacies are set up in the East Room. More bars and a similar feast are found in the State Dining Room, where, off to one side, shines the annual gingerbread White House and a table brimming over with special Christmas cookies.

Upon arrival, each guest is given a red, blue, or white card, indicating what time you must be downstairs, in line, to have your photo taken with the president and First Lady in the Diplomatic Reception Room. It's all extremely well organized. Once downstairs, you're given another card with your name on it. The line moves fast. As you reach the doorway, a marine takes your card and escorts you to the president and First Lady, where he announces your name, so the president knows who's coming up next.

And there you are! Your time "alone" with the most powerful couple on the planet. You have maybe thirty seconds to say hello and grip and grin for the camera before you're ushered along and the next couple moves in.

Of course, everybody in line's preoccupied with what to say to the Leader of the Free World in those thirty seconds. You can't wait till you're introduced. You've got to have something ready ahead of time. At Christmas 2012, shortly after his reelection, I told Obama, "Mr. President, don't let anybody tell you you're a lame duck."

He shot back, "Am I acting like one?"

Carol did better. I was greeting First Lady Michelle Obama when I heard the president laughing out loud behind me. "Michelle, you've got to hear this," he said. Carol had just told him about our granddaughter Prairie, then two-years old, who lives in Inverness, California, near the Point Reyes Lighthouse. Every time she sees the lighthouse, Carol related, Prairie says, "That's where Barack Obama lives." The lighthouse, not the White House.

"That's the funniest story I've heard all night," Obama roared.

PROM NIGHT

Everybody remembers his or her senior prom. It's a once-in-a-lifetime event, except for Washington journalists. We have a senior prom every April. It's called the White House Correspondents' Dinner.

The first dinner of the White House Correspondents' Association was held in 1920. Four years later, Calvin Coolidge became the first president to attend the dinner, as has every president since. Except Donald Trump. Who, of course, hates the media.

It's a festive affair, the one time a year when journalists, politicians, and newsmakers, who are more often at one another's throats, gather in the same room to eat, drink, gossip, make nice, and be merry.

For over sixty years, the dinner was a relatively staid event, but that changed in 1987 when the late Michael Kelly, then with *The Baltimore Sun*, invited as his guest Fawn Hall, bombshell White House secretary for Ollie North, who was notorious for following North's orders to shred all documents establishing any White House role in providing illegal arms to the Contras in Nicaragua. One year later, Kelly topped himself by squiring Donna Rice, onetime mistress of presidential candidate Gary Hart.

With Fawn Hall's appearance, the serious journalistic nature of the Correspondents' Dinner gave way to a race among all media outlets for the most famous or most notorious celebrity guests. At one dinner during the Clinton years, for example, I remember yukking it up with Whitewater character Susan McDougal while she was sitting on the lap of *Hustler* publisher Larry Flynt—in his gold wheelchair! My first year, I invited Senator Barbara Boxer as my guest. Another year, I took California governor Jerry Brown, who spent a good part of the evening huddled with a fellow Catholic, Supreme Court Justice Antonin Scalia.

The funniest time occurred at the 2010 WHCD, long before he ran for president, when I invited Bernie Sanders, then just a little-known Independent senator from Vermont, as my guest. Before dinner, the senator, his wife, Jane, and I were mingling in the giant CNN party when Bernie exclaimed, "Oh, my god, there's Rupert Murdoch!" Sure enough, halfway across the room stood Murdoch himself, drink in hand, chatting with another guest. "I can't stand to be in the same room with him," Bernie fumed. "Get me out of here!" I thought he was kidding. He wasn't.

My most embarrassing experience came a couple of years later when I showed up with Eliot Spitzer, former governor of New York and host of Current TV's *Viewpoint*. Spitzer was best known for resigning as governor after it was revealed that he'd traveled to Washington's Mayflower Hotel with a prostitute from a New York escort service he frequented, where he was known as Client Number Nine.

Traffic was not moving as we approached the Washington Hilton, so we hopped out of the car and walked the last block. Gawkers soon spotted Spitzer and started chanting, "Client Number Nine, Client Number Nine!"

I asked Spitzer, "You okay?"

"Don't worry," he said with a grim smile. "You don't think I've heard this before?" You had to admire his thick skin, if not his bad judgment.

By tradition, entertainment for the WHCA dinner is provided by a stand-up comic. Two of the best, in my opinion, were Wanda Sykes in 2009, and Seth Meyers in 2010.

Sykes, the first African American woman and first lesbian to headline prom night, saluted President Obama as "the first black president." "I'm proud to be able to say that," she told him from the podium. "Unless you screw up. Then it's, 'What's up with that half-white guy?'" Sykes absolutely killed with her jabs at Rush Limbaugh, Sean Hannity, and Sarah Palin, among many others. Limbaugh, she suggested, hates America so much he might have been the twentieth terrorist, "but he was so strung out on Oxycontin he missed his flight." She accused Palin of "pulling out at the last minute" from attending the dinner, adding, "Somebody should tell her that's not how you practice abstinence." And she brought down the house when she talked about how scary Dick Cheney was: "I tell my kids, 'Look, if two cars pull up, and one car has a stranger in it, and the other has Dick Cheney . . . you get in the car with the stranger!'"

Two years later, *Saturday Night Live*'s Seth Meyers famously blistered

Donald Trump. "He says he's considering running for president as a Republican," Meyers noted. "Which is surprising, since I just assumed he was running as a joke." Meyers added it was ironic that Donald Trump's head appears so often on Fox "because a fox so often appears on Donald Trump's head." As to Trump's assurance that he had a great relationship with "the blacks"? "Unless the Blacks are a family of white people down the street, I'll bet he's mistaken."

Trump, sitting with his wife Melania about halfway back in the enormous ballroom, just glared at the podium. Some people surmise that he was so pissed off at being mocked by the Washington establishment that night that he decided to run for president—just to get even.

Even more lively than the Correspondents' Dinner itself are the after-parties sponsored by various media organizations. For years, the Bloomberg party was the toughest to get into. I crashed it several years in a row with colleagues Susan Toffler and Bill Hemmer. Bloomberg's since been overtaken by *Vanity Fair* and MSNBC.

One night I was chatting with fellow liberal talk show host Ed Schultz when New Jersey governor Chris Christie sauntered in. "Jesus, I can't believe Chris Christie's here!" Ed exclaimed. "I wouldn't even shake hands with that bastard." Then he changed his mind. "Do you have a camera? Let's go say hello to him."

A few moments later, the two of them were arm in arm, posing for my camera. Christie looked up and said, "I can't believe it. Here I am with my arm around Ed Schultz, having my picture taken by Bill Press!"

Now, in the immortal words of Richard Nixon, I think it's important at this point to make one point perfectly clear: There's nothing wrong with hanging out, having a drink, and shooting the bull with your political enemies. Sure, on one level, it's phony. But not entirely. In fact, it's too bad it's only one night a year. We ought to do more of it. It's a good reminder that we're all human. It's evidence of the fact that, in the end, as Americans, we're all on the same team. And it's an important statement that while we may disagree on politics and policy, we can still remain civil toward each other. There should be more socializing like that in Washington.

But here's the problem with Washington today. Not only is across-party-line socializing in the evenings so rare, there's almost no across-party-line problem-solving during the day. If there were, if Republicans and Democrats met regularly to hammer out important legislation or just to have lunch, Congress would not be so hopelessly broken today, mired in partisan gridlock, and unable to accomplish anything.

BROKEN POLITICS

It wasn't always this way. Not so long ago, it was a lot different. Both sides would fight like hell at election time. But once the dust had settled, leaders of both parties would get together, figure out what big issues they faced that year, and get down to work on the necessary fixes.

It's the kind of enlightened, pragmatic leadership we expected and received from Democrats like Tip O'Neill, George Mitchell, and Tom Daschle, or Republicans like Howard Baker, Bob Dole, and Trent Lott. As Tip O'Neill quipped, "House Republicans were only the opposition; the Senate was the enemy."

But all that changed in 1994, when Newt Gingrich was elected Speaker. Newt's primary goal was never to get things done. It was to destroy the opposition. He introduced the practice of permanent campaigning with no time off in between for governing.

Gingrich even gave Republicans a list of pejorative terms to use whenever talking about Democrats, including *betray, destructive, greed, hypocrisy, liberal, pathetic, radical, self-serving, shallow*, and *traitors*. And, of course, a companion list of words to use when talking about Republicans: *citizen, courage, fair, family, freedom, liberty, moral, opportunity, pro-flag, prosperity, protect*, and *truth*.

Today, Congress is a disaster zone. Never have the two major parties been so far apart. Never has the debate been so ugly and personal. Never before have so many members of Congress put what's good for their party ahead of what's good for the country. And never has so little been accomplished. We might as well send all members of Congress home on permanent leave. True, they don't get anything done in their home districts. But they don't get anything done in Washington, either, because this is the era of nonstop politicking.

Nobody personifies this "politics first" approach to Congress more than Senate majority leader Mitch McConnell, who famously told the *National*

Journal in October 2010 that the number-one legislative goal of Republicans was "for President Obama to be a one-term president." By following McConnell's political, not legislative, agenda, Senate Republicans earned their reputation as "the Party of No" by opposing everything President Obama proposed—even legislation, like immigration reform and an individual mandate for health insurance, which they themselves had sponsored just a couple of years earlier. And, for that all-out, do-nothing opposition, they were rewarded with the White House, both houses of Congress, and a Supreme Court seat stolen from Merrick Garland.

There's no denying it: The political system in Washington is broken. The problem is, most people believe both parties are equally at fault. Which is simply not the case.

I'm not saying Democrats are perfect. They're not. But you can't accuse them of refusing to compromise. In fact, starting with President Obama, Democrats are often too willing to compromise, as I bemoaned in my book *Buyer's Remorse.*

No, the real reason politics in Washington today is broken is because Republicans decided that their role is to stand in the way of progress on any issue. They have no ideas. They're against everything, but they're for nothing, with the possible exception of even more tax cuts for the rich.

Some people used to complain about congressional gridlock. That's so twentieth century. The problem today is not gridlock. It's total blockade. And only one party is responsible: the Republican Party—with its worthless, impotent Congress and embarrassingly inept president

Don't take my word for it. In their book *It's Even Worse Than It Looks: How the American Constitutional System Collided with the New Politics of Extremism*, Norm Ornstein and Thomas Mann, two of the most respected congressional experts in the country, pull no punches on which party's to blame:

> However awkward it may be for the traditional press and nonpartisan analysts to acknowledge, one of the two major parties, the Republican Party, has become an insurgent outlier: ideologically extreme; contemptuous of the inherited social and economic policy regime; scornful of compromise; unpersuaded by conventional understanding of facts, evidence, and science; and dismissive of the legitimacy of its

political opposition. When one party moves this far from the center of American politics, it is extremely difficult to enact policies responsive to the country's most pressing challenges.

The sad but ultimate reality, of course, is that, after being total obstructionists for eight years, when Republicans finally took over the House, Senate, and White House in 2017, they still couldn't get anything done. They couldn't even round up enough Republican votes to repeal Obamacare, even though that's all they'd talked about for seven years. Instead, they blamed Democrats for being obstructionists.

Again, the end result of such a total political breakdown is the failure to make progress on any of the critical policy challenges facing this nation. Those problems are not that difficult. They could easily be fixed. But they'll never be fixed unless politicians of both parties are once again willing to sit down together and get to work solving problems. For my grandchildren's sake, I hope that happens in my lifetime. But I'm not holding my breath.

CLEAN FOR GENE

One of the unexpected and very special advantages of moving to Washington was the opportunity to reconnect with Senator Eugene McCarthy, who propelled my interest in politics decades earlier.

As noted earlier, Carol and I met in 1968 during the McCarthy for President campaign in San Francisco. I'd shaken hands with Senator McCarthy a couple of times while he was campaigning in California but had never really met him. In fact, I didn't even know he was still alive until one day Chuck Conconi casually mentioned that he'd just had lunch with the senator. My jaw dropped. McCarthy's still alive? He lives here? You know him? When can I meet him?

Chuck soon organized lunch for the three of us at Sam & Harry's on Nineteenth Street. I was thrilled just to see this tall, distinguished, silver-haired gentleman walk in the door. Gene moved slowly, but he was still in good form and in great spirits. We had a long, laugh-filled lunch as he regaled us with stories about Lyndon Johnson, Bobby Kennedy, and Hubert

Humphrey, whom he derided as having "the soul of a vice president." That lunch was the first of many.

Later, Chuck and I interviewed the senator in his Kalorama apartment for the January 2000 edition of *Washingtonian* magazine. But most of the time we got together, it was just for fun, usually at the Palm, with a rotating band of McCarthy friends and former staffers.

On April 5, 2003, Carol and I hosted McCarthy's eighty-seventh birthday at our home. Before dinner, standing in front of the fireplace, Gene proudly recited a few favorite poems by William Butler Yeats, as well as a couple of his own.

McCarthy then took his place at the head of the table and entertained us the entire evening. After dinner, then Senate majority leader Tom Daschle saluted McCarthy for the entire generation of young men and women, including all of us present, he had brought into politics. Around the table, in addition to Tom and Linda Daschle, were Chuck and Janelle Conconi; Marie Arana, then editor of *The Washington Post* book review; her husband, Jonathan Yardley, leading book critic for *The Washington Post*; Al Eisele, editor of *The Hill*, and his wife, Moira; John MacArthur, editor of *Harper's*; and McCarthy's former press secretary, investigative journalist Seymour Hersh.

After he grew too weak to live alone, McCarthy moved to the Georgetown, an assisted living facility. I'd occasionally pick him up there in my car and drive him to lunch at the Four Seasons or some other place nearby that was easily accessible. But soon, as Gene's mobility declined, those outings, too, became impossible. So I'd just go to the Georgetown, sometimes alone, sometimes with Chuck Conconi, and sit and talk until McCarthy grew too tired.

Gene slowly went downhill, requiring more and more personal care, but toward the end of his life, he had one last hurrah. When Sam Scinta, head of Fulcrum Publishing, read a *New Yorker* article about McCarthy's yet-unpublished poetry, he called the senator and offered to publish the entire collection. The result was McCarthy's last book, *Parting Shots from My Brittle Brow*, which we celebrated the evening of January 22, 2005, at the National Press Club. McCarthy, in his wheelchair, was thrilled to have one more moment in the spotlight. It was his last public event.

McCarthy died the night of December 10, 2005. Three days later, Carol

and I joined a small group of friends at his burial in the cemetery of Wood-
ville, Rappahannock County, Virginia, where McCarthy had a country
home. His daughter Mary and former girlfriend Marya McLaughlin are
also buried there.

It was a bitter, cold, windy day. Presbyterian minister John Boyles officiated over the graveside service. Then Peter Yarrow—of Peter, Paul, and
Mary fame—unpacked his guitar, donned a pair of gloves with the fingers
cut off, and sang two of Gene's favorite songs: "The Magi" and "Sweet Survivor." We recited the Lord's Prayer as Gene's coffin was lowered into the
ground, after which we all took turns, in the true Irish tradition, of tossing
shovels of dirt onto his grave. It was a very moving ceremony and a very
private farewell for such an important American political leader.

The public celebration of Eugene McCarthy's life came before a packed
house on January 14, 2006, at Washington's magnificent National Cathedral. Many current and former members of Congress were there, as well as
many leading journalists. Sasha Callahan, daughter of Lewis & Clark professor and longtime McCarthy friend and supporter John Callahan, played
a beautiful cello sonata. Heartfelt eulogies were given by McCarthy's
daughter Ellen, former Minnesota congressman Jim Oberstar, and former
CNN anchor Mary Alice Williams. Peter Yarrow, this time with his
daughter, Bethany, again sang "The Magi" and "Sweet Survivor," and concluded the service by leading the congregation in a rousing rendition of
"This Land Is Your Land."

But as always, Bill Clinton stole the show, this time with his account of
the first time he met McCarthy. While serving as a congressional intern,
Clinton lived with a family in northwest Washington. One day, his host offered Clinton a ticket to a black-tie dinner where President Nixon was to
be the guest of honor. When Clinton hesitated, explaining that while he
could easily rent a tux, he didn't know where he'd find a pair of size 12 black
shoes, his host said he'd check with a big-footed friend who lived nearby.

Sure enough, as Clinton told the story, he was sitting on the front steps
the next day when Senator Eugene McCarthy walked up the driveway and
said, "I hear you're looking for a pair of big black shoes." The senator sat
down and entertained Clinton with political stories for an hour, then handed
him the shoes. That evening, Clinton continued, he was standing in line to
shake the president's hand, when he suddenly had second thoughts and

turned away. "I just couldn't bring myself to shake Richard Nixon's hand while wearing Gene McCarthy's shoes!"

I felt so blessed to have the opportunity to reconnect with Senator Gene McCarthy and on such a personal level. He was my first political hero. To me, his 1968 campaign was as good as politics ever gets: genuine excitement, huge crowds, big ideas, millions of young people volunteering for a candidate they could believe in.

Surely, I never thought I'd see anything like that political whirlwind again. But that was before I met Senator Bernie Sanders.

10

FEEL THE BERN

Just when we think we have it all figured out, politics has a way of surprising us. That certainly proved true in 2016.

Early in 2015, it looked like the die was already cast for the presidential election of 2016. Republicans had settled on yet another member of the only Republican family that knew how to win the White House. Democrats were eager to hand the crown to Hillary Clinton without a primary, because everybody knew she'd end up the nominee anyway. And both sides complained about having to suffer through another Bush-versus-Clinton presidential contest; was America's political gene pool really that small?

But voters had a different plan in mind. Republicans rejected presumed front-runner Jeb Bush and fifteen other candidates in favor of brash outsider Donald Trump, while Democrats came close to taking the nomination away from Hillary and handing it to the most unlikely of challengers, Vermont Independent senator Bernie Sanders, who wasn't even a Democrat.

And I found myself right in the middle of it—as a Bernie Bro.

It was, I admit, a big change for me to go from a longtime Clinton supporter to a Sanders supporter. As noted earlier, I became close to both Bill and Hillary when I was Democratic state chair of California. I enjoyed their hospitality often at the White House. I supported Hillary Clinton over Barack Obama in 2008. At the same time, it wasn't a hard choice to decide to support Bernie over Hillary in the primary. Not because I'd fallen out of love with Hillary. My decision was very straightforward. One, I believed a vigorous primary would be good for the Democratic Party. I strongly disagreed with those who wanted to hand the nomination to Hillary without a Democratic primary, especially since she hadn't proved to be a very effective candidate in 2008. Two, I believed the party needed a new face, somebody who could create a lot of excitement among new and, especially, younger voters. I just never expected the Pied Piper to turn out to be a seventy-four-year-old Democratic Socialist from Vermont. And three, I knew I could always support Hillary Clinton in the general election if she won the nomination.

I originally got to know Senator Sanders in my role as a talk show host. Unfortunately, as noted earlier, progressive talk radio has never really taken off, mainly because conservative network owners, who control the airwaves, refuse to include any liberal hosts as part of their programming.

When I launched *The Bill Press Show* in July 2005, for example, there were some two thousand news-talk radio stations in the country, of which only some one hundred were progressive talk. The rest were right-wing propaganda outlets, 24–7, all with the same cast of blowhards: Rush Limbaugh, Sean Hannity, Michael Savage, Mark Levin, Laura Ingraham, and others.

To correct that imbalance, a few of us turned to Democratic senators for help. Our allies included majority leader Harry Reid and Senators Debbie Stabenow and Byron Dorgan. But nobody was more helpful than Senator Bernie Sanders.

The Vermont Independent not only preached the importance of progressive talk radio, he practiced it. He appeared for an entire hour every Friday on Thom Hartmann's show. He was a regular guest on Ed Schultz's radio and TV broadcasts. He also appeared frequently on my radio show and spoke at a lecture series I host at the Hill Center on Capitol Hill. For a year, I even served as one of Bernie's Senate interns—so I could occasionally cover Congress.

And so it was with special interest, early in 2014, that I started hearing rumors that Senator Sanders was thinking about running for president in 2016. I checked in with press secretary Michael Briggs, who suggested I stop by the senator's office the next afternoon.

"What's all this talk about 2016?" I asked Bernie as we settled into his office.

"My life doesn't depend on running for president," Bernie wanted me to know up front. Even though, he admitted, he'd discovered that nobody really took you or your ideas seriously until you ran for president. Then he went on to explain: His goal was to make sure that the progressive issues he'd championed so aggressively for so many years were front and center in the Democratic primary. He knew Hillary wouldn't raise them on her own, so somebody else had to run in order to promote the progressive agenda and get those issues into the mix. He'd already talked to Elizabeth Warren and didn't believe she would jump in. If nobody else did, Bernie said, he was thinking about it.

It sounded good to me, except for my fear that Bernie, running as an Independent, would just siphon votes from Hillary and help elect a Republican president. "I won't do that," Bernie pledged. "I won't become another Ralph Nader." He was determined, he assured me, to make sure the White House stayed in Democratic hands. He'd never do anything that might in any way help Republicans recapture the White House.

Thus reassured, "It's not crazy," I told Bernie. But if he were really serious, I suggested he pull together a few veteran campaign strategists to seek their advice. As they say, "Be careful what you ask for, 'cause you just might get it."

"That's a good idea," Bernie responded. "Could you organize that for me?"

How could I say no? I immediately contacted friends who'd worked in presidential campaigns, inviting them to a private conversation with Senator Sanders about a possible run for president. The entire discussion would be off the record, I assured them, with no endorsement implied. They were invited simply to listen to the senator's plans and offer their advice, no strings attached.

Putting that group together was when I first sensed the resistance Senator Sanders would later face from establishment Democrats. Some declined because they said they wanted to avoid a divisive primary. Others begged off because they were already committed to Hillary. One veteran strategist vowed he'd love to attend but was afraid the Clintons would learn he'd been there.

And so it happened that on the evening of April 9, 2014—as first reported by Jonathan Allen and Amie Parnes in their book *Shattered*—a group of us sat down with Senator Sanders in my home on Capitol Hill. Joining me and Carol with the senator were his wife, Jane Sanders; Democratic strategist Tad Devine; his business partner Mark Longabaugh; veteran campaign strategist Peter Fenn; Brad Woodhouse, former communications director of the Democratic National Committee; and Susan McCue, former chief of staff to Senate majority leader Harry Reid. Also present were Michael Briggs, the senator's press secretary, and Michaeleen Crowell, his chief of staff.

We gathered in the living room over Carol's beef stew, salad, red wine, and cookies for dessert. Senator Sanders opened by essentially repeating what he'd told me a couple of weeks earlier. He was determined that progressive issues be central to the 2016 presidential primary campaign; he knew Hillary Clinton would not raise those issues on her own, and if nobody else stepped forward to do so, he was contemplating jumping in. But again, he emphasized, he had made no decision to run.

Next, Tad Devine presented a memo he'd prepared at the senator's request, outlining the potential challenges and opportunities an insurgent, outsider campaign would face. Tad concluded with his optimistic assessment of raising enough money online, with no PAC money, to fund a serious presidential campaign. But nobody dreamed the Sanders campaign would prove so successful in fundraising it would actually surpass Barack Obama's 2008 record.

Sanders then asked each of us for our thoughts, turning to me first.

"I have only three words for you, Senator," I said. Bernie furrowed his brow, wondering what was coming next. "Ambassador to France!"

Bernie roared, and after that moment of levity, we all chimed in with more serious observations, which added up to the idea that a Sanders campaign wasn't as crazy as it might seem. There was a real discontent among voters with politics as usual, which created the opening for a serious challenge to Hillary. Everyone also agreed on one other important point: If he did run, Sanders would have to run as a Democrat—not only to be taken seriously but to be included in the debates and have his name on the ballot in all fifty states. The senator readily agreed, and that's where we left it.

Until . . .

A few months later, I received another call from the good senator from Vermont with a significant request. "That was a good meeting we had at your house," he said. "I learned a lot. Do you think we could schedule another one?"

Which we did. On November 19, 2014, over Carol's chicken cacciatore this time, with almost the same cast of characters: Senator and Mrs. Sanders; Carol and me; Tad Devine and Mark Longabaugh; Susan McCue, Michael Briggs, and Michaeleen Crowell. Peter Fenn was out of town. Brad Woodhouse declined. This time we were also joined by Congressman Keith Ellison and Congresswoman Barbara Lee; Alyssa Mastromonaco, former deputy chief of staff for the Obama White House; and Phil Fiermonte, director of Sanders's Vermont district office.

Second time around, the conversation was more pointed and more serious. By this time, it was clear that neither Elizabeth Warren nor any other progressive planned to run. Tad Devine again opened by outlining a potential national primary campaign: when to launch, what states to target, what the message should be, how to build a grassroots organization, and how much money could be raised online. Ever the optimist, Tad projected $40–50 million, which seemed highly ambitious at the time, but turned out to be way too conservative.

Again, the consensus was that Bernie's running for president wasn't crazy, that there was a real opening for an alternative to Hillary, and that if Bernie didn't mount a truly progressive challenge, nobody else would. Barbara Lee added a sober note by warning that Bernie would face a serious challenge in the African American community because he'd represented a predominately white state for so long and because, despite his early involvement in the civil rights movement, he had nowhere near the long history enjoyed by Bill and Hillary Clinton with African American voters—a warning that would prove to be prophetic.

Overall, our little "kitchen cabinet" felt very positive about a possible Sanders candidacy, which now looked more and more likely, especially when the senator ended our meeting by reminding us that he had not yet made a final decision, but then asked, "If I do decide to run, will each of you be with me?" In my memory, with the exception of Barbara Lee, who had left early, everybody else said yes.

BERNIE FOR PRESIDENT

The rest is now familiar history. On April 30, 2015, in a low-key and hurried press availability outside the Capitol—"We don't have an endless amount of time; I've got to get back for votes"—Bernie Sanders announced that he was, indeed, running for the Democratic nomination for president. He cited middle-class angst as the driving force of his candidacy: "For most Americans, their reality is that they're working longer hours for lower wages. In inflation-adjusted income, they're earning less money than they used to years ago, despite a huge increase in technology and productivity. While at exactly the same time, 99 percent of all new income generated in this country is going to the top 1 percent. And my conclusion is that that type of economics is not only immoral, it's not only wrong, it's unsustainable."

"The major issue" for 2016, Sanders told the small group of reporters, is: "How do we create an economy that works for all of our people rather than a small number of billionaires? And the second issue, directly related, is the fact that as a result of the disastrous Supreme Court decision on Citizens United, we now have a political situation where billionaires are literally able to buy elections and candidates." Add climate change, breaking up the big banks, single-payer health insurance, and prison reform and you have the gist of every Sanders campaign speech, building and expanding on progressive issues he'd championed for the last forty years.

Bernie went on to surprise everyone, starting with himself, by the amazing success of his campaign. He won 21 primary contests, received over 13 million votes, amassed a total of 1,876 delegates, and raised an astounding $232 million, $216 million of which came from small donations averaging $27. Overall, 2.3 million supporters made a total of 8 million contributions to the Sanders campaign. No political candidate ever has raised anywhere near that amount of grassroots money.

It didn't take long for those pundits who'd dismissed Bernie as a gadfly and "message only" candidate to be proven wrong. On July 2, over ten thousand enthusiastic fans turned out to see him in Madison, Wisconsin—the biggest crowd of any 2016 candidate up to that point, and double the number who turned out for Hillary's launch of her official candidacy on New York's Roosevelt Island the month before. He went on to draw record-making crowds everywhere he went: Boston, twenty-five thousand; Portland, Oregon, twenty-eight thousand; Seattle, thirty thousand.

Twice that summer of 2016, I experienced Bernie's newfound celebrity. In July, I attended the summer meeting of the Democratic National Committee in Minneapolis, where all five Democratic candidates at the time spoke: Hillary Clinton, Bernie Sanders, Martin O'Malley, Jim Webb, and Lincoln Chafee. Before leaving Washington, I'd arranged with press secretary Michael Briggs to have dinner with Bernie and Jane the night before at Manny's Steakhouse on Marquette Avenue.

After stopping by a couple of receptions at the hotel, Bernie and I walked out of the Hilton Hotel—he then had no Secret Service protection—and headed for the restaurant, accompanied by Jane, campaign manager Jeff Weaver, and press secretary Briggs. We were immediately mobbed by fans wanting to take selfies. It was like walking with a rock star. It took almost an hour to walk the one block to Manny's. When we walked in and headed to our table, the entire restaurant stood up and applauded. What a dramatic change from the last time Bernie and I had gone out for dinner, at Acqua Al 2 on Capitol Hill, after which we had simply said good night and both walked home alone.

At dinner that evening in Minneapolis, while talking about his chances in California, Bernie asked me to set up a meeting for him with my friend and former boss, Governor Jerry Brown. I jokingly told him that Jerry owed me because the last time he was in Washington, Carol and I hosted an off-the-record lunch at our home for him and twelve political journalists.

Bingo! Bernie's eyes lit up, and again he pounced. "That sounds like a good idea. Could you put something like that together for me?" Of course, I would, and could, and did, which provided my second window into Bernie's newfound celebrity. This time, it was not like pulling teeth to get people to meet with Bernie; it was more like posting guards at the door to keep them away.

On Thursday, September 17, over delicious chicken-curry salad prepared by Carol, Bernie sat on our living room couch and fielded questions from some of Washington's best political journalists: Karen Tumulty, *The Washington Post*; Bill Hamilton, *The New York Times*; Doyle McManus, *Los Angeles Times*; Sam Stein, *Huffington Post*; Alex Seitz-Wald, MSNBC; Nancy Cordes, CBS News; Kelly O'Donnell, NBC News; Brianna Keilar, CNN; Alexander Bolton, *The Hill*; Peter Nicholas, *The Wall Street Journal*; Tamara Keith, NPR; Steven Shepard, *Politico*; and Evan McMorris-Santoro, *BuzzFeed*. Bernie then moved out to the patio for an interview with *Los Angeles Times* reporter Ted Rall, while campaign manager Jeff Weaver stayed behind to outline and answer questions on campaign strategy and logistics.

It was a very productive session. Reporters left with a better understanding of Bernie's message and a greater impression of how serious a campaign he was mounting.

Perhaps most important, through the primaries, Bernie not only won millions of votes, he also succeeded in prompting Hillary Clinton to address key progressive issues, and even to change her position on some of them. As secretary of state, she supported the Keystone Pipeline; as a candidate, she opposed it. As secretary of state, she supported the Trans-Pacific Partnership, or TPP; as a candidate, she opposed it. She started her campaign by calling for a twelve-dollar minimum wage; by the end of her campaign, she joined Senator Sanders in urging a fifteen-dollar minimum wage. She never embraced a single-payer health care system, but she did endorse adding a "public plan option" to Obamacare, widely considered the first step toward single payer. By the end of the primary, she had endorsed tuition-free college for all high school graduates, not just debt-free college. She also began talking about the issue of income inequality, which even Vice President Joe Biden noted was a new issue for her.

Clearly, Bernie grasped a political reality that the entire Democratic political establishment had missed: a sense of alienation, frustration, and even anger that had been building for years among millions and millions of Americans who feel left behind or ignored in today's economy. Globalization, the online economy, and new trade deals may have helped the top 1 or 2 percent of American households. But for the vast majority of Americans, it meant only the loss of good jobs, stagnant or lower wages, loss of savings, both parents working, sometimes both at more than one job, and still unable to pay their bills at the end of the month, let alone put anything aside for their kids' college education.

Again, Bernie's initial goal was not so much to win the nomination as it was to inject those progressive issues into the Democratic primary. But a funny thing happened along the way: Given the size of his crowds and his early wins in a couple of key primaries, Bernie soon realized that Hillary Clinton was a weaker candidate than anybody thought and that he actually had a shot at winning the nomination. For a while, it turned into a real horse race. Bernie's criticism of Hillary, and hers of him, became a lot sharper—until the delegate math, boosted in large part by the party's superdelegates, shifted irreversibly in her favor.

Which, in a perverse way, came as something of a relief to me. I still wanted Bernie to win, but for a couple of weeks, I was afraid that I alone might inadvertently cause Bernie to lose—all because of "the blurb heard 'round the world."

Here's the backstory. I was a big fan of President Obama's. Nonetheless, like many progressives, I was disappointed in his failure to deliver on many progressive issues. So disappointed, in fact, that I wrote a book about it, *Buyer's Remorse: How Obama Let Progressives Down*, in which I dutifully gave Obama credit for all the good things he'd done but also criticized him for the many issues on which he either failed to deliver or failed to fight the good fight.

Months before publication, I asked Bernie's press secretary, Michael Briggs, if the senator might be willing to provide a blurb for the back of the book. Bernie agreed, and Mike and I, well aware that Bernie might be announcing his candidacy for president, worked out what we thought was a totally innocuous blurb nobody could object to.

What we didn't anticipate was that, without checking with me, the publisher took one line out of Bernie's blurb and blasted it on the front cover of the book: "Bill Press makes the case . . . read this book. Senator Bernie Sanders." As soon as I saw it, I called Briggs and Tad Devine and warned them we might have a problem. When the book came out, Bernie might be accused of attacking President Obama. "Be ready in case the shit hits the fan," I told them. Sure enough, it did.

Publication date was Tuesday, February 2. Two days before, on *Meet the Press*, Chuck Todd showed Bernie a copy of the book and asked him why he was so critical of Obama. Shortly thereafter, the Clinton campaign put out a statement attacking Bernie for attacking Obama, arguing that this proved he wasn't a real Democrat. "We expect that kind of criticism from Republicans, but not from Democrats." Hillary pounced.

Whenever Bernie was asked about the blurb over the next couple of weeks, he patiently explained that he was a big supporter of Obama, even though he didn't agree with him on every issue. And, besides, he'd only written a blurb for a book written by somebody else.

Meanwhile, I was worried and torn. On the one hand, I was pleased with all the free publicity generated for the book, and so was the publisher. On the other, I hated creating such a problem for Bernie.

Then, on February 11, just when I thought things were quieting down, along came the first debate where only Bernie and Hillary Clinton were onstage together, hosted from Milwaukee by PBS anchors Judy Woodruff and Gwen Ifill. I was in New York, sitting on the set of CNN's *AC360*, one of a panel of commentators assembled to provide post-debate analysis.

I almost fell off my chair when I heard Secretary Clinton say, "Today Senator Sanders said that President Obama failed the presidential leadership test. And this is not the first time that he has criticized President Obama. In the past, he has called him weak. He has called him a disappointment. He wrote a foreword for a book that basically argued voters should have buyer's remorse when it comes to President Obama's leadership and legacy."

All I could think was: *Oh, shit.*

Anderson Cooper shot me a look that said: *What the fuck?*

To his credit, Bernie was ready for Hillary's line of attack. "You ran against Barack Obama," he shot back. "I was not that candidate." Then he went on to explain, "So I have voiced criticisms. You're right. Maybe you haven't. I have. But I think to suggest that I have voiced criticism, this blurb that you talk about, you know what the blurb said? The blurb said that the next president of the United States has got to be aggressive in bringing people into the political process. That's what I said. That is what I believe."

Of course, no sooner was the debate over than Anderson asked me what the flap over the blurb was all about. Fortunately, Paul Begala had handed me his copy of the book. I didn't have mine with me. I held it up, said it praised President Obama where appropriate but also criticized him where he deserved it—and pointed out that Senator Sanders had actually only provided a blurb for the back of the book. He had not, as Hillary charged, written the book's foreword.

Not only that, I added, the now-famous blurb, which Clinton had obviously not read, was harmless, as I proved by reading in on the air:

> "Bill Press makes the case why, long after taking the oath of office, the next president of the United States must keep rallying the people who elected him or her on behalf of progressive causes. That is the only way real change will happen. Read this book."

To close the show, Anderson asked each of us our final thoughts. There was no doubt in my mind who'd won the debate. Again holding up a copy of the book, I summed up: "A good night for Hillary, a great night for my book."

Even though Bernie did not win the nomination, he and his supporters did shake up the Democratic Party by forcing party leaders to explore radical changes in party rules governing elections, including same-day voter registration, getting rid of closed primaries and caucuses, and changing the status of superdelegates. They also succeeded in adopting was what was hailed as "the most progressive platform in the party's history."

THE REVOLUTION

Win or lose, Sanders was never going to just walk away from the 2016 primaries without continuing the battle. His goal was not just to organize a campaign. He wanted to start a movement—to ignite a revolution—and he immediately proceeded to do so.

First, he launched a new political organization called Our Revolution to recruit and support progressive candidates across the country for city council, state legislature, House, and Senate—and to promote a progressive agenda in Congress. Today, former Ohio State Senator Nina Turner and Larry Cohen, former president of the Communication Workers of America, lead the movement.

Second, he quickly published a book by the same name. *Our Revolution*, a 450-page manuscript that Bernie personally pounded out in eight weeks, could be considered in many ways the new progressive Bible. It's actually two books in one: a candid account of the Sanders campaign from Iowa through the national convention, and a progressive road map for solving the major issues facing the nation today, from campaign finance reform to climate change.

Third, he continues to campaign across the country on behalf of progressive candidates and causes, and is leading opposition to the policies of Donald Trump.

Of the Bernie Sanders campaign of 2016, I believe history will say few have ever lost a campaign while winning so much.

As for me, here's what I learned:

My experience with Bernie Sanders only reinforced one of the main lessons I take away from my years of political activism; I know it sounds like contradiction, but in politics, you don't always have to win in order to make a difference. Sometimes, in fact, you win by losing.

That's certainly true of the three candidates for president I was most passionate about: Gene McCarthy in 1968; Jerry Brown in 1976; and Bernie Sanders in 2016. Each of them lost, but each came out a winner.

McCarthy launched a movement that changed the course of a nation and ended the war in Vietnam. Brown established himself as the most visionary politician in American and went on to serve as mayor of Oakland and California attorney general before being reelected governor of California. And Bernie Sanders is now one of the most powerful members of the Senate and leader of his own reform movement.

The same is true of many issues I've fought for. We lost many battles with utilities over nuclear power plants, for example, before public opinion turned against them and nuclear reactors began to be dismantled. It took several attempts to pass an initiative legalizing the recreational use of marijuana in California before one measure finally passed in 2016.

So, yes, it's still better to win than lose. But losing isn't necessarily the end of the road. It's better to fight for someone or some good cause you believe in, even if you lose, than to surrender your principles and go along with the crowd. Indeed, I'm prouder of the candidates I supported who lost than many of those who won.

Out of the Democrats' loss in 2016 also came a lot of good—in the form of a revitalized political left. In fact, I haven't seen so much excitement and energy in politics since the anti-war protests of the late '60s—as first manifested in the great Women's March on Washington on January 21, 2017, the day after Donald Trump's inauguration. Despite Trump's first big lie as president, that march attracted far, far more people to the Washington Mall than he had the day before, not counting the hundreds of thousands who showed up for sister marches around the country. In the first six months of 2017 alone, the Tax Protest March, the March for Science, and the People's Climate March also drew hundreds of thousands of activists. That new-born energy also burst forth in huge crowds at congressional town halls, protesting Trump's plans to repeal Obamacare, and in an outpouring of new members and contributors to progressive organizations EMILY's List, MoveOn.org, the ACLU, Our Revolution, Indivisible, and others.

And the most exciting thing about this surge of political action on the left is: It's not being organized by any national powerhouse. Not by the Democratic National Committee, labor unions, or big PACs. It's happening spontaneously. It's totally grassroots-driven. Which is why it's so genuine.

The challenge, of course, is to bottle, focus, or direct that energy into electing progressive candidates to state legislatures, governorships, the House, and the Senate in 2018. But for the first time in fifty years, the raw political force is there, ready to be harnessed—driven, in part, by disgust with the policies and person of Donald Trump, but also driven by the real-ization that progressives came so close in 2016 and could have produced a better result if they'd only worked harder.

And none of that dynamic new political energy on the left would exist today were it not for the unlikely yet sensational and inspiring candidacy of Bernie Sanders of Vermont.

Looking back on the 2016 presidential election, there's no doubt in my mind that Bernie Sanders best understood the political reality of the day, the angst millions of Americans were experiencing, what issues were most important to them, which voters were important to target, and how Demo-crats could win. Unfortunately, the Democratic Party establishment didn't listen. They dismissed him as an oddball. They made up their mind to crown Hillary with the nomination long before she even announced she was running. They totally misread the voter mood of the moment. They downplayed people's disgust with politics as usual. They ignored the powerful desire for change. And then they ended up nominating the wrong candidate.

Democrats should never have lost the 2016 election. And Bernie Sanders would have won it.

Sadly, the most pathetic take on the 2016 campaign came from Hillary Clinton herself, in her book *What Happened?*

Rather than accepting full responsibility for her own defeat, after a miserably-run campaign, Hillary blamed a handful of others, including James Comey, Joe Biden, Jill Stein, Wikileaks, the Russians—and, of course, and especially, Bernie Sanders.

"Bernie couldn't make an argument against me in this area on policy," she complained, "so he had to resort to innuendo and impugning my character." And those attacks "caused lasting damage," Hillary charged, "making it harder to unify progressives in the general election and paving the way for Trump's 'Crooked Hillary' campaign."

Not only that, she questioned Bernie's loyalty as a Democrat: "(Sanders) didn't get into the race to make sure a Democrat won the White House, he got in to disrupt the Democratic Party."

Hillary is dead wrong on all three counts. First, as recounted above, promoting progressive policies was what drove Bernie Sanders to run for president in the first place, and that's what his campaign was all about. Every campaign speech was an hour-long recitation of progressive policy goals, including: single-payer health care; campaign reform; immigration reform; sentencing reform; climate change; and living wage.

Second, you can't blame Bernie for Trump's anti-Clinton smear "Crooked Hillary," any more than you can blame him for "Lyin' Ted" or "Little Marco." And, of course, Trump was talking about Hillary's use of a private email server, which Bernie Sanders, to the dismay of many of his supporters, refused to make an issue by famously asserting: "The American people are sick and tired of hearing about your damn emails."

Third, as Senator Sanders told me early on, his primary goal was to make sure a Democrat won the White House. He just thought he had a better formula for getting there, and that's what primaries are all about. After losing the primary, Bernie barnstormed the country, warning his supporters about Donald Trump and stressing the importance of getting out to vote for Hillary Clinton. And, ever since the election, he still continues to campaign nonstop across the country for progressive candidates for mayor, city council, state legislature, governor, Congress, and Senate. His goal is not to "disrupt" the Democratic Party. It's to rebuild, revitalize, and reenergize the Democratic Party and restore its original mandate as the party of working-class Americans, the party of Main Street, not Wall Street.

I still love and respect Hillary Clinton. I wish she were President of the United States. She would have made a great president. But she never should have written that book. Nobody likes a sore loser.

"THIS IS CNN"

Meanwhile, a funny thing happened on the way to the White House. Bernie Sanders may not have won the nomination but, thanks to Bernie, I got a new job on CNN.

So, in effect, this book comes full circle. It begins with my landing at CNN in 1996 as cohost of *Crossfire*. It ends with my returning to CNN twenty years later as a political contributor and Bernie Sanders supporter.

The job offer came in an email from CNN's Washington bureau chief, Sam Feist, following a guest appearance early in 2016 on *State of the Union*. But it wasn't until my first official appearance as a paid contributor on *The Lead* with host Jake Tapper that I understood why. Moments before we went live, Tapper asked if, in fact, I had endorsed Bernie Sanders. No, I hadn't, I told him. He was a friend. I had encouraged him to run for president, but I hadn't actually endorsed anyone.

"Well, can we at least identify you as a Bernie Sanders supporter?" Jake asked.

"Of course," I said. And that was it.

I realized that CNN's existing band of Democratic contributors were all supporting Hillary or pretending to be neutral in the primary. They needed somebody who would stand up for Bernie. That was me. And I was proud and happy to fill that role as best I could.

It was a great experience, a real privilege, and a fun ride to be part of CNN's coverage of the 2016 election, which came to an end for me at the end of the year.

"And that's the way it is," as Saint Walter Cronkite used to say and as I wrap this memoir. There's still a lot on my plate: four daily broadcasts of the nationally syndicated *The Bill Press Show*, which you can catch at You-

Tube.com/thebillpressshow or on Free Speech TV. Plus, two weekly columns, one for the Tribune Content Agency, the other for *The Hill*; frequent appearances on CNN and MSNBC; daily White House briefings; and, as always, another book or two in preparation.

It's been a great run so far—from a small town in Delaware, with a brief detour in the seminary, to San Francisco City Hall, the California State Senate, the California governor's office, two presidential campaigns, Los Angeles TV, radio talk show host, candidate for insurance commissioner, California Democratic chairman, CNN, MSNBC, Free Speech TV, and the White House Briefing Room—and it ain't over yet.

Yes, I've grown in years, but I believe I've grown in other ways, too. Ways that matter a lot more: a better sense of what's right and what's wrong; a greater understanding of what's important and what's not; a deeper set of core principles; and a stronger determination to fight the good fight and make this a better world for those who are still left out and left behind.

In those battles—for social justice, economic justice, universal health care, a clean environment, strong unions, public education, an end to all forms of discrimination against anybody for any reason—I apply the values I learned as a student of theology to the causes I embrace politically as a proud progressive.

Indeed, I don't know how you can read and accept the message of the Gospels and *not* be a progressive. To me, that's where it all comes together: the fusion of the social gospel with the progressive movement. It's the real-life application of the most important line in the New Testament, as taught by Jesus himself in the Lord's Prayer (Matthew 6:10): "Thy kingdom come, thy will be done, *on earth* as it is in heaven."

Note that the challenge to improve the human condition *on earth* comes first. Because the first priority is to deliver equal opportunity for all here *on earth*—where we're still running the show—before worrying about what, if anything, comes next. Even for nonbelievers, that's what political activism is all about.

And so I go on, looking forward, not backward, enriched by the great experiences I've had so far and excited by the challenges that lie ahead. I may have rounded first and second base and be nearing third, but there's a long way to go, and many more glorious adventures ahead, before I reach home plate.

ACKNOWLEDGMENTS

How do you acknowledge or thank everybody who's helped you out in your entire life and career? You can't! All you can do is take the best shot your memory allows and hope you don't leave too many people out.

So, with a blanket apology to all those I've missed, here's a toast to some very special friends who haven't already been mentioned in this tome.

Unlike some people, I love spending time with my siblings, because we have so many laughs together. Thanks for all the support and love from brothers Dave, Joe, and Patrick and sisters-in-law Nancy, Chris, and Rosie. Ditto to sisters Margie and Mary, and brothers-in-law Herb and Steve. And a special thanks to Margie, the family historian, for refreshing my memory about Delaware City days and tracking down family photos.

The joy of seeing them all is made even more special by getting together with their extended offspring, a great gang of nieces and nephews and their families.

From my adopted French family, Dominique Lesterlin continues to watch over me with her son and my godson, Gael; his wife, Lovisa; and their daughters, Tove and Moa.

Carol and I left California at least temporarily behind when we relocated to Washington, but still count many close friends there, from one end of the state to the other, including Betty and John Moulds in Sacramento; Bob Weisman and Ruth Ross, now moved to Portland; Jim and Pam Campe, Elizabeth Ptak, and Carlos and Rebecca Porrata in Inverness; Barbara and John Martin, Bukowski's publisher, in Santa Rosa; and former congressman Sam Farr and his wife, Shary, in Carmel.

In the Southland: Bruce and Norah Broillet, Paul and Dana Kiesel, Gary and Terry Paul, plus the entire Siciliano family, in Los Angeles; Milan Panić, Newport Beach; and Laurie Black, Lynn Schenk, Sol and Lauren Lizerbram, and Bill and Michelle Lerach in San Diego.

Of early investors in my radio show, several have become close personal friends and political soul mates: Susie and Mark Buell; Pat and Bearnice Patterson; Dick and Sue Wollack; Chase Mishkin; George and Judy Marcus; Joe and Abigail Azrack; Dick Blum; and Ben Lap.

And I can't mention California without a special shout-out to Governor Jerry Brown, who is still the most visionary and effective governor in the United States, and whose friendship and support over the years means so much to me. Thank you, Jerry.

As noted, Washington can be a tough town to crack but, once you break through, you discover some truly wonderful, talented, and dedicated people, many of whom are now our closest friends: John Phillips and Linda Douglass; Melissa Moss and Jonathan Silver; Bonny Wolf and Michael Levy; Elizabeth Bagley; Lanny and Carolyn Davis; Robert and Jane Siegel; Jay and Pam Feldman; Arlene Holt and Willie Baker; Jean-Max Guieu and Jean-François Thibault; Martha Honey and Tony Avirgan; Craig Kellerman and Tom Hill; Michael Tubbs; Mara Liasson and Jon Cuneo; Daniel Stone; Lucie Gikovich; and Michael Lotus.

An important subset of the Washington crowd is a group of Sacramento transplants who still love hanging out together. We call ourselves the California Mafia. Charter members: Larry and Joan Naake; Steve and Suzanne Swendiman; Bruce and Margareta Yarwood; Vic Fazio and Kathy Sawyer; Jan Denton and John Andrews, now moved to Santa Fe; and adopted Arkansan Patsy Thomasson.

Thanks also to our talented production team at *The Bill Press Show,* led by Executive Producer Peter Ogburn, with Associate Producer Jamie Benson; videographer Cyprian Bowlding; production assistant Rachael Lung Rogers; and business partner Paul Woodhull. I know I'm biased, but they are the best in the business. They make me look like I know what I'm doing.

A very special tribute to editor Kevin Murphy and literary agent Ron Goldfarb. This is the eighth book we've worked on together, and whatever limitations I have as a writer are more than compensated for by Kevin's genius as editor and writer and Ron's editorial advice and widely respected skills at representation. Plus, Ron and Joanne Goldfarb count among our closest friends. Daniel Stone helped shape the manuscript. This time, I'm fortunate to be back in the expert hands of publisher Tom Dunne, a political junkie like me, and his capable new senior editor, Stephen Power, with the assistance of editorial assistant Samantha Zukergood and the entire team at Thomas Dunne Books. It's an honor to publish under the banner of St. Martin's Press.

Of course, none of this would be possible without the love and support of such an incredible, fun, warm, and loving family. Thank you, Mark and Cari, Milo, and Silas. And thank you, David and Hez, Prairie, Willow, and Django. Every day, in every way, you make Mema and Granddad proud and happy.

And thanks, most of all, to Carol, who has loved and sustained me, and put up with my nonsense, for so many years. More than anyone, with her razor-sharp memory, she helped with this book. She is the rock on which our family is built. It is her love and counsel that keeps me going.

INDEX